SPORTS BETTING AND BOOKMAKING

SPORTS BETTING AND BOOKMAKING

An American History

Arne K. Lang

ROWMAN & LITTLEFIELD
Lanham • Boulder • New York • London

Published by Rowman & Littlefield
A wholly owned subsidary of The Rowman & Littlefield Publishing Group,
Inc.
4501 Forbes Boulevard, Suite 200, Lanham, Maryland 20706
www.rowman.com

Unit A, Whitacre Mews, 26-34 Stannary Street, London SE11 4AB

British Library Cataloguing in Publication Information Available

Library of Congress Cataloging-in-Publication Data

Names: Lang, Arne K., author.
Title: Sports betting and bookmaking : an American history / Arne K. Lang.
Description: Lanham, Maryland : Rowman & Littlefield, 2016. | Includes bibliographical refer-
    ences and index.
Identifiers: LCCN 2015047132 (print) | LCCN 2016008782 (ebook) | ISBN 9781442265530 (hard-
    back : alk. paper) | ISBN 9781442265547 (electronic)
Subjects: LCSH: Horse racing—Betting—United States—History. | Sports betting—United
    States—History. | Book-making (Betting)—United States—History.
Classification: LCC SF332 .L36 2016 (print) | LCC SF332 (ebook) | DDC 798.4010973—dc23
LC record available at http://lccn.loc.gov/2015047132

♾ ™ The paper used in this publication meets the minimum requirements of
American National Standard for Information Sciences Permanence of Paper
for Printed Library Materials, ANSI/NISO Z39.48-1992.

Printed in the United States of America

CONTENTS

ACKNOWLEDGMENTS

I couldn't have written this book if I hadn't spent the bulk of my adult years in Las Vegas where I got to know many interesting people involved in sports wagering. A number of these people helped shape this book, if only by sharing their insights. I have known Dana Parham for more than twenty-five years. Through him I got to meet the fabled Bill Benter, who was generous in sharing his remarkable story. Kirk Brooks, Rob Terry, Dion Frayle, Brian Kist, and Arturo O'Connor provided keys that opened more doors.

In my younger days after leaving the academic world, I had a sideline as a "personality" in the emerging wave of sports talk radio. I feel a special debt to Russ Culver, the noted oddsmaker, who got the ball rolling, and to David Malinsky, the longest-tenured of my various co-hosts. They taught me plenty, as did Michael Roxborough, another friend of long standing, who bubbled forth during the dawn of those inspiriting days.

I have been privileged to know Lem Banker, a man of good cheer with a wealth of good stories. Howard Schwartz, the marketing director of Gamblers Book Club, has been a longtime supporter. Eileen DiRocco provided me open access to the back files of *Gaming Today*. Christen Karniski of Rowman & Littlefield believed in this book and was a good shepherd, navigating the manuscript through the protocols of her publishing house. Thanks to Alan Shaw, Mike Kerzetski, Doug Dunlap, Helen Salinas, and Art Rubin for being good neighbors. I'm grateful to Shane Langvad and Jessica Welman for their technical support. And here's a toast to the many absent friends who encouraged me to keep writing. In memoriam, thank you Mike Lee, Huey Mahl, Harvey Rothman, Lee Pete, Bobby Bryde, and John and Edna Luckman.

The Department of Special Collections at the UNLV Lied Library is a terrific resource, and the people working there are always pleasant and helpful. The department houses the invaluable Center for Gaming Research.

How does one begin to thank all the people who enlightened me as I was surfing the web? It's impossible. However, with due respect to all the unnamed, I'd like to say that I enjoy reading the threads on "Colin's Ghost," the horse racing history site that Kevin Martin founded. Mr. Martin understands that all those long-gone racetracks were something more than homes for gambling. For many they were homes in the hearth sense; communal gathering places that gave rise to lasting memories.

My life has been enriched by a very special lady, my wife, Kitt. This book is for her.

INTRODUCTION

In 1922 a young reporter named Herbert Asbury, later a noted author, made an interesting observation about bookmaking. "It is the biggest business in the United States," he said, "that is operated on credit without collateral."

Bookmakers in those days dealt primarily with horseplayers. They operated behind a veil of secrecy, as they had been forced into the shadows, expelled from the racetrack betting enclosures where their profession had taken flight. In the pages of this book we lift that veil to examine the nuts and bolts, and explore the historical roots, of a largely obscure field of commerce.

A historical analysis of bookmaking necessarily pots it against the backdrop of thoroughbred racing, an enterprise that rose from the ashes to become America's leading spectator sport, only to dwindle to where loyal racetrack patrons came to be seen as remnants of a lost tribe. As the racing game was fraying, team sports—football and basketball and such—became a bigger and bigger betting attraction, eventually swamping horse racing as the bread-and-butter of the bookmaking community. These were not unrelated developments. The shift was spurred in some small measure by disaffected horseplayers.

When I started this book I didn't know where it would take me, but I knew where I didn't want to go. I didn't want to write a book about the racing game that focused on rogues and scandals and I didn't want to explore the history of bookmaking through the prism of organized crime.

Rogues and scandals were common themes in early writings about horse racing, when the prevailing viewpoint was that racetracks, by virtue of being hives of gambling, fostered behavior that aggravated a host of social problems. Writers of later years who wrote about illegal, off-track betting were, by and large, dismayed by the specter of it and contemptuous of the men that steered the ship. It became an article of faith that bookmakers were agents of organized crime; not merely struts in a polymorphous criminal enterprise, but the pillars without which the enterprise would crumble. The lurid title of a 1961 book, *A Two-Dollar Bet Means Murder*, exemplifies this mind-set.

These persistent themes have produced a body of literature that barely recognizes that "playing the ponies" is an enterprise well fitted to many fields of inquiry—probability theory, entrepreneurial studies, and the sociology of leisure to name but a few. And it wasn't as if bookmakers and their emissaries were hard to find. At various times and places they burst out of the shadows in great profusion. In 1949, there were reportedly 443 places in New Orleans where a fellow could consign a bet on a horse race. Evansville, Indiana, which then had a population of about a hundred twenty-five thousand, had forty bookie joints. Steubenville, Ohio, which had a peak population of about forty thousand, once housed eleven full-fledged bookmaking establishments.

These figures, culled from *Life* magazine, *Sports Illustrated*, and the biography of Steubenville native Jimmy the Greek, lack supporting documentation, but, inflated or not, they paint a picture of a robust industry. In some communities, horse parlors, in the aggregate, were as well patronized as movie theatres, notwithstanding the fact that the parlors appealed to a narrow demographic: adult men with a smattering of adult women.

Writing an honest history of race and sports betting without touching on the dark side proved to be impossible. By their very nature, activities defined as illicit will attract shady characters. Until recent times, off-track betting and municipal corruption were inseparable. And commentators prone to see only the dark side shaped public policy. The early reformers, armed with the sword of righteousness, succeeded in getting laws passed that shuttered nearly all of America's thoroughbred tracks. Reformers of later years, although disburdened of puritan dogma, gestated laws that remain vital today, bedeviling gambler-businessmen working outside approved channels.

When I set sail on this project, my interests were twofold. I was curious about America's first bookmakers, the men that built the foundation on which the modern Nevada sports book stands. Secondly, I was fascinated by the New York racing scene in the first decade of the twentieth century, a scene at once so buoyant and then suddenly so dead. The upheaval wasn't unique to New York, but New York was the cynosure of American thoroughbred racing. Before the unraveling, more than 40 percent of the money distributed to horsemen in the United States and Canada was generated by racetracks in New York. Developments there had far-reaching effects.

Our story begins in New York, the primary stomping ground, with detours to Chicago, Las Vegas, Atlantic City, and to that vast, borderless global village called Cyberspace. Toward the end we touch down in Basseterre, a small city on a Caribbean Island so quaint that it has no traffic lights.

Basseterre wasn't on the itinerary when the journey started. I had no knowledge of it. But there I found a most remarkable colony, a group of bet takers and bet makers who have pumped millions of dollars into the pari-mutuel pools that are the lifeblood of thoroughbred racing. The bet makers have taken Damon Runyon's famous dictum—"all horse-players die broke"—and punctured it with such acuity that it was as if Runyon had said that the sun rises in the west.

LEONARD JEROME

The Towering Pillar of the Horsey Set

If one set out to write a broad history of horse racing in America, one could begin with descriptions of street races in the colonial era. They were a recurrent feature of life in towns that served as the hubs of rural counties. If the emphasis was on horse racing as a form of mass entertainment, a logical starting point would be the great North-South intersectional match races that bobbed up sporadically during the third, fourth, and fifth decades of the nineteenth century. The Union Course on the Hempstead plains of Long Island and the Metairie Course in New Orleans were the leading destinations.

These were America's first sporting spectacles. The 1823 race at the Union Course between American Eclipse, the pride of the North, and Sir Henry, the pride of the South, attracted a crowd estimated at sixty thousand, perhaps one-third from out of state. As John Eisenberg notes, a gathering of this magnitude was unprecedented. The turnout was larger than the combined population of Illinois and Delaware and larger than all but three American cities.[1] Named for the great British racehorse Eclipse, American Eclipse proved to be worthy of the name, winning the second and third heats after a jockey change to claim the $10,000 purse.

The race between Fashion and Peytona at the Union Course in 1845 was an even bigger event. "When two men meet on the street," said a writer for the *New Orleans Times-Picayune*, "the *first* question is which of the mares is bound to win; the next whether it be fact that Mexico has declared war (on the United States). The (horse race) is deemed vastly more interesting."[2] The Long Island Railroad ran ten excursion trains to the racecourse, the first of which arrived shortly after dawn.[3] The crowd numbered seventy thousand according to the most conservative estimate.

Peytona, foaled in Alabama, defeated her New Jersey–bred rival in two closely contested heats. As had been the case when American Eclipse ran against Sir Henry, each heat was four miles long. This emphasis on stamina was consistent with other athletic competitions. In pedestrianism, long-distance runners were held in higher esteem, and competed for larger purses, than sprinters. In prizefighting, bouts had no time limit. Some lasted for hours.

John Cox Stevens, whose father owned most of what is now Hoboken, was the guiding spirit behind the big races on the Union Course but his legacy as a prime mover in the commercialization of American horse racing was diminished by the fact that racing in and around New York City never took a firm hold during his lifetime (he died in 1857). Racing at the Union Course eventually staggered to a stop, ceasing after 1847, by which time Stevens, a great go-getter, was immersed in yachting, the sport with which he became most closely identified. In the decade leading up to the Civil War, harness racing was a vastly greater enterprise than thoroughbred racing, although it too languished as the drumbeats of war became louder.

Leonard W. Jerome (1817–1891) was a far more important figure in the history of the turf. Indeed, he was the man most responsible for elevating thoroughbred racing in the United States into a mainstream sport. Recognized posthumously as the American financier who was Winston Churchill's maternal grandfather, Jerome's legacy as a great sportsman somehow got lost in the shadow of his famous descendent.

Leonard Jerome left a large footprint in Saratoga Springs, New York, where he helped lay the foundation for America's most prestigious summer meet. He played a role in the establishment of Morris Park, which was hailed as the finest racing plant in the world when it opened in 1889. He spearheaded the establishment of the Coney Island Racing Association, the custodian of the Sheepshead Bay track, which for many years was the top track in the country, attracting the best talent with the highest purses. And he made a huge contribution to American popular culture at the thoroughbred track in Westchester County that bore his name. Two innovations imported from Europe—the bookmakers' ring and pari-mutuel betting—made their first appearance in the United States at Jerome Park.

A distant relative of George Washington, Leonard Jerome was born on a farm near Syracuse, New York. He attended Princeton, but money was tight and he left after a year to finish his schooling at a less expensive college closer to his home, Union College in Schenectady, where he pursued a law degree. At age twenty-two, he was admitted to the New York State bar and joined a firm in Albany.

Several years later, while practicing law in Rochester, Jerome and his younger brother Lawrence "Larry" Jerome pooled their life savings to acquire a local newspaper, the *Daily American*. Their paper championed the Whig Party, which sent Zachary Taylor to the White House in 1848. As a reward for his advocacy, Leonard Jerome was appointed ambassador to Trieste, a nation-state that was then part of the sprawling Austro-Hungarian Empire. Jerome had acquired an interest in a trotter while living in Rochester, but his great passion for racing—more specifically the spectacle of racing—took flight in Europe, particularly in Paris, where he spent most of his time while representing his country in a job that was largely a paid vacation.

Jerome was very fond of Europe, as were his children, daughters Jeanette, Clarita, and Leonie. Each of them married a British nobleman. Jeanette Jerome, conventionally called Jennie, bagged the biggest prize. In 1874, at age twenty, she married Randolph Henry Spencer-Churchill, the second son of the second Duke of Marlborough. She bore him two children, the oldest a boy they named Winston.

In Leonard Jerome's obituary in the *New York Times*, it was noted that there were "previous manifestations of a strong speculative turn in the Jerome family." One of Leonard's older brothers struck it rich speculating in mulberry trees while studying theology at Princeton. Another brother, Addison G. Jerome, a stock broker turned merchant banker, had the sort of meteoric rise and fall on Wall Street that was the stuff of legend. It was a day when great fortunes were made and lost speculating in mining and railroad stocks.

Addison Jerome was going great guns in 1850 when Leonard decided to join him. Lawrence Jerome followed close behind. The three brothers shared a house in Brooklyn before moving to Manhattan, where, in the words of a biographer, they lived like tornadoes, "accepting occasional ruin as a good steeplechaser does a fall—just a passing event to learn from."[4]

The volatility eventually caught up with Leonard Jerome and he lost most of his fortune, but en route to this doleful denouement he lived the high life, sharing the good times with life-long friends that shared his interests and his sense of style, a personification of the Gilded Age. The Jerome mansion on Twenty-Sixth Street at the corner of Madison Avenue, a six-story beauty built in 1859, was said to be the most opulent home in the city. The building in the courtyard with stained glass windows and interior walls paneled in black walnut was a horse shed.

Jerome rubbed elbows and occasionally butted heads with three generations of Vanderbilt men. The great robber baron Cornelius "Commodore" Vanderbilt and his son William Henry Vanderbilt—they died nine years apart—were both lionized as America's wealthiest man. William's son William Kissam Vanderbilt assumed control of the family's railroad empire but attracted less notice for his business dealings than for his contributions to yachting and thoroughbred racing. Among other things, he was one of the founding members of the Jockey Club.

Leonard Jerome had a great deal in common with the Commodore's grandson. William Kissam Vanderbilt was educated in Geneva, supported the opera, and had social graces that were sorely lacking in his forebears. But Jerome's best buddies were men in his age bracket, notably William R. Travers and August Belmont. Their friendship was cemented by an appreciation for fast horses and a felt need to impose structure and hopefully commercialize what was then a weak and disorganized sport.

Born in the Rhineland, August Belmont was twenty-two years old when he arrived in New York in 1837 as an emissary of the Frankfurt branch of the Rothschild banking family. Quick to shed his foreignness, Belmont opened his own firm, took an active interest in politics, married the daughter of a U.S. naval hero, and became a pillar of society, renowned for his epicurean tastes and lavish dinner parties. Although politically his views and those of Leonard Jerome often diverged, the two men enjoyed each other's company.

William Travers, born into a Baltimore mercantile family, was a lawyer by training and a Wall Street daredevil by instinct. After making the acquaintance of the Jerome brothers, he was invited to join their firm.

His love of horses was manifested in the large Westchester County stud farm that he co-owned with prominent horsemen John R. Hunter and George Osgood, a Vanderbilt by marriage. An inveterate joiner—at one time he held membership in twenty-seven clubs—Travers had a speech impediment, a stammer that enhanced the punch of his droll humor. When he died in 1887, it was written that "his brilliancy and wit were family proverbs in thousands of homes."[5]

Travers's boon companion Larry Jerome was knit from the same cloth. The most adventurous of the Jerome brothers, Larry would be eulogized as the greatest wit and practical joker that this country ever produced. The two mirth makers were regulars at Delmonico's, the most renowned of America's great restaurants. They were there on the night that Larry Jerome's wife bore him a son that he named William— William Travers Jerome in the full corpus—a boy who would go on to exert considerable sway over the sport of horse racing, but in a manner that was totally at variance with his lineage (more about him later).

2

SARATOGA AND JEROME PARK

The Fountainheads

Situated in the pine-scented foothills of the Adirondack Mountains, Saratoga Springs was already an internationally known resort when Leonard Jerome and his friends set about implanting a racing meet there in the summer of 1863. People were drawn there by the water that bubbled out of the mineral springs; it was widely believed to have medicinal properties. Saratoga had no shortage of accommodations for invalids on a tight budget, but regular visitors, in the main, were men of considerable wealth, more so in the summer months when the mornings and evenings were considerably cooler than in the sweltering cities from which they came. In the argot of these nabobs, Saratoga, shorthand for Saratoga Springs, was simply "The Spa."

At the time of the first Saratoga meet, horse racing in the Northern states was exhibiting signs of a renaissance. New Jersey was in the forefront. The Passaic County Agricultural Society held a three-day meet at a newly formed track in Paterson in 1862 and efforts were afoot to establish meets in Hoboken and Secaucus and in the seaside community of Long Branch. Many of the prime movers behind these meets were war profiteers. Milton H. Sanford, who established a major breeding farm in the Preakness hills of Passaic County, owned textile mills and was already a rich man when the war broke out, but he increased his fortune many times over selling blankets to the Union army and was thus able to participate in the racing game on a much larger scale.

The true father of Saratoga racing was John "Old Smoke" Morrissey. Born in Tipperary County, Ireland, and raised on the wrong side of the tracks in Troy, New York, Morrissey was a bare-knuckle boxing champion—he acquired his nickname after an impromptu fight in a saloon in which he was burned by an overturned stove—who went on to run a chain of gambling dens in New York City, concessions granted to him by friends high up in the hierarchy of the political machine known as Tammany Hall. In 1861, at age thirty, he expanded his holdings with a room in Saratoga Springs, the precursor to his famous "club house," a gambling emporium that drew favorable comparisons to the most ornate gambling palaces in Europe. With silk curtains, velvet tapestry, expensive artwork, and furnishings inlaid with gold, the three-story, red-brick building, whose games of chance were off-limits to the townsfolk, was painstakingly plush: "a gorgeous, gilded, glittering trap-door to perdition" as one visitor described it.[1]

The inauguration of thoroughbred racing on August 3, 1863, predated the opening of Morrissey's club house by almost seven years. He would have preferred to launch both ventures simultaneously, but a short racing meet required less attention to detail and he was persuaded by his friend and benefactor Cornelius Vanderbilt to put the grand casino on the back burner. The Commodore, who had recently acquired controlling interest in the New York Central Railroad, had a vested interest in the growth of tourism in Saratoga. For most people, a visit there entailed a ride on one of his excursion trains. In later years, when racetracks came under siege, track operators would find that railway companies were their strongest allies. Racegoers were an important revenue stream and railroad tycoons were well represented in the "horsey set."

Morrissey looked to the Bluegrass State of Kentucky for his key employees. Charles Wheatly, the track's superintendent, was considered America's leading authority on thoroughbred genealogy and had experience running the Lexington track. Another Lexington man, Dublin-born Robert Underwood, a veterinarian by training but best known as an auctioneer, was awarded the pool-selling privilege. In those days, racetrack betting took the form of Calcutta pools. An amusing chap with a photographic memory who salted his soliloquy with witty side remarks and morsels of information about each horse, delivered with a tinge of an Irish brogue, Dr. Underwood was known as the "prince of pool sellers." He acquired this reputation while running pools at Meta-irie and at the Magnolia course in Mobile, Alabama.

The first Saratoga meet consisted of only eight races spaced across four days. Some of the races were best-of-three heats. Good purses drew entries from fourteen stables representing four states and Canada. Betting was brisk. At the ornate United States Hotel, the pool selling on the eves of the races drew lively crowds. According to a report in a popular sports journal, the *Spirit of the Times*, the shouts of the bidders in the basement room carried into the ballroom upstairs where there was "a magnificent display of female loveliness, in costly ornaments and sumptuous attire, moving to stirring music in the mazy dance."[2] At the track, the vacationers were more subdued. Morrissey insisted that people remain seated while a race was in progress and patrolled the grandstand to ensure that his edict was adhered to.

Gambling was stitched into the fabric of Saratoga, but so was piety—Saratoga was the birthplace of the Christian temperance movement—and gambling in this homonymous environment had previously taken a more dignified form. The old guard was partial to card games like baccarat, where etiquette dictated that one mask his excitement with a taciturn demeanor. The noisy dither in the pool-selling salon was symbolic of a new era. Saratoga was attracting a more raffish element.

John Morrissey went on to become a United States congressman and then, after breaking with Tammany Hall, a New York state senator, but a portion of the population always viewed him as a loutish fellow of questionable morals and his foray into Saratoga discomfited many of the old-timers. Morrissey intuitively understood that if he wanted to grow his thoroughbred meet into a larger spectacle, he couldn't do it alone, and that he needed more than financial assistance; he needed the imprimatur of "gentlemen." Leonard Jerome wasn't exactly old money, but in certain settings he exuded old world refinement—a patron of the arts, he was particularly fond of grand opera—and it didn't hurt that two of his eight brothers were Presbyterian clergymen.

The inaugural racing meet was an unexpected bonanza for the Saratoga business community. According to Saratoga historian Edward Hotaling, the occupancy rate at the hotels and boardinghouses on the final day of the inaugural meet, a Thursday, was 25 percent higher than the busiest day of the previous year.[3] This was more remarkable considering that the country was in the grip of a terrible war, and that the racing facility, which sat about a half mile from the center of town, was lacking. Formerly a trotting course, the track had no grandstand and those watching the races from the comfort of their carriages had their views obstructed by trees, barns, and sheds.

The final day of racing was barely finished when the Saratoga Racing Association was born. When the meet resumed the following summer, racegoers witnessed the races from the comfort of a more modern facility situated across from the original track. One of the highlights of the meet was a race called the Travers Stakes. The race was won by a bay mare named Kentucky, a horse partly owned by none other than Mr. Travers himself.

The Saratoga Racing Association was stamped an official entity on March 21, 1865—nineteen days before the signing of the peace treaty that marked the end of the Civil War—when it was incorporated under the bylaws of the state of New York under the formal name "Saratoga Association for the Improvement of the Breed of Horses." William R. Travers, Leonard Jerome, and John Hunter assumed key posts, respectively president, vice president, and chairman of the executive committee. John Morrissey was a major stockholder, presumptively the leading stockholder, but his name appeared nowhere on the papers of incorporation.

Improving the breed of horses was a noble undertaking. Images of soldiers on horseback dueling with sabers were images from an earlier era, but many cavalrymen still carried sabers and cavalry units were an essential component of a well-equipped military. In the civilian world, many occupations required good horses. Southern plantation owners, Yankee traders, and western ranchers often spent the greater part of a day on a horse, as did country doctors, country lawyers, circuit judges, and circuit preachers. Farmers used horses to plow their fields and till their crops. Horses powered streetcars, fire trucks, and ambulances. In 1865, a letter traveling coast-to-coast by Pony Express took ten days. Breeding horses that were more resistant to disease and could run faster across longer distances was an investment in energy efficiency and a prod to greater productivity. Work horses with a thoroughbred strain out-performed other work horses and racing was seen as the best way to identify the horses most likely to pass on favorable traits.

The phrase "improving the breed of horses"—which the Saratoga association co-opted from the charters of older jockey clubs—came to be an object of derision. As the sport drifted away from long-distance races to sprints, and as motorized vehicles supplanted horse-drawn conveyances, it became obvious that the breeding of racehorses had little utility for improving the lot of mankind. Racetrack owners that justified racing as an invaluable tool for selective breeding were lampooned for their hypocrisy:

> "Tell me: That fellow over there taking bets. What purpose does he serve?"

> "Why he has come here to assist us in improving the breed of horses."

The grandstand was lengthened for the third Saratoga meeting in 1865 and a second stand was built to handle the overflow, expansions that proved insufficient as the turnout was fantastic. In the aggregate, the crowd for the six days of racing approached fifty thousand, an enlargement attributed to the end of the Civil War; the cessation of hostilities supposedly unleashed a pent-up need for communal merrymaking. High-ranking army officers from both sides of the conflict were spotted among the racegoers.

On the opening day of the meet, a Monday, the crowd arriving for the races was laden with young men whose appearance suggested trouble, two thousand hard-boiled characters in all, said one report. But there was no trouble whatsoever. "There was no loud talking, no vulgar expressions . . . not a pocket was picked, or a man knocked down, so far as could be ascertained," said a piece in the *New York Times*.[4]

Leonard Jerome had observed the same phenomenon at the Chantilly course in France where the presence of nobility had a soothing affect that swayed young toughs into behaving like gentlemen. He now had one more reason to think that he could bring Saratoga-style racing to the metropolis, potting a track within easy reach of people living in America's most densely populated city without creating a hive for disturbances that would cause him grief.

Jerome set his plans in motion by establishing a real estate investment company. Named the Villa Park Site and Improvement Association, it was formed for the purpose of acquiring the Bathgate farm, a 230-acre spread well-suited to harboring a large racing plant. The list of stockholders was laden with names that would live long in the annals of

American thoroughbred racing: Belmont, Travers, Withers, Lorillard, and so on. Jerome then leased the property to an entity of his own making, the American Jockey Club. Incorporated as a nonprofit organization, the club was formed on April 17, 1866, at a meeting in Jerome's office. At the meeting, August Belmont accepted the position of president, a post he would retain for the next twenty-one years. (The very first jockey clubs were formed in an age when gentlemen raced their own horses. Oddly, the label stuck, never becoming antiquated.)

Situated approximately four miles north of what is now Yankee Stadium, Jerome Park was the first racetrack in the metropolitan area that one could get to from Manhattan straightaway without breaking up the trip with a ferryboat ride. And it was much more than a racetrack. The luxurious clubhouse with its wide veranda had all the amenities of a five-star hotel. Open year-around, it became a popular destination for society balls. The food served in the members' dining room rivaled the fare at Delmonico's. The first home of the Westchester Polo Club, America's first formal polo club, the track had many restricted areas that bespoke of a caste system—members had their own private entrance—but adults and children of all social ranks were welcome to use the property in the wintertime for ice skating, sledding, and tobogganing.

September 25, 1866, marked the grand opening of Jerome Park. The *New York Times*, a Whig Party organ when it was founded in 1851 (Leonard Jerome was an investor), gave the event a fawning review, describing the scene as a brilliant display of fashion and equipage. General Ulysses S. Grant was among the estimated twenty-five thousand attendees. The house band met him as he entered the gates, trumpeting his arrival with Handel's *See the Conquering Hero Comes*. The feature race, called the Inauguration Stakes, was won by Kentucky, the prohibitive favorite in a field whittled by multiple scratches to only four horses.

3

POOL SELLERS, BOOKMAKERS, AND PARI-MUTUELS

In the days preceding Jerome Park's inaugural meet, newspaper readers were informed that no betting would be conducted on the premises. This was a lie. Dr. Underwood was in action as were several unauthorized pool sellers.

The big pools were conducted off-site on the eve of the races. Members of the sporting press were on hand to log the results. At John Chamberlin's Broadway clubhouse, reminisced a reporter, the scenes "were dramatic for the personages present and the sums of money adventured."[1]

Auction pools were also conducted at hotels popular among visiting horsemen. In New York, the Fifth Avenue Hotel and the Astor House were the top destinations. On racing days at Jerome Park, both hotels displayed flags representing the track. If bad weather forced a postponement, the flags were positioned at half-mast to inform racegoers of this development.

Pool selling was associated with men with large bankrolls. Inevitably, the enterprise diffused into the ranks of the hoi polloi. In the city, rooms were opened to accommodate men of lesser means. These establishments, hangouts for the sporting crowd, were called *poolrooms*, a term that eventually took on a different meaning.

Allowing pool selling on-site was risky. Embedded in the New York Constitution was a law that prohibited keeping or occupying a place for the purpose of gambling. Defined broadly, the stand set aside for

Underwood fit under this definition. But several years would elapse before the authorities were drawn to take action, and in the meantime, Doc Underwood, with his distinctive style, became one of the most recognizable characters on the racing scene. "No meeting seems complete without his cheery voice," noted a turf reporter for the *New York Times*.[2]

When a horse was pulled from a race, a pool seller such as Underwood merely canceled the wager and readjusted the payout. However, race-day scratches were more than annoying to bettors whose forecasts rested on visualizations of how each race would unfold. Eliminating one or more contenders altered the picture, particularly if it knocked out the likely pacesetter. Holding pools on the eve of a race forced one to lock in a wager before all the variables were known. The condition of the track's surface might change in the interim, as might jockey assignments and the number of entrants.

Pools conducted before a day of racing were useful in one regard. They established what a professional sports bettor would call an "overnight line," a base price for each entrant that became a bargaining chip for man-to-man wagers. The conversion of auction results into odds was a relatively simple matter, as indicated by this example:

	Winning Bids	Odds
Favorite	$4000	3/1
Second Choice	$3000	4/1
Third Choice	$1000	12/1
Fourth Choice	$500	24/1
Field	$1500	8/1

Pool selling was already on unsteady legs when Jerome Park opened to rave reviews. It was a cumbersome method of satisfying the gambling urge, and there were flaws inherent in the paradigm. Foremost, a man who successfully bid on a horse couldn't calculate his potential winnings until all the other bids were in. In terms of getting value—in horse racing lingo, securing an *overlay*, a situation where the odds were longer than the probability of winning—a man was betting on the blind, unless he happened to go last, and by then all the good horses were taken. (Sometimes two or more horses had to be aggregated into one entity to attract a buyer. The combination was called "the field.")

"French pools" (pari-mutuel wagering), and the bookmaker's ring, a British construct, led to the demise of pool selling. The first pari-mutuel machines seen in the United States were put to use at Jerome Park in 1871. There were initially four of these curious contraptions, three requiring a $5 wager and the other a $25 wager. Other amounts necessitated multiple transactions; for example, a man wagering $20 left the counter with four tickets. Later that same year, a new track in New Jersey, Monmouth Park, introduced French pools at its summer meet. The following year, the experiment spread to the Fair Grounds in New Orleans.

The father of pari-mutuel wagering was Pierre Oller, a Parisian perfume maker with a knack for devising schemes that rested on mathematical principles. Leonard Jerome saw the potential for pari-mutuel betting while attending the races at Longchamps and imported the innovation to America. An alternate form of wagering, the English system of bookmaking, was reportedly adopted at the urging of Pierre Lorillard IV, who was exposed to the concept during his many trips to England where he kept an annex of his famous Rancocas, New Jersey, racing stable. The heir to a vast tobacco fortune—lore has it that the word "millionaire" first appeared in his father's obituary—Lorillard sponsored Henry Stanton, who crossed the pond in 1872 to organize the bookmaking pitch at Jerome Park. The initial crew consisted of only nine men. They were conspicuous by the knapsacks slung over their shoulders.[3]

In England, racetrack bookmakers were known for their flamboyance. They operated under gaily colored umbrellas and some dressed outlandishly to set them apart from their rivals. Stanton was conspicuous by his frock coat and gray beard, but his appearance would have attracted little notice in his native country. American bookmakers were never as gaudy as their British cousins, but the most resourceful adopted a *shtick* that served to ingrain their "brand." The bookmaker "Virginia" Carroll kept bettors in stitches with his wisecracks. "He is a Punch and Judy show all by himself," said a reporter.[4]

Bookmaking wasn't rocket science, but rare was the man who mastered it without taking his lumps. Unlike pool sellers, bookmakers were at risk of paying out more than they took in, as was frequently the case. A certain segment of bettors were drawn to bookmakers when they had other alternatives for this very reason. Taking money from a bookmaker instilled a feeling of triumph. Having a winning ticket cashed by a mutuel clerk wasn't as satisfying.

A good bookmaker had a knack for figures. He could glance at the odds chalked on his slate and calculate his jeopardy in his head while performing other tasks. The odds that he internalized were mentally transformed into the pieces of a pie. Some of the pieces were large (the favorites) and some were slivers (the longshots). If a bookie wasn't careful, the sum of the various segments would grow larger than the whole and he would be in danger of being "dutched." A bettor playing into a "dutch book" can lock in a predetermined profit by wagering on every horse, sizing each wager in direct proportion to the odds.

At the core of bookmaking is the notion of a *round book*. A bookmaker achieves a round book when he juggles the odds in such a fashion that he stands to win regardless of how the race plays out. A round book that is perfectly round—where each entrant is backed in exact proportion to the opening odds—is an ideal construct, seldom if ever realized, and in truth a bookmaker would be disappointed if he achieved it, as it would mean that his earnings were "par for the course" when his hopes were higher.

As sports historian John Dizikes has noted, the first pari-mutuel machines were bulky and primitive. Each horse in a race was assigned a number. When a person made a wager, he was given a pasteboard bearing the number of the horse that he picked. The pasteboard was pulled from a rack and the force used in extracting it activated a counter that recorded the bet. Those picking the winning horse divided up the entire pool, less a commission for the operator.[5]

The pasteboards were serially numbered in large print so that a punter scanning the rack could see how many tickets had been written on each entrant, affording him a rough estimation of his payoff if he picked the winning horse. Needless to say, this was a very rough estimation, virtually useless if done early in the betting cycle. However, the pari-mutuel system had several advantages over betting with bookmakers. Foremost, a man backing a rank outsider had a chance of making a big score. A bookmaker was at risk of being ruined if a longshot romped home at fantastic odds, so he kept the odds artificially low on the horses that in theory had no chance of winning. If overextended beyond his comfort zone because of heavy wagering on a particular horse, a bookmaker might simply refuse to take any more bets on that horse. He erased the odds and chalked in the word "out" on his slate, a maneuver that caused him to be scorned as a man with a weak spine. The pari-mutuel operator, by contrast, was indifferent. The outcome of a race had no bearing on his commission. In 1872, six lucky persons visiting Jerome Park placed $5 on a nag named Nickajack and won $1,178 (adjusted for inflation, roughly $22,000). Several years later, a longshot returned $1,080 on a $5 laydown at Saratoga.[6]

In the early days of pari-mutuel betting, the calculators were slow and mistake prone. Payouts were sometimes richer and sometimes lighter than what they should have been, and often well below expectations, fueling talk of skullduggery. There were never any surprises of this sort when betting with a bookmaker because the odds that one obtained were fixed. The bookies were constantly reconfiguring the odds to diminish their jeopardy, but a man's wager was locked in at the time that he made it, making subsequent revisions of no consequence to him.

Fixed-odds betting made the game of trying to beat the races a more cerebral game. Good selections were the key to showing a long-term profit, but an astute forecaster could increase his returns and boost his earnings by the judicious timing of his wagers. A fellow who was attuned to the rhythms of the marketplace or was privy to inside information was able to lock in a wager at generous odds before the odds were flattened out. Moreover, a man holding "the best of it" had options that would not have existed had he placed his money in a pari-mutuel pool. For example, he could sell off his bet at a premium, locking in a small but guaranteed profit before the race was run. He could hedge under any circumstance, but hedging (betting on more than one runner) took on an added dimension because there were more situations where hedging was the proper strategy. The result was that some very smart people were drawn into the ranks of horseplayers, individuals adept at solving puzzles by the application of mathematical principles. Many of these individuals became bookmakers. The dichotomy between bookies and big bettors was often blurred.

At racetracks, bookmakers flocked together in designated areas. The centralization promoted comparison shopping, as the odds on a particular horse weren't uniform. Maximizing winnings was thus a function of exploiting variations occurring in both time and space. The sophisticated player looked to hit up the bet taker offering the best odds on the horse that he fancied, and then timed his wager to receive the optimal return. This was easier said than done in a fluid environment, and extremely difficult if a man was acting alone.

Pari-mutuel betting was more impersonal than betting with bookmakers and for many less intimidating. The machines were most popular with small-fry bettors and novices. But all that changed in 1877 when the New York legislature abolished auction and pari-mutuel pools, an action spurred by an "outrageous" amount of betting on political races (more about that in the next chapter). The new law did not specifically mention bookmaking, a loophole for the management of Jerome Park, the first track affected, whose attorneys would argue that bookmaking was a fundamentally different enterprise than pool selling and thereby outside the scope of the statute. Hence, the bookmakers were allowed to stay and enjoyed all the benefits of a monopoly. Punters that had bet pari-mutuels exclusively had no choice but to intrude upon the bookmakers' turf where they were exposed to the methods of more sophisticated handicappers. The bookmakers accommodated them by accepting smaller bets than was their custom and eventually a separate phalanx of bet takers emerged to accommodate the "pikers" (small bettors).

Jerome Park absorbed the brunt of the anti-pool-selling law. Pool selling continued at thoroughbred and harness tracks in other parts of the state without repercussions. Leonard Jerome eventually persuaded the authorities to rescind the embargo. Reporters cheered the return of the auctioneers whose loud patter brightened the ambience.

During most of the racing seasons at Jerome Park, all three betting formats were on display. The scene would be replicated elsewhere. At Chicago's Washington Park in 1887, a reporter counted thirty-six bookmaking stalls, four pari-mutuel machines, and two auction pools.[7] Pick your poison, quipped the jokesters, but a horseplayer never had it so good.

4

OFF-TRACK BETTING

The Poolroom Scene

John Morrissey wasn't the first gambler-businessman in America to run scrupulously honest games in an elegant setting, but no one did more to advance the image of what a high-stakes gambling house should look like. His emporium in Manhattan near Union Square was magnificently furnished. The storerooms were stocked with the finest wines, liquors, and cigars, items provided free to his best customers. The place raised the bar and then he went and surpassed it with his sumptuously appointed gambling palace in Saratoga. But these were merely the brightest jewels in his galaxy. Morrissey had an ownership stake in many other gambling establishments and they ran the gamut from sawdust joint to hifalutin.

The racetrack-building boom in the years following the Civil War was accompanied by a parallel boom in off-track betting. Some rooms that sheltered card and dice games were modified to allow horse betting and new places opened that were designed specifically for horseplayers. Pools were sold in these haunts in the same manner as they were sold at the racetrack, so naturally these places came to be called poolrooms. Poolroom keepers, however, were partial to "turf exchange," a term of British origin that carried a more dignified coloration. The New York Turf Exchange, the formal name of the house commonly identified as Kelly and Bliss, sold auction pools on the big races in England, popular items in a day when many of the residents of

New York City were immigrants from the British Isles, where betting the races was a popular working-class diversion. (The label "poolroom" obscured the fact that the big operators derived most of their income from brokering man-to-man bets. They held the stakes and deducted a commission from the winner's proceeds as payment for their services.)

In the poolrooms, one could wager on various kinds of competitions. The annual Harvard-Yale rowing race was a big betting event. Sailing regattas were popular, as were international rifle-shooting contests, high-stakes billiards matches, and long-distance foot races. But nothing attracted as much action as an election, in particular a presidential election. The most highly publicized horse race was a minnow by comparison.

Important elections spawned a spate of unconventional propositions. Races with a virtual shoo-in were infused with intrigue by the expedient of a handicap; to be considered the winner for betting purposes, the winner had to out-distance his opponent by exceeding a specified minimum number of votes. Combination pools were grafted to presidential elections, marking the first heavy use of these instruments. The pools were formed by bunching races that were judged to be toss-ups into a single entity, typically a group of four. As in a parlay, a bettor needed to select all of the winning candidates or the bet was lost. The exact payoff for each of the possible combinations couldn't be determined until all the bets were in, as this was a pari-mutuel setup. In some places, the presidential race was coupled with the gubernatorial race, creating a betting proposition with four possible outcomes. Poolrooms always stayed open late on election days. As the returns dribbled in on the ticker, there was considerable hedging of wagers. (In hedging, a bettor effectively buys insurance by wagering opposite his initial wager. He sacrifices a percentage of his potential winnings to eliminate the possibility of losing it all.)

Poolroom activity was a recurrent theme in news stories surrounding the presidential election of 1876. The race between New York governor Samuel J. Tilden, an anti-Tammany Democrat and Ohio governor Rutherford B. Hayes, the Republican standard-bearer, left bet-takers in an awkward position. Tilden won 51.5 percent of the popular vote, but twenty disputed electoral votes put the outcome in limbo. The stalemate, lasting nearly four months, wasn't broken until March 2, 1877, the Friday before Inauguration Day, when concessions were made that led a congressional commission to award the disputed votes to Hayes, sending him off to the White House.

In New York, there were several extraordinarily large bets on Tilden, who closed a slight favorite. But there were suspicions that these bets weren't genuine. It was thought that the men making them were friends of Tilden throwing chum on the water in hopes of inducing voters without a firm conviction to follow the smart money. The perpetrators then supposedly hedged their bets with multiple wagers on Hayes that were too small to attract notice. The fact that most of the large bets were made at Morrissey's place added fuel to the scuttlebutt, as Morrissey, who accompanied Tilden to the Democratic National Convention in St. Louis, was a Tilden man. A reporter estimated that $400,000 was wagered on the 1876 presidential election in his room alone.[1]

The stories about the betting in family newspapers were precisely what the poolroom operators didn't need. And more unwelcome attention came their way when Morrissey, in exasperation, declared all bets off. His decision, reached thirty-four days after the election, had a domino effect as other bet takers did likewise; they were waiting for Senator Morrissey to make the first move.

While many agreed that this was the proper course of action, Morrissey was castigated for imposing a handling fee, deducting 2 percent from each of the wagers he was holding (perhaps the derivation of the expression "dirty pool"). Reporters wrote that this was contrary to the rules of gambling, but there were no formal rules addressing this exigency and there was actually a precedent for it, a precedent rooted in prizefighting, ironically the sport that was John Morrissey's bootstrap to high finance. Prizefights were constantly ending in controversy, leading referees to declare all bets off, and some poolroom operators had taken to holding back a small commission when returning nullified wagers to compensate for their time and trouble.

Some of the election bets had come in early and were presumably parked in an interest-bearing account. Imposing a levy on these holdings was held to be especially unfair, amounting to double-dipping. News reports were scathing. "There has been a growing impression that the pool business . . . was little better than swindling, an impression which the events of the past few days has greatly strengthened," said a *New York Times* writer.[2] His counterpart at the *Tribune* condemned Morrissey's conduct, but shed no tears for the bettors, feeling they debased the democratic ideal by reducing a presidential election to a gambling proposition. Morrissey's decision to declare all bets off, he quipped, "amounts to a declaration that nobody has been elected to the Presidency; and a pretty (sad) condition we shall be in, if it be so."[3]

At the next session of the state legislature, several bills were introduced to outlaw pool selling. The lawmakers chose the bill with the widest scope. It prohibited pool selling everywhere, on and off the track. The larger poolroom concerns in New York City, Morrissey's included, shifted their operations to New Jersey, most setting up shop in Hoboken, a short hop by ferry from several points in Manhattan. In the Garden State, it was illegal to keep a gambling house, but the law wasn't enforced.

Safe havens didn't remain safe indefinitely, so the uprooting and relocation of poolrooms and other types of gambling houses was an exertion that would be repeated over and over again. In 1881, a crackdown on poolrooms in lower Manhattan sent operators scurrying across the East River to Long Island City, where they resumed operations in buildings close by the Hunter's Point ferry landing. The spur for this diaspora was a letter to the mayor that was published in the *New York Times*. The writer, Arthur Briesen, an attorney, implored the mayor to clean up a stretch of Barclay Street near Broadway that was honeycombed with poolrooms: "Ladies on their way to and from the Hoboken ferry avoid the street because of the hundreds of gamblers, loafers, and drunkards who crowd the sidewalks opposite the poolrooms," he wrote, noting that the situation was hurting legitimate businesses in the neighborhood.[4] The letter touched a nerve with Mayor William Grace who had been elected on a reform ticket. Within a few days after it was published, the Barclay Street rooms were dark.

The poolroom had then evolved to where it was more than just a place to make a bet; it was a place where a man could kill a few hours betting the races and kibitzing with men of a similar bent. This was the product of a revolutionary technology, the telegraph, and the corollary device that it spawned, the "ticker."

Prior to the telegraph, the time it took to disseminate news was a function of distance. The telegraph—hailed as the greatest advancement in mass communication since the invention of the printing press—made it possible to get race results from faraway tracks in a matter of minutes. The ticker, which appeared in 1867, displayed reams of horse racing information and official race results on a rolling strip of paper. In time, poolroom operators hired men to recreate the races from the ticker, an occupation ideally suited to an out-of-work actor. The best of them injected drama into their race calls and fabricated information that potted the races against a more vivid backdrop. Running commentaries of races were provided in poolrooms roughly fifty years before they became standard at racetracks. Gambling historian David G. Schwartz notes that poolrooms were likely the first places to offer live entertainment originating from a remote location.[5] Descriptions of races, initially hollered into a megaphone, were eventually piped into multiple poolrooms simultaneously, transmitted over a loudspeaker, an early adaptation of closed-circuit technology.

With the telegraph, news stories of general interest arrived not only faster but at more frequent intervals. This encouraged the growth of afternoon papers, and of evening editions of morning papers, many of which were driven by their sports coverage. With few exceptions, all major sporting events were contested outdoors in the sunlight, enabling a man to grab a late edition paper on his way home from work and digest the day's results before he sat down to supper. The expanded coverage, coupled with the rise in literacy, enhanced the popularity of horse racing and other spectator sports and indirectly brought more business to the poolrooms.

Horse racing on a high plane was then expanding into areas that experienced mild winters, notably southern Louisiana and coastal California, a boon to poolroom operators who could now keep their doors open nearly year-round. And inevitably it heightened the backlash. Reformers were more tolerant of gambling when it was cubby-holed into short periods of time bounded by strict parameters. This was consistent with the tradition in some western societies of holding annual festivals during which citizens were allowed to blow off steam, celebrating in ways that bent social norms.

Poolrooms were convenient. They accommodated bettors that lacked the time or the resources to visit the track. They accommodated workers on lunch breaks. During periods when there was little fear of police harassment, the operators competed openly for customers, running ads in racing publications and employing sidewalk hawkers to steer in passersby. Uniformed policemen were sometimes seen assisting poolroom owners in keeping an orderly house.[6]

An even greater level of convenience was provided by runners. Enterprising young men, some working independently but most in the service of poolrooms, established routes, much like milkmen and ice men, taking bets in office buildings, factories, hotels, billiard parlors, bowling alleys, and so on. Their operations were called *handbooks*. The term, which was first ascribed to freelance racetrack bookmakers, evolved into a catch-all term that, in general, referenced a person or place at the bottom rung of the bookmaking hierarchy. If someone were to say "there's a handbook over on Second Avenue," he may have in mind an actual person, a curbstone bookmaker, but more than likely he was referencing a place that accepted wagers on the sly, perhaps a barber shop, a cigar store, the concierge desk of a hotel, or a street-corner newsstand—a place where taking bets was not the primary business or ostensibly not the primary business. Poolrooms accommodated men with leisure time. A handbook accommodated men at work or men on the go.[7]

One of the more moderate arguments against poolrooms was that they engendered inefficiency in the workplace, fostering an underproductive society. A man contemplating a bet was distracted from his labors. But a more cutting argument was that they were gateways to a life of dissipation. "[Poolrooms] are a demoralizing influence upon the young and the weak, for whom they become most dangerous schools of vice and crime," said an editorial writer, echoing a widely shared opinion. A *New York Tribune* writer claimed that cases of destitution, beggary, and dishonesty were a thousand times more prevalent among poolroom habitués than among those that confined their betting to the racetrack.[8]

Betting the races would come to be seen as an old man's game—wags say the median age of today's died-in-the-wool horseplayer is deceased—but this wasn't true in the early years. Indeed, many reformers regarded off-track betting as the most pernicious form of gambling because of its hold upon the young. "The faces of the young, so many of them beardless, showed that they were advancing fast in the downward career," said a reporter after visiting a crowded New York poolroom in 1880. The young men were spiraling, he said, to "the lowest depths of degradation which marks a gambler's life." A reporter visiting a crowded Chicago poolroom in 1890 guessed that half the patrons were no older than nineteen.[9]

During the heyday of Tammany Hall, periodic drives to shut down New York poolrooms were stifled by an uncooperative enforcement detail. The police department was then governed by a panel of six commissioners. The commissioners whined that they got little support from precinct captains, the precinct captains, in turn, faulted unnamed insubordinates, and policemen at all levels in the chain-of-command averred that arresting pool sellers was an exercise in futility because the magistrates were disinclined to mete out any punishment beyond a slap on the wrist. Corruption was pervasive, energizing anti-poolroom do-gooders who would eventually widen their crusade to shutting down the racetracks.

In the bigger cities, some poolroom operators established separate rooms for women. Reformers were especially outraged by these accommodations. There was a general feeling that women were more vulnerable to losing their money because they were more inclined to base their picks on superstitions. "To chronicle all of their idiosyncrasies," said a turf writer, "would be a task of vast magnitude." A Chicago clergyman, writing in 1895, claimed that women traveling alone to a racetrack or a poolroom often stopped along the way to consult with a fortune teller. [10]

Campaigns to shut down the poolrooms eventually focused on shutting down their information providers. Reformers zeroed in on the Western Union Telegraph Company, which had acquired a national poolroom monopoly. Indeed, poolrooms were the backbone of their business.

A Western Union command post at a racetrack was no penny-ante operation. A network of employees worked in close harmony under harsh time constraints. One man would gather up the particulars essential for mapping out the race—scratches, post positions, jockeys, weights, etc.—and keep abreast of any changes. Another would monitor the activity of the big bookmakers in the betting ring to keep abreast of fluctuations in the odds. They were updated at intervals. The snapshots were called quotations. Yet another man would chart the race so that it could be recreated. Assisting them were assorted runners and a supervisor and at the hub, the linchpin of it all, the telegrapher who would punch the information into the system and send it out across the wire.

The cost of labor was high, but a larger expense was the "privilege" fee. Western Union paid some racetracks more than $1,000 a week for the right to keep an office on the premises. But the profits were yet enormous. In 1890, the New York office of Western Union reportedly took in $700,000 (roughly $18 million in 2015 dollars) from poolrooms and other places that catered to the sporting crowd.[11] Each subscriber paid a fee that varied according to how many tracks were purchased.

Periodically the privilege fee became a bone of contention. A stand-off at Gravesend in 1891, when Western Union balked at a rate increase, resulted in one of the more absurd cat-and-mouse games in the annals of gambling.

Banished from the track, Western Union leased a room in a nearby building and set up a relay team. Workers inside the track scrawled notes on slips of paper that were inserted into hollow wooden balls that were hurled over the fence to confederates waiting on the outside. This arrangement proved inadequate. Although some of the inside men were dressed as stable boys to mask the true nature of their task, the guards weren't fooled and were quick to evict them. One of the wooden missiles was errant. A man walking on the street was hit on the head and suffered a concussion.[12]

The standoff persisted into the fall meet. This time, Western Union perched a man on a wooden tower erected just outside the grounds. Coworkers inside the fence communicated with him using an elaborate system of semaphores based on the Morse alphabet. But once again the security guards were quick to spoil the soup. A young woman took to signaling the man in the tower from an open window in the ladies room, but she eventually came out, whereupon the security guards took her into custody and had the window fastened shut.

A rumor circulated that Western Union planned to conduct their surveillance from a hot-air balloon. Word came from the track that a team of sharpshooters would be hired to shoot it down. In this chaotic environment, mistakes were inevitable and the poolrooms were often fed wrong information. On one occasion, the designated winner of a race was actually the horse that finished last. Bets were settled before the mistake was discovered. In time, the telegraph company and the racetrack reached a truce and the poolroom operators had one less thing to worry about, but another round of adversity was always just around the corner.[13]

Prior to 1894, when the last of the original Bell patents expired, the telephone was found almost exclusively in places of business and in the homes of the business elite. In short order, it became a common appliance. The instrument would fundamentally change the bookmaking business. It increased the efficiency of hedging, allowing poolroom operators to lay off wagers on over-bet horses closer to post time and across a broader landscape. Interstate alliances evolved. It spurred consolidations. The smaller rooms, where the costs associated with telegraphy were a major burden, were swallowed up and became branch offices that took their information via the telephone from a central clearinghouse. And, of course, the telephone encouraged more betting by making it more convenient. A man with good credit could wager from his home or his workplace.

But telegraph service was still essential; a poolroom where bettors gathered to while away an afternoon was rudderless without it. Accurate information was vital, and with the telegraph there were fewer errors in conveying a large body of data. Equally important, information supplied by a ticker provided a written record of the event that was bet on.

In New York City, Western Union came under great scrutiny following the elections of 1901. Columbia University president Seth Low won the mayor's race on an anti-Tammany platform and a new district attorney, William Travers Jerome, was swept into office with him. Western Union would be forced to relinquish their race wire monopoly, a development with enormous ramifications.

5

NEW YORK'S
RACETRACK-BUILDING BOOM

The years 1879–1907 witnessed the opening of eight thoroughbred tracks in metropolitan New York (exclusive of New Jersey). The first three emerged on Coney Island, a barrier island separated from the main body of Brooklyn by a narrow strand of water. Brooklyn was then an independent city, America's third-largest in 1880, ranking between Philadelphia and Chicago. Thought to have more houses of Christian worship per capita than any other major city, it was informally known as the City of Churches. Coney Island, smeared with the catchphrase Sodom by the Sea, was loosely appended to it but a world apart.

Brighton Beach, the first of the Coney Island racetracks, was built by William Engeman. A ship's carpenter by trade, Engeman made his first fortune selling pack mules to the Union army. In 1873, he acquired two hundred acres of oceanfront property in a section of Coney Island that would take the name Brighton Beach. He put up a hotel, the cornerstone of a compound that would include the area's first pier, a commodious bathing pavilion, and then the racetrack.

The Manhattan Beach Hotel, the first of Coney Island's luxury hotels, opened in 1877, sparking a building boom that turned the barrier island into America's national summer playground, a development hastened by the consolidation and expansion of railroad lines. The seminal moment occurred on September 24, 1883, when cable cars began regular service across the Brooklyn Bridge. A project that consumed more than two decades, the bridge was considered one of the great wonders of the world.

Brighton Beach racetrack, built in only six weeks, opened on June 28, 1879. The first card of what would be a thirty-four-day meet consisted of only three events, one of which was a steeplechase. The spectators numbered only a few thousand, but the races were soon drawing big crowds. On July 4, 1881, more than twenty thousand turned up, undeterred by intermittent showers. The crowd was so thick around the pool sellers and the pari-mutuel machines that hundreds were unable to place their bets.[1] In 1884, the peak year, the racing meet lasted 125 days, and the money wagered was thought to be higher than at all the other racetracks in the country combined.

Brighton Beach, notes sports historian Steven A. Riess, was America's first successful *proprietary* racetrack. The track wasn't intended as a semi-exclusive playground for the social elite and didn't operate under a charter that paid homage to improving the breed; William Engeman built it to make money and would have quickly found some other use for the land if it had failed to deliver a profit. The track was open only five years when Engeman died of Bright's disease. His brother George Engeman and William's son of the same name inherited the operation, toning down the number of racing days to gain favor with the Jockey Club. In 1887, the Engemans opened a sister track in Clifton, New Jersey.

William Engeman Sr. was influenced by the example of Long Branch, New Jersey, the outline of which was visible from parts of Coney Island on a clear day. Prior to the Civil War, Long Branch, a seaside community on the North Jersey Shore, was a place where a traveler might stop to eat some fish. The transition of Long Branch into a summer resort accelerated with the opening of Monmouth Park in 1870, and within a few years Long Branch was touted as "the Brighton of America," a reference to the beach town in England that had become a popular summer retreat for pleasure seekers from London. Engeman purloined the evocation. The territory where he planted his complex was christened Brighton Beach in 1878.[2]

Leonard Jerome and his friends were also bullish on Coney Island. For all its grandeur, Jerome Park was poorly situated for holding meets during the hottest months of the year. By contrast, Coney Island with its balmy ocean breezes was ideal. The racing enthusiasts in Jerome's circle included many traction magnates who were keenly aware that visitor volume would increase dramatically once the bridge was completed and wanted in before property values soared.

In 1879, the newly constituted Coney Island Jockey Club, of which Leonard Jerome was president, acquired a barren piece of land on the Coney Island mainland, a 112-acre tract that sat between the bay and the little village of Sheepshead. The track they built upon it, taking the name Sheepshead Bay, opened on June 19, 1880. The plant soon reflected Jerome's sensibility, boasting well-manicured lawns, lovely flower gardens, big shade trees, good restaurants, and a music pavilion. Barely a year after its opening, a reporter wrote that the track at Saratoga looked stale by comparison.[3]

In the late summer of 1886, a third Coney Island racetrack opened in the township of Gravesend, taking that name. For rail passengers, it was the most accessible track of the three. The spur of an elevated railroad stopped directly within the facility, funneling passengers into a walkway that led directly to the grandstand. The home of the Preakness Stakes from 1894 to 1908, Gravesend was a proprietary track like Brighton Beach—"everyone was welcome so long as he kept reasonably sober, and (kept) his hands in his own pockets," noted turf historian Charles Palmer—but a cut above, offering better racing in a more upscale racing plant.[4]

Gravesend's principal owners, brothers Michael and Philip Dwyer, were second-generation butchers who built a Brooklyn meat market into a large wholesale operation. Men of different temperament, they were frequently at loggerheads. Michael Dwyer's big bets were legendary. He reportedly wagered $135,000 to win $100,000 on the 1892 presidential election, the largest-winning wager on Grover Cleveland. Philip rarely bet more than $100. Their racing stable, which consistently ranked at or near the top in annual earnings, consisted of very few horses purchased as yearlings; their preference was for ready-made racing stock that could pay immediate dividends. An early acquisition, a horse named Hindoo, was a great coup. Purchased as a two-year-old, Hindoo won eighteen straight races, including the 1881 Kentucky Derby.

The Dwyer brothers picked a bad year to open a racetrack. Coney Island political boss John Y. McKane—his various titles included chief of police—was under pressure to stifle racetrack gambling and there were sporadic crackdowns on open betting to mollify the reformers. But Gravesend, which opened with sixty authorized bookmakers on the premises, weathered the storm and became an equal cohort in what became a Coney Island triumvirate.

During the early years, Gravesend's summer meet ran concurrently with the Sheepshead Bay summer meet, but on alternate days. Gravesend had Mondays, Wednesdays, and Fridays; Sheepshead ran Tuesdays, Thursdays, and Saturdays. Coney Island was never more fashionable. The three big races at Sheepshead Bay—the Suburban, the Futurity, and the Realization Stakes—and the richest race at Gravesend, the Brooklyn Handicap, attracted scads of famous people, so many that run-of-the-mill celebrities got lost in the crowd.

The food courts at Sheepshead Bay complemented the rich accouterments. At the inaugural running of the Futurity Stakes in 1888, patrons consumed twelve hundred pounds of lobster and emptied nearly four hundred cases of champagne.[5] After the races, if insufficiently sated, you could walk to one of several five-star restaurants. But there was a seamy underbelly to Coney Island. After dark, portions of the seaside community morphed into an annex of New York's Bowery, with all its attendant vices.

In 1889, John A. Morris opened a racetrack two miles east of Jerome Park. The facility, named Morris Park, wasn't as picturesque as Jerome Park or Sheepshead Bay, but it was larger and better equipped. Reporters were bowled over by the restrooms, as nice as those found in the fanciest hotels, and took note of the fair prices at the concession stands; a glass of beer was only a nickel. The betting ring was situated under the grandstand. The pari-mutuel machines, electrically powered, were off in a separate area. They were configured to take "win" and "place" bets in amounts as small as $2, a departure from the $5 norm.

John A. Morris inherited his love of horse racing from his father, Francis Morris, who had the distinction of owning the filly Ruthless, the winner of the first Belmont Stakes, run during the inaugural meet at Jerome Park. Francis Morris was one of the largest landowners in Texas, but his wealth came to pale beside that of his Harvard-educated son, who raked in a fortune as the largest individual stockholder in the Louisiana Lottery Company.

Chartered in 1866, the lottery was promoted as the solution to freeing Louisiana from the choke-hold of Civil War debt. Special provisions were made for disabled veterans and for the widows and orphans of soldiers killed on the battlefield. Lottery tickets were sold to ticket brokers at a discount, giving the Louisiana Lottery a national distribution network. The aggregate of monthly and semi-annual drawings reached an annual gross of $28 million with more than 90 percent coming from out of state. With stock dividends amounting to 80 percent in an average year, John A. Morris acquired so much loot that the members of the royal family of Monaco were said to be minimum-wage workers by comparison. He manifested that wealth in the park that bore his name.[6]

During the early days of Morris Park, races were sometimes held on days when there was racing "down the block" at Jerome Park. When dates conflicted, Leonard Jerome's loyalty was to the newcomer. This odd situation owed to two factors. A financial reversal had compelled him to divest his stock in the Villa Park Improvement Association and he could see that Jerome Park's days were numbered. The city coveted the site for a reservoir. The deal was finally sealed in 1894 and the glory that was Jerome Park was submerged under a lake of water. In his end days, before he retired to England in poor health, Leonard Jerome served as the president of the racing association that ran Morris Park. His former partners bore him no malice. Some joined him in the new venture.

John A. Morris and his son John Hennen Morris were instrumental in the restructuring of the Jockey Club. The bylaws of the new organization achieved the rule of law in 1894 when the newly formed New York State Racing Commission ordained the Jockey Club the sport's governing body. While the ordination carried no legal sway outside New York, the Jockey Club regulated racing up and down the Eastern Seaboard. The following year, John A. Morris suffered a fatal stroke at the family ranch in Texas.

Morris Park was barely three years old when plans were laid for a racetrack in Queens, which was then an independent county (Queens was swept into the city of New York along with Brooklyn in 1898). The Queens County Jockey Club, chartered in 1892, built their facility, named Aqueduct Park, near a reservoir in the Ozone Park neighborhood on the shores of Jamaica Bay. Little fanfare attended the opening on September 27, 1894, but the track was destined to become one of the most important in the country.

Nine years after the opening of Aqueduct, another racetrack opened in Queens. The guiding spirits behind Jamaica Racetrack were Tammany chieftains Timothy "Big Tim" Sullivan and Patrick H. McCarren and prominent Long Island land developer William H. Reynolds, a former state senator. The leading stockholder, Eugene D. Wood, was an Albany lobbyist who amassed a fortune investing in utility companies. (The Wood Memorial, one of America's most prestigious races, is named for him.)

Jamaica was even less well appointed than unpretentious Aqueduct, but it acquired a loyal core of patrons. In its early years, it was often called "the people's track." Big Tim Sullivan set the tone. A former New York State senator and active U.S. congressman (1903–1906), the charismatic Sullivan was practically a king in his densely populated district, an area that included the polyglot Lower East Side, but he never lost the common touch. At the races, Big Tim customarily shunned his box in the clubhouse to sit with the "regular folks" in the cheap seats. (According to the *New York Tribune*, seventy thousand people lined the sidewalk for Sullivan's funeral procession in 1913. The mourners at his funeral mass included "United States Senators and Representatives in Congress, prize fighters, justices of the Supreme Court, clergymen, gangsters, thugs, saloonkeepers, lawyers . . . good women and otherwise.")[7]

Belmont Park arrived in 1905. The track, which straddled the border where Queens abutted the town of Elmont in Nassau County, Long Island, was owned and operated by the Westchester Racing Association, which had leased Morris Park from the heirs of John A. Morris. Belmont Park would be the last major thoroughbred track built in metropolitan New York, marking the end of a building boom that birthed eight racetracks in a span of only twenty-six years. Amplifying the hubbub, several short-lived "bush tracks" bobbed up within an easy commute of New York in northern New Jersey in the late 1880s.

Belmont Park stood as a testament to the late August Belmont and his son of the same name. The middle boy of August Belmont's three sons, August II (he was never referenced as August Belmont *Jr.* in his lifetime) was the successor to his father as the head of the family banking house and a shrewd businessman in his own right. A company in which he held a big interest built New York City's first subway and acquired a near-monopoly over rapid transit in Manhattan. And to an even greater degree than his father, he came to be lauded as a great patron of the turf. He was named the first president of the Jockey Club, making him the de facto head of racing in New York and other places where the organization held sway.

Belmont Park replaced Morris Park, which lay fallow after the 1904 fall meet and was reborn as a short-lived auto-racing oval before developers subdivided the property into a housing tract. During the final years of thoroughbred racing at Morris Park, racetracks lost favor with New York's society doyens. When the Westchester Polo Club chose to make Newport, Rhode Island, its permanent home, Newport became the place to be. The grand opening of Belmont Park on Thursday, May 4, 1905, reanimated the gleam. The major dailies—the *Times, Herald, Tribune, Sun, Post, World,* and *Telegram*—gave the event big play. Most had three reporters covering the event: a feature writer, a racing correspondent, and a society reporter.

The grand opening of Belmont Park was one of the last great spectacles of the Gilded Age. High society arrived in a stammering procession of carriages and luxury automobiles. The convergence near the entrance produced Long Island's first recorded traffic jam, and many of the vehicles wound up being left outside the track. The starting time of the first race was pushed back thirty minutes to accommodate late arrivals. Three bands entertained the crowd during the wait.

In the throng, more than forty thousand, there was a good smattering of European blue bloods and those that mimicked their Brahmin ways. Tall hats and frock coats were the norm for the men that gathered in the clubhouse. The women they squired wore ensembles "manifestly fresh from Paris."[8] During the card, a stiff wind ignited roiling dust storms, but the races were highly entertaining, mitigating the unpleasantness. The feature race, the Metropolitan Handicap, ended in a dead heat between 4/5 favorite Sysonby and lightly regarded Race King. "Their names will endure, and the present generation of turf folk will cherish the picture they made as they fought it out side by side in that desperate struggle as one of the most valuable reminiscences in their entire sporting repertory," read a report on the front page of the next day's *Tribune*.[9]

The sheer size of Belmont Park, which sat on 640 acres, was astonishing. The semi-circular betting ring could accommodate two hundred bookmakers. One hundred eighty were in action on opening day. A reporter described the scene inside the betting enclosure as a seething pandemonium.[10]

Twenty-seven months after the opening of Belmont Park, horseplayers in metropolitan New York had yet another thoroughbred track vying for their patronage. Originally a harness racing facility, the Empire City racetrack, sitting on the border of the Westchester County towns of Yonkers and Mount Vernon, opened for thoroughbred racing on August 10, 1907. The track's principal owner, grocery magnate James Butler, launched the twenty-three-day meet in defiance of the racing commission, which in theory operated independently of the Jockey Club but in reality was little more than an extension of it. Under the bylaws of the Percy-Gray law, the commission could turn down a license seeker if his proposal was deemed not in the best interest of the established order. Butler refused to knuckle under and the courts granted him an injunction while the case was under appeal.

Butler ran his inaugural meet on a shoestring. It could not be otherwise, as he had struggled to stave off bankruptcy with poorly attended harness and automobile races while awaiting a favorable legal outcome in his long-running battle with the racing trust. His detractors thought that his thoroughbred meet had little chance of turning a profit, but twenty thousand people were in the house for opening day and the meet was so successful that there was a nice cache left over for capital improvements. After a wobbly start, the layers in the betting ring also did well. Favorites were infrequent visitors to the winners circle, a boon to the bet takers.[11]

In the world of horse racing, gambling was the straw that stirred the drink. But the social climate forced track operators into a difficult balancing act, for gambling was both a lifeline and a hanging rope.

6

BOOKMAKERS AND THEIR MODUS OPERANDI

At Jerome Park, auction pools, pari-mutuel pools, and the bookmakers' ring were separate concessions. The men that ran them were independent contractors. Management maintained an air of detachment. This was prudent for legal purposes.

The track took a percentage of the action from auction pools and pari-mutuel pools; the lessees received a sub-percentage. Bookmaking was trickier. The action in the ring was helter-skelter, the play impossible to measure, and so the lessee was dunned a flat rate. He sublet the booths in the enclosure, reserving one or more for his own use.

NEW YORK BOOKMAKING AND THE LAW

There was no specific reference to bookmaking in the New York Penal Code, but a law passed in 1851 made gambling a misdemeanor and bookmaking violated the spirit of it. The Ives Pool law, which took effect on May 25, 1887, removed the cloud.

The Ives Pool Law

Named for a Saratoga assemblyman, the Ives Pool law legalized betting within the confines of a race course on races run that day on that particular course. The law did not overturn the anti-betting statute in the New York Penal Code but merely suspended it when certain conditions were met. Similar laws passed in Missouri and Tennessee were called breeder's laws. The sponsors chose the name to suggest that racetrack gambling played an important role in shoring up agriculture and military preparedness.

The Ives law hatched unlikely bedfellows. Reformers wanted gambling shut down everywhere. The poolroom men, chafing at the double standard, joined them in fighting to have the law repealed. Their attorneys challenged the law on the grounds that it discriminated against citizens in the lower income brackets, violating the equal protection clause of the Fourteenth Amendment. "So long as the opulent are permitted to gamble at Morris Park, I don't see why other citizens should not be permitted to lay odds in Manhattan," said Benjamin Steinhardt, the attorney for poolroom keeper Peter De Lacy, a relentless opponent of the Ives law.[1]

The Ives law was ruled unconstitutional in 1893. Racetrack operators secured an injunction that kept the law in place through the end of the racing season and then set their lawyers to work drafting a new law that they—and hopefully their enemies—could live with. The upshot was the Percy-Gray law, which fomented an even bigger backlash than the law that it replaced.

The Percy-Gray Law

Approved on May 22, 1895, the Percy-Gray law affirmed that betting was lawful in the enclosures of state-sanctioned racetracks with the proviso that no tokens or memoranda be displayed. This meant that the slates on which the odds were posted had to go and that a bookie could not keep a ledger in full view of those hovering about him. Additionally, the tracks were required to post "no betting" signs and furnish patrolmen to deter would-be violators.

The directives accomplished nothing. A guard would look the other way as bets were made. The "no-betting" sign posted where the bookmakers congregated served as a beacon to strangers in search of a place to make wagers. But the signs served an important purpose, absolving racetrack operators of any liability for allowing gambling on their premises. The Percy-Gray law also established a state racing commission, elongated the racing calendar, forbade night racing and racing during the winter months, and boosted the tax on racing associations by charging a 5 percent tax on gross receipts—including programs, refreshments, and so on—whereas previously the tariff applied only to admission tickets. The tax money went to the operators of agricultural fairs to be used as premiums for agricultural and mechanical improvements.

What made the Percy-Gray law such a cunning deception was a proviso that said a man recording a bet was guilty of a felony *except when another penalty was provided by law*. In the New York Penal Code, it was written that a bet taker was to "forfeit the value of any money or property so wagered . . . to be recovered in a civil action by the person making the bet." In layman's terms, a man could sue his bookie to recover a lost wager. As there was little chance of this happening—for an ordinary bettor, the cost of litigation would exceed the refund—racetrack bookmakers, assuming they were relatively discreet, were in the clear. There was scant chance that they would be summoned to appear as defendants in a court of law. As for poolroom operators, a companion bill passed the same day, the Wilds bill, reaffirmed the illegality of off-track betting.

The curious new law, which allowed bookmaking but not tangible evidence of it, begat the sham called *oral betting*. The chalkboards came down, but bettors were supplied with postcard-size pasteboards that displayed the opening odds. When a patron entered the betting enclosure, he was given a numbered badge that he wore on his lapel or tied to a buttonhole of his shirt. When he made a bet, his badge number and the details of the wager were furtively recorded by the bookmaker's clerk. He was encouraged to leave his business card with his wager written down on the back of it to reduce the likelihood of a misunderstanding. The badge served as his identification when it was time to square accounts. The settlement was customarily done outside the racetrack at the conclusion of the last race. Bookmakers took to returning the proceeds of winning wagers in a small brown envelope.

The drawbacks were manifest. Since no receipts were given, bettors and bookmakers were on the honor system, an encouragement to welshing. Bookies compensated by offering less generous odds, which translated into writing less business. Bet takers took to dealing only with men that they knew to be trustworthy or men recommended to them by a trusted third party. That eroded the patronage of casual fans. Delaying payouts until after the final race depressed the churn and imposed a hardship on racegoers who had to leave early, perhaps because of an important dinner engagement. Tourists were less likely to build a day of racing into their itinerary.

The degree to which bookmakers conformed to the stricture varied according to the pressure to conform. When enforcement was lax, it was business as usual. Some bookmakers were less submissive than others, more willing to tempt fate by conducting their affairs openly.

BOOKMAKING OPERATIONS

During the early days of racing, the bookmakers operated within an open-air enclosure marked off by a short fence. Enclosures of later vintage were usually covered with a roof but open on all sides. These were far more commodious than the original compound at Jerome Park. (At various places, the bookmaking pitch was underneath the grandstand or in the infield, accessible via a tunnel.)

Within the betting enclosure, each bookmaker had a booth, a compartment perhaps six feet wide and eight feet deep. In the booth, the bookmaker stood on a platform so that he could look over the crowd and see what his neighbors were up to. A sign on the railing displayed his name or the name of the firm that he represented. The items that he was selling and their prices, namely the names of the horses entered in the next race and their current odds, were displayed on a blackboard attached to a pole.

At a minimum, a racetrack bookmaker of the first order operated with three assistants—a clerk who took money and gave out receipts (slips of paper that were color coded for each race, on which the bet was recorded in indelible ink); a man to record each transaction, called a sheet writer; and a runner whose job it was to keep him abreast of any significant shift in the odds. A bookmaker invited trouble if he left his prices unruffled to where they deviated substantially from the consensus. And besides, why let a man get down on a horse at 12/1 if one's competitors were less generous and the fellow would have been quite content with getting just 10/1?

The sheet writer worked with a sheet of ruled paper roughly the size of an unfolded newspaper. He entered each bet and kept a running tally so that his boss could see at a glance the best- and worst-case scenarios.

A good sheet writer could make fast mathematical calculations in his head. A good runner was good at sniffing out the source of the money that was driving down the odds on a particular horse. It was especially important to stay in line if big bets were being spread around the ring by representatives of a man known for having a sharp opinion. During the course of a race day, a runner might also act as a "lay-off" man, wagering his employer's money on over-bet horses as a means of achieving a better-balanced book, but as a rule the men entrusted with this responsibility performed no other tasks. The lay-off men, and men empowered to move money for big bettors, were called betting commissioners.

The betting commissioner for high roller John A. Drake was described as a burly colored man who glided around the ring "as if athletics had been part of his early training."[2] Others were conspicuously less nimble: "In their eagerness to keep their employers well informed, [the runners] rush about the ring like football players on the gridiron, knocking people down in their mad dashes." A turf writer, likening the runners to catapults, implored the authorities to "curtail their bumptiousness."[3]

Bookmakers with high limits and those that opened for business ahead of the herd kept more workers on their payrolls. In the case of the latter, the bookie required the services of an odds consultant. It was also prudent to employ a spy, a person snooping about the back lots with his antennae always attuned to signs of chicanery. It was widely assumed that these spies were not above arranging a betting coup, either on behalf of a bookmaker or as a henchman for a betting syndicate.

AMERICA'S FIRST ODDSMAKER

America's leading sports weekly, the *Spirit of the Times*, estimated that $500,000 changed hands when Peytona met Fashion in their great race in 1845. The victorious Peytona closed as the favorite, with most of the late bets sealed at odds of 10/7. A more popular wager was on the time of the opening heat. Races fashioned into a race against the clock were the first "over/under" propositions in sports gambling.

The great antebellum match races predated the advent of oddsmakers. Individuals bet man-to-man, haggling over the terms of the wager until an accord was reached. The stakes were often consigned to a third party. In time, stakes holders began to solicit bets, with no guarantee of a matching bet on the other side—pivotal moments in the evolution of bookmaking.

James Kelly, the cofounder of the Kelly and Bliss firm in New York, is credited with developing America's first *winter books*, a form of antepost betting that originated in England. In these propositions, odds are posted on all the horses nominated for a big race months in advance of the actual race. The list of nominees is long, making for juicy odds, but the great majority of the horses on the list will be waylaid by intervening developments and a man betting on a horse that doesn't run is out of luck, as all bets are action—that is, no refunds. In an ordinary year, the bet taker's hold is enormous, but one miscalculation can wipe out the profits accumulated over several years. An early example occurred in 1886 when Troubadour, a consensus 5/1 shot at post, won the Suburban Handicap. The horse's owner, Captain Sam Brown of Pittsburgh, locked in his bets six months before the race was run, securing 50/1 odds, and reportedly won $85,000, an amount thought to be the largest windfall on a single race in the history of the American turf to that point in time.[4]

Several big bookmakers formulated their own odds, but most leaned on the expertise of others. The first odds consultant to emerge from the shadow of his employer was Auguste "Tex" Grenet. Born into a prosperous family in San Antonio—his father was the largest retailer of dry goods in southern Texas and owned the territory's finest restaurant—Grenet had been selling his odds for fifty years when A. J. Liebling wrote a lengthy profile of him for the *New Yorker* in 1937.[5]

Grenet was the first person from Texas to attend Manhattan College, a school where the curriculum was steeped in the French Catholic tradition. He was enrolled there when his father died, breaking off his monthly allowance. In need of an income until the estate was settled, he took to playing the horses at Jerome Park. His inherent aptitude for mathematics—he could perform complicated equations in his head—served him well, but he found the ups and downs of a gambler's life unsettling and gravitated toward steadier employment. Dave Johnson, one of the leading bookmakers, hired him as a consultant and eventually other bookies procured his services. His chief client came to be the news agency that distributed his odds to newspapers around the country.

Grenet weaved his odds from many threads. He kept meticulous logs, but was also a keen observer who could detect in the running of a race all sorts of minutia that could not be distilled into past performance charts. A brief stint as a sheet writer was instructive, giving him a greater understanding of the horseplayer's mentality. "You must know your horses and you must know your tracks, but the important thing is to know your mugs," was one of his favorite sayings.

Compiling trustworthy odds for a full card of racing was a time-consuming chore. To lighten his load, Grenet had his own consultants, most prominently a clocker named Ollie Thomas. An African American in an age when African Americans were well represented at all levels in the hierarchy of racetrack workers, Thomas, an ex-Pullman porter, was on the go before sunset each racing day, off to monitor the workouts with the tool of his trade, a dependable stopwatch. There were too many workouts for him to catch them all, but clockers were a close-knit fraternity, sharing information willingly.

Ollie Thomas also had keen powers of observation and a gift for remembering minute details. He was sensitive to a horse's markings and could identify a horse at a distance by its confirmation and its gait. These were important attributes, as trainers were forever sending out false signals. It was common for them to cover a horse's unique leg markings with bandages. (The prizefighting term "under wraps" derived from this practice; a boxer fighting under wraps is holding something back. As in horse racing, the motivation might be to build up the odds on a future go.)

Tex Grenet's odds, cribbed by bookmakers outside his tiny circle of paid subscribers, diffused across the betting ring. In time, he had a competitor, a man named Gene Austin. Some bookmakers utilized both of them. Whenever there was a significant difference of opinion, the odds would be shaded toward the middle ground.

Grenet continued to bet, but his wagers were modest. It was his habit to wander about the bookmaking ring between races. If he found odds on any particular horse that were substantially higher than what he had arrived at, he stepped in and made a play. His behavior was guided by the ethos of the racetrack where a man's opinion was derided as worthless if he lacked the gumption to bet on it. Grenet felt that his role obligated him to make some bets, if only for token amounts. In the act of betting, he nipped any aspersions on his integrity.

COMPETITION AND ALLIANCES

In America, as in England, a pecking order emerged in the betting arena. The bookmakers accorded the highest status were those that were less squeamish about taking a big wager. They were easy to find, as they invariably occupied a choice spot. Then there were the back-line bookies. The tracks always reserved spaces for independent operators, an elastic amount that expanded on holidays when the races were certain to be well patronized. These irregular bet takers drew most of their action from unsophisticated players. The holiday racegoer, said a reporter, was just as willing to accept the shorter odds as the longer, and some were so lacking in mathematics that they couldn't tell the difference.[6]

The irregulars at the back of the back line typically worked without an assistant. They displayed their odds on a slate that hung by a rope around their necks. One couldn't work at this game in New York without the consent of Robert Pinkerton. The grandson of the founder of the famous detective agency, Pinkerton was in charge of security at all the Jockey Club tracks. He also vetted the messenger bettors that plied the grandstand serving unescorted women.

Women weren't permitted to enter the betting ring. The pushing and shoving provided a cover for inappropriate touching ("copping a feel" in the vernacular) and gallantry demanded that women be shielded from the course language overheard there. The restriction endowed the messenger bettors with a captive audience.

Unable to roam about as freely as the men, the women were systematically cheated. The messenger bettors, at least most of them, shaved down the odds that were available in the ring, sometimes in collusion with a shady bookmaker who kicked back a piece of the action. Some of the messengers took liberties by holding some of the bets that they handled. Inevitably, there were occasions when a longshot romped home and the messenger lacked sufficient funds to meet his obligation. Pinkerton would ostracize a proxy caught welshing, but that was of little consolation to a woman whose money was stolen. It was no use complaining to the directors of the racing association that ran the track. They wouldn't intercede, as that would compromise the fiction that they took no cognizance of gambling.[7]

The relationship between bookmakers and track owners was symbiotic, yet often strained. In their public posturing, the owners acted as if the bookies were from a separate universe, but they treated them as tenants and were constantly looking to increase the rent, a daily tariff ostensibly meant to cover the cost of Pinkerton guards and cleanup crews. If the bookies succeeded in making them hold the line, the owners had other ways of dredging more money out of the ring, most obviously by cramming more "tenants" into it. Persistently threatened with higher overhead or the prospect of less business owing to heightened competition, the leading bookies formed alliances. The first alliances fell apart, but an organization founded in 1896 achieved stability and became an effective voice. It was called the Metropolitan Turf Association and its members came to be called the "Mets" (a term that faded into antiquity and was then reborn in 1962 as the nickname of New York's National League baseball team). The initiation fee for members, initially $500, went into an escrow account that served as a bond, protecting bettors from welshing. A man who confined his dealings to MTA bookies had no reason to fear being stiffed.

The MTA staged a wildcat strike at Aqueduct in 1897. Management was left with a motley crew of back-line bookmakers. They were herded into the favorable spots, but moving them into a better neighborhood merely magnified their shortcomings. As was their habit, they offered less generous odds than the men they were replacing and were averse to accepting large wagers. The inept work of the starter, who left the heavily backed favorite at the post in the fourth race, caused more dissatisfaction. When the racegoers left the track on their homeward journey, "disgust was depicted on almost every face."[8]

At the grand opening of Belmont Park in 1905, nearly half the bookmakers, eighty-six in all, belonged to the Metropolitan Turf Association. Occupying the most prominent booths—a rotation system prevented anyone from usurping an especially prized location—they emblazoned their MTA membership with lapel buttons and other insignia that set them apart from the others. The insignia conveyed a message akin to a Better Business Bureau seal of approval.

In the maelstrom of the betting ring, however, disputes were inevitable. Track owners could not openly mediate these disputes and still maintain the façade that the bookies were an independent body, but keeping brouhahas to a minimum was a matter of utmost importance. Protection against welshing addressed one side of the coin, but problems more commonly arose from miscommunications and misunderstandings, and a wrangle born from an honest mistake was just as likely to redound into a public relations crisis.

The superintendent of the betting ring was vested with the power to settle all disputes. No one performed this role as famously as John G. Cavanagh. Orphaned at a young age, Cavanagh had a series of menial racetrack jobs before graduating to this post at Sheepshead Bay in 1894. A self-educated man who collected books about Abraham Lincoln, he went on to work at all the big eastern tracks in a career that consumed parts of five decades.[9]

Cavanagh was the liaison between the track secretary and the bookies. It was his responsibility to keep the bet takers abreast of any adjustments, such as jockey changes and late scratches. But sometimes there was a breakdown in communication and then the bookies and bettors turned to Cavanagh, whose rulings set precedents that stood for many years. Cavanagh couldn't toss a bookie off the course without consulting with the racing stewards, but he was duty-bound to report any unethical behavior and it was his responsibility to enforce whatever sanctions were imposed.

Cavanagh was cozy with the bookmakers but rendered enough decisions against them that his impartiality was seldom questioned. During the days of oral betting, punters sometimes made the mistake of attempting to cash a winning wager at a station other than where they actually made the bet. Cavanagh was known to go out of his way to get things sorted out. Beginning in 1901, he took to arranging the annual pilgrimage to Saratoga. The chartered train that brought the Mets there each August came to be dubbed the Cavanagh Special. The scene at Grand Central Station, the point of departure, was rollicking, and the scene at the Saratoga depot had even more of a holiday feel. The locals welcomed the bookies with a brass band.

On the surface, racetrack bookmakers and track operators were on the same page when it came to the poolrooms. Racetrack operators profited from poolrooms indirectly from the fee imposed on Western

Union and found poolrooms useful in keeping away the rougher element, but poolrooms siphoned away business, and in the operator's perfect world there would be no poolrooms whatsoever. Michael Dwyer's long-running feud with poolroom baron Peter De Lacy exemplified this discord. But in reality things were never that unambiguous. At some racetracks, the man that leased the bookmaking concession was a prominent poolroom keeper. His opportunities weren't limited to racing plants. The betting concession was a source of ancillary revenue for promoters of important prizefights and indoor pedestrian competitions such as those held at Madison Square Garden.

During the early years of the post–Civil War racing revival, on-track bookmaking was of necessity an avocation. There simply weren't enough races to provide steady employment. A poolroom allowed a bookmaker to diversify and stay active during lulls between racing meets. Moreover, a poolroom connection was advantageous to a man operating on the race course. Being a bookie was less risky if one dealt to a broad customer mix; poolrooms attracted more of a longshot-oriented crowd, drawing in punters that leveled out the betting by putting their coin on horses that got little or no play at the track. Some MTA bookmakers had investments in poolrooms and also owned racing stables, a triple conflict of interest that wasn't lost on the enemies of racetrack gambling.

Relations between racetrack operators and bookmakers' alliances were persistently contentious. At various times, the operators were roused to keep the betting ring pure by ostracizing bookmakers known to be in league with local poolroom keepers. These crackdowns were difficult to enforce.

7

TIPSTERS AND TOUTS

In 1888, a reporter covering the races at Monmouth Park was contemptuous of the touts that crossed his path, calling them the most offensive of all the nuisances that one encounters on a race course: "These tipsters haunt the betting ring and in case they ever happen to mention the name of a winner to a man who bets on a race he has a hard time of it until he has crossed the palm of the tout with some of Uncle Sam's greenbacks."[1]

The reporter used the terms "tout" and "tipster" interchangeably, but a few years earlier these terms had different meanings. A tout (the term originated in England) was understood to be a detective who prowled about the inner sanctums of race courses, sniffing out skullduggery, but more generally keeping tabs on the fitness of the horses being prepped for upcoming races. A horse was a fragile animal, prone to tendinitis, lung disorders, hoof cracks, and so forth. Of all the variables in the handicapping equation, none was more salient than a horse's physical condition. A good tout developed a sixth sense for recognizing when a horse felt out of sorts, information prized by his employer—a bookmaker or a bettor that risked large sums. A tipster, by contrast, sold his picks to whomever he could wheedle into buying them. The image of a tipster was that of a knave who buttonholed strangers with hot tips and was not above giving out more than one horse in a race.

Tipsters working outside the track packaged their selections in "sheets," little bulletins tucked inside sealed envelopes. They too attracted complaints for their aggressiveness, forcing the police to periodically take steps to thin their ranks. Racegoers arriving by train were likely to find the exits clogged by sheet sellers. Twenty-five sellers arrested at the Gravesend rail station on June 8, 1904, were charged with violating the law that prohibited blocking a public thoroughfare.[2]

Most sporting papers of the period and some of the less respectable dailies carried tipster advertisements, a practice with deeper roots in Britain. In 1904, a muckraking paper called *The Truth* exposed the shady dealings of tipsters that advertised extensively in papers published in England and Ireland. Most tipsters had more than one handle. Their credentials were embellished. One man posed as a veterinary surgeon employed by a large racing stable. All of them made extravagant claims, gilding their top picks with names like the Peerless Special. Some sent out literature containing endorsements from prominent men in the racing industry—endorsements contrived without the consent of the men being quoted—and one tipster even had the audacity to claim that he had received a certificate of merit from *The Truth* itself![3]

The tipsters weren't very sharp. The *London Daily News* did a survey of newspaper and sporting tabloid selections for thoroughbred races run over a period of eight months in 1903. Of the eighteen correspondents in the survey, only one showed a profit, a modest profit at that. Their American counterparts likely fared no better. In an informal survey, the top-rated newspaper handicapper in America in 1914 correctly named 272 winners in 871 races. However, because he had a penchant for picking big favorites, those that followed his selections still finished in the red. And as for the tipsters with the loudest advertisements, it doesn't appear that any of them exhibited a degree of proficiency that set them apart from the herd for any sustained period of time. In the estimation of Mark Clapson, an authority on the history of bookmaking in Great Britain, tipsters probably had little influence on the formulation or modification of odds offered by bookmakers.[4]

Charles Mackenzie, an English immigrant who covered horse racing for St. Louis papers, was one of the first pick sellers in the United States to develop a national clientele. Calling himself a turf advisor, Mackenzie burst out of the blocks like a demon with a spectacular run of winning selections but couldn't sustain the momentum. He kept at it by creating new identities, a process he repeated whenever he fell into a slump. In common with his counterparts in England, he was partial to pseudonyms that smacked of an aristocratic lineage.[5] That Mackenzie was able to persevere said a great deal about the psychology that governed his enterprise. Within the universe of those that purchase gambling advice there is a core group of "repeat offenders," individuals quick to sever ties with a tipster performing poorly, but easily swayed into giving another pick seller a chance to make things right. In this milieu, a tipster's sucker list may be the most valuable thing that he owns.

The most prominent tipsters were the bunco artists peddling a sure thing. The following paragraphs were excerpted from a mailer that circulated in 1907:

> You probably read in the daily papers of the killing made by our clients on the Fiddler. We were on the inside then and we cleaned up $200,000 for our clients. The odds were 20 to 1. They said the Fiddler was a ringer and if he was, don't that show the class of information we give? We were in the know. These pippins don't come along often, but when they do you can plunge to the limit.
>
> Now we have another that will be along in about a week. It ought to be as good as 20 to 1, for even the wisest have got no line on this one. It is bottled tight, ripe and ready for our clients. When we get through with this trick the bank rolls of the bookies will look like a train had run over them . . . this trick is so good that we are sending it out to only a limited number of clients and to get in you must be among the first.

It cost only a dollar to purchase the name of the hot horse, but the person receiving the wire was instructed to make a separate $5 wager for the tipster and remit the winnings "or else we will cut you off of our list and you will not be able to get any more of these sweet ones." The reporter that shared this epistle with his readers noted that if the recipient was foolish enough to take the bait, he was certain to receive "literature" for years to come.[6]

Many tipsters peddled systems in addition to their daily plays. Conventionally simple formulas for unearthing winning selections, there were literally hundreds of systems in the marketplace, some bundled into booklets and others sold individually. These too were promoted with extravagant claims. A system called the Infallible System presumably never lost.

Postal authorities took a dim view of get-rich-quick schemes but lacked the manpower to fumigate on a regular basis. In 1908, they were sufficiently roused to blacklist fifty tipsters. Their circulars were seized and destroyed.[7] Federal laws governing mail fraud were vague, so attorneys for the accused were normally able to negotiate a token punishment in the form of a small fine. Prosecutors were hampered by the reluctance of victims to come forth and expose their gullibility.

During the early years of the twentieth century, several tipsters formed investment bureaus, companies that ostensibly placed bets on horse races for their "shareholders." Maxim & Gay and the E.J. Arnold Company emerged as the leaders in the field. Both spent a fortune on newspaper advertisements.

Maxim & Gay was founded in New York by Simon Herzig, an ex-felon who had served two stints in prison following convictions for larceny and forgery. Better known by his pseudonym, George Graham Rice, Herzig paid top dollar for wordsmiths. His newspaper ads, conventionally filling three-fourths of a page in a standard broadsheet, ran continuously for weeks before the advent of an important racing meet and then popped up again at intervals while the meet was in progress. They were carried by papers in such far-flung places as Hopkinsville, Kentucky; Ocala, Florida; Guthrie, Oklahoma; and Bisbee, Arizona. Herzig was partial to the hinterlands.

Maxim & Gay managed the accounts of their clients, taking a 25 percent commission on any earnings. Compared with some of their competitors, their methods were prim and proper. Herzig employed a team of well-paid consultants to handicap the races. His agents actually placed bets on behalf of his clients. Dividend checks were generated after a run of good fortune. Account holders weren't informed of their plays until after the fact, but there was no fudging—reports were sent out in envelopes that were time-stamped before the start of the races.

For accounting purposes, payouts on winning selections were pegged to the odds at post time as displayed in the next day's edition of a designated newspaper. This is where the firm made its money. Bets were placed early and in such large sums that the odds plummeted. On winning selections, the company's customers were short-changed. Herzig claimed responders to his ads provided him with $1.3 million in working capital for the 1903–1904 New Orleans winter meet and that when the one-hundred-day meet was finished he had churned this bankroll into a $700,000 profit.[8]

Whatever money Herzig/Rice earned from his racetrack endeavors was likely dwarfed by the money he made selling worthless mining stock. For a time his operation was headquartered in the boomtown of Goldfield in desolate Esmeralda County, Nevada. He wrote a book about his escapades titled *My Adventures with Your Money* and served three more terms in prison for fraudulent dealings before disappearing into thin air.

The E.J. Arnold Company, founded in St. Louis in 1899, was a more complex operation. Styled a turf investment cooperative, the company owned a racing stable, a breeding farm, and a poolroom in Hot Springs, Arkansas, and operated bookmaking stands at various race courses. Investors received a handsome certificate. It promised a 3 percent dividend paid weekly. The dividend was eventually cut to 2 percent, but even then a man stood to double his money in less than a year.

The prospectuses of the E.J. Arnold Company were also gems of inveiglement. "Whoever wrote his circulars and letters was an artist," said a reporter. "They are dreams of epistolary beauty, concise, complete, and convincing." The company reportedly had more than two thousand shareholders when it and five other similarly structured bureaus in St. Louis were shut down by Missouri authorities at the behest of federal postal inspectors. What followed was a classic "run" of the sort associated with the crash of Ponzi schemes. Police in riot gear were called in to keep the peace as victims scrambled to withdraw their funds. "Collapse of Turf Investment Bubble wipes out the Savings of Thousands," read the front-page headline in the *St. Louis Republic*.[9]

The expansion of horse racing during the Great Depression was accompanied by a surge in the number of racing papers. Some of the newcomers were little more than wrappers for tipster advertisements. In 1935, the New York attorney general, working with postal authorities, launched an investigation of the tipster industry that resulted in eighty-six indictments. The operation had the support of New York racing commissioners. The frequent allusion to fixed races in tipster advertisements bespattered the industry that they regulated.

The investigation brought few convictions, but the facts presented to the grand jury made for good reading. Consistent with earlier findings, most tipsters had multiple aliases. Claiming to be the brother or broth-

er-in-law of a well-known jockey was a common ploy. The tipsters pursued new clients from a "sucker list" that circulated in-house until it had
outlived its usefulness, whereupon it was sold or traded for a list with
fresh names. Customers that purchased a package of selections, such as
buying a full race meet, would be pitched "specials" that weren't included in the package. To justify the extra fee, they were told that the
firm had gone to considerable expense to rig the outcome.

A bill to outlaw phony newspaper advertisements was then working
its way through the New York legislature. Introduced in 1935, the bill
would have forced tipsters to be truthful when publishing the names
and returns of the daily specials they released on previous days. The
phony scratch sheets that were pressed into the hands of racetrack
patrons as they were leaving the track would be no more. Ostensibly
leftovers, these were second editions run off on a fast press at a nearby
print shop after the early races had been run. A logjam at the end of the
legislative session kept the anti-tipster bill from advancing to the Senate
floor.[10]

Anti-tipster drives would continue sporadically in the ensuing years.
In March of 1938, the United States attorney for the Southern District
of New York orchestrated a series of raids on firms that placed deceitful
ads in racing papers, resulting in sixty-eight arrests for mail fraud. The
firm that took the biggest hit was run by five brothers from Brooklyn.
They were linked to 107 aliases and reportedly had a sucker list with
more than fifteen thousand names.[11]

Throughout most of the twentieth century, long-distance calls were
expensive. As late as 1950, most intercity calls were routed through a
third party. The person initiating the call spoke to a switchboard operator. When the process was automated, rates fell, the telephone became
the primary medium through which a tipster reached out to a potential
client, and there was a proliferation of boiler rooms. (The term, which
came into widespread use in the late 1950s, is thought to have originated in the persistent din that characterized a room in which multiple
telephones were in use simultaneously, a din not unlike that found in a
boiler room.) Boiler rooms were places where high-pressure salesmen
working on commission hawked products, typically investment opportunities, of dubious value.

In their dealings with potential clients, telephone salesmen in the
employ of tipsters were told to elicit the normal bet size of the potential

pigeon with whom they were talking. This established the base price for the negotiable fee. When racing tipsters of the boiler room stripe were supplanted by telemarketers hawking sports selections, this policy became more deeply ingrained. The transition from racing to sports was seamless; the technology changed, but not the gambit. And because outcomes in both are often impacted by highly unusual occurrences, a tipster always had a good alibi for the "anomaly" of a wrong selection.

American Sports Advisors, a consortium of four boiler rooms, was the industry leader in the sports selection field during the 1980s when virtually every football and basketball annual was chock full of tipster advertisements. Founded in New York by Royce Kanofsky and "Professor" Ed Horowitz, the company reportedly grossed $114,000 a week during the 1981 football season. Three years later, the company was publically traded and reportedly had an annual gross of $6 million dollars.[12]

The company and an unrelated company in Baltimore, Mike Warren Sports, attracted the attention of the FBI because of numerous complaints of unscrupulous practices. Former ASA employees alleged that potential customers were harassed with high-pressure sales tactics, that the company failed to honor money-back guarantees, and that some customers were over-charged on their credit cards. The companies were never prosecuted—"misunderstandings" were blamed on rogue salesmen—but in 1990 the New York City Department of Consumer Affairs leveled fines against eight handicapping services for deceptive newspaper advertisements. In announcing the fines, NYC Consumer Affairs commissioner Angelo Aponte assailed the hypocrisy of papers that exposed scams on the front page and then promoted scams at the back of the sports section. America's national newspaper, *USA Today*, was a leading offender.[13]

From scattered evidence, it appears that sports betting consultants, in the main, are no smarter than their cousins of earlier generations who tailored their selections to horse racing. Sports monitor Mike McCusker, quoted in the *Wall Street Journal*, reported that only seventeen of the seventy services that he monitored had a win-proficiency of 54 percent or higher for the 1984 football season. Another study conducted over a three-year period found that sports tipsters in the aggregate hit 51 percent of their NFL plays. Releases designated "best bets" performed slightly higher. In yet another study, Roland Anderson found that only nine of thirty-two services maintained an average of 52.4 percent or better across three consecutive football seasons (1989–1991) and that none of them exceeded this benchmark in every season (at 11/10 odds, the break-even point is 52.38). Because the consultants in his survey paid a fee to be monitored, the findings were not necessarily representative of all pick sellers.[14]

These studies were conducted before the Internet age was in full bloom. Modern handicappers are logically more proficient as they have more information at their disposal, a larger body of accumulated wisdom, and a richer repository of data from which to test hypotheses. But adroitness within the pick-selling fraternity remains an elusive quality.

Data provided by an Oklahoma monitoring service for the years 2002–2006 showed very little difference between NFL and college football selections, both averaging between 50 and 51 percent. In none of the five years did the sum of all the picks exceed the 52.4 percent threshold.[15]

More recent data comes from the *Las Vegas Review-Journal*. In 2013 and 2014, twenty individuals divided into two ten-member panels submitted college and pro football selections. Predominantly professional handicappers with a smattering of local sports journalists and one sports book director, the panelists submitted five plays each week, sixty-five plays overall for the college contingent and eighty-five for the pro. The picks appeared in the Saturday (college) and Sunday editions of the paper using betting lines culled from a leading sports book for grading purposes.

The prognosticators picking NFL games fared slightly better, a finding inconsistent with earlier surveys which found that college selections tended to be somewhat stronger. In 2013, the NFL panelists in the aggregate hit 53.4 percent of their plays, a figure that dropped to 51.9 percent in 2014. The corresponding figures for the college panels were 48 percent and 52.3 percent. The top performer hit 60.5 percent of his NFL plays in 2013.

If nothing else, these surveys point out the great challenge facing a man who hopes to make a good living wagering on sporting events. And they lay bare the lies perpetuated by the boiler room services that shout "absolutely free" as bait to rope in the unsuspecting and the pathologically masochistic.[16]

8

BIG PLUNGERS AND OUTLAWS

Contrary to the conventional wisdom, there were devoted horseplayers—a select few, to be certain—that came out ahead over the long haul. Congruently, during the course of every race meet, some bookmakers fell by the wayside. Fourteen weeks into the 1902 New York racing season, roughly 25 percent of the bookmakers in action on opening day had quit, their bankrolls wiped out. In 1907, at the Meadows track in Seattle, bookmakers in the aggregate were down $150,000 after nine weeks of the 11-week meet with scant chance of finishing in the black.[1]

Some of the bookmakers had only themselves to blame for their bad fortune. Bad money management by bettors is the bookmaker's hidden edge, but some bookmakers were possessed of the same frailty. They could minimize their losses only by cutting down their possible winnings, but some lacked the discipline to keep a steady hand and were knocked off their pins in pursuit of the big score. By and large, however, attrition in their ranks was attributed to the growing sophistication of the everyday horseplayer. Writing in 1901, a reporter noted that punters had become more well-informed and were using more sophisticated methods of analysis.[2] Bettors with respected opinions—in particular those that embraced handicapping as a science, eschewing inside information for empirical data—were dubbed "wise ones" or "knowing ones" in newspaper reports, but more commonly referenced as "the talent." A turf writer might write "the talent got the best of the bookies today at

Brighton Beach" or "the talent was dumbfounded when three longshots romped home at Sheepshead Bay."

The most aggressive bookmakers walked the narrowest tightropes. They and the big plungers with whom they jousted were great grist for turf writers.

With no federal income tax, a man who bet heavily had less reason to be discreet. When a big plunger made a big score, it made the papers. Few men could realistically hope to someday emulate these leviathans of the turf, but their well-publicized exploits suggested that the racing game was beatable and enhanced its allure. Turn of the century stalwarts such as John "Bet-a-Million" Gates, John A. Drake, "Pittsburgh Phil" Smith, Elias "Lucky" Baldwin, Charles "Riley" Grannan, Joe "The Boy Plunger" Yeager, Thomas "Chicago" O'Brien, and copper king Marcus Daly were as much a part of the American racing scene as the most celebrated racehorses.[3]

No one bet more than Gates, who acquired his sobriquet betting the races in England. On his most extravagant afternoons, he put six figures into play. Born on a farm in Illinois, Gates began his business career selling barbed wire to Texas ranchers and went on to control several thriving steel mills. Encouraged to tone down his betting by August Belmont II, Gates reportedly said: "For me there's no fun in betting just a few thousand; I want to lay down enough to hurt the other fellow if he loses, and enough to hurt me if I lose."[4] Like all of the big plungers, Gates bet through proxies, but he often ventured into the betting ring, if only to dress down a bookmaker who shied away from bettors of his stripe.

"Bet-a-Million" Gates was a born gambler. Anything with an uncertain outcome, be it a friendly game of cards, a round of golf, or a race between raindrops sliding down a window pane, was fair game for a wager. But despite his many triumphs, there's reason to think that he actually lost more money at gambling than he won. Reports of big scores are invariably skewed toward the high side, and Gates's compulsive behavior was inconsistent with the profile of a long-term winner, albeit it served him well on Wall Street where the biggest fortunes were made.

Gates's boon companion John A. Drake was cut from the same cloth. The son of a railroad tycoon who became the governor of Iowa—Drake University in Des Moines is named for him—Drake enlarged the family fortune while serving on the Chicago Board of Trade. An expert bridge and backgammon player, he reportedly had a run in 1902 where he won $381,000 betting the races in a span of only five weeks.[5] He partnered with Gates in building Rockingham Park in New Hampshire, an ill-advised venture, as the races played to a sea of empty seats, but a misadventure that was a mere speed bump for men of their means. They had better success with their racing stable. Horses owned or co-owned by Drake won several big races in Europe. He spent his golden years in France.

There's no doubt that Pittsburgh Phil finished a winner. Born in Sewickley, Pennsylvania, with the unassuming name George Edward Smith, Phil began betting in the poolrooms of Pittsburgh while working as a cork cutter. When he died in 1905 at age forty-three, he left an estate valued at $600,000 (roughly $15 million in today's dollars). His entire fortune reportedly came from winning wagers.

Pittsburgh Phil has been called the first modern handicapper-bettor because he kept his own performance charts and valued hard data above inside information. However, he also developed a sixth sense for gleaning how badly a trainer wanted to win from his body language in the paddock, a heightened sensitivity to what poker players call "tells." He sleuthed out winners with such keen powers of observation that he was likened to Sherlock Holmes.[6]

As the size of his bets increased, Phil became more meticulous, employing spotters to study horses in training and to keep him abreast of any suspicious activities. One of the young men that he employed, Frank M. Kelley, went on to have a long career as a racing official, ending his days in California as the track superintendent at Hollywood Park.[7]

In common with most other big plungers, Pittsburgh Phil owned race horses, but he disbanded his little stable when he felt that it compromised his objectivity. Away from the bookmakers ring, his nondescript appearance and taciturn demeanor made it easy for him to blend in with the crowd. He adhered religiously to the British admonition that a man should handle adversity with a stiff upper lip. When watching a race, Pittsburgh Phil never displayed any emotion. He kept his field glasses trained on the horses after they crossed the finish line to gauge how much energy they expended. In his day, horses raced more frequently. Interest in his exploits surged with the publication of "Racing

Maxims and Methods of Pittsburgh Phil," a primer for novice bettors released three years after his death. The book (a timeless classic) was born from conversations with his friend Edward W. Cole, the turf editor of the *New York Evening Telegram*.

No one left a larger estate than Lucky Baldwin, who acquired an immense tract of land in the San Gabriel Valley of Los Angeles County where he located his famous stud farm at Rancho Santa Anita. The son of an Ohio farmer, Baldwin was born into humble circumstances, but he was already a wealthy man when he set out to conquer the racing game, having profited from shrewd investments in gold and silver mines, utility companies, hotels, and railroads. Horses owned by him won a record four American Derbys. The signature event at Chicago's Washington Park, the American Derby was briefly the richest race in the country. The high point came in 1893, the year that Chicago hosted a world's fair, the Columbian Exposition.

The sagas of Riley Grannan and Joe Yeager resonated more strongly with race-goers of modest means because they started with almost nothing. The son of a poor tailor, Grannan was born in Paris, Kentucky, in the heart of Bluegrass Country. He was working as a bellboy at a New Orleans hotel and attending the races in his spare time when he caught the eye of bookmaker Edward G. Boté, one of several men credited with inventing the form chart. Grannan had an uncanny knack for re-creating a race from memory and supposedly had no peer when it came to discerning the winner of a race in progress if all the horses were tightly bunched heading into the final turn. Grannan worked briefly for Boté and then for a prominent Kentucky bookmaker before branching out on his own. In 1895, at age twenty-seven, he reportedly parlayed a $30 stake into $195,000 betting the races at Saratoga and Coney Island.[8]

Joe Yeager was even more precocious. The Boy Plunger learned the basics as a teenager working as a clerk in a Cincinnati poolroom and was a full-fledged high-roller while still in his early twenties. Reportedly the first person ever barred from the poolrooms of Hot Springs, Yeager periodically went broke and his heyday was here and gone in a flash. In this regard, his saga was somewhat similar to that of Riley Grannan, who was reduced to booking small at California tracks before surfacing in Rawhide, Nevada, his final destination, where he ran a saloon. Joe Yeager died young (age thirty-eight), as did Grannan (thirty-nine) and

Pittsburgh Phil (forty-three). Armchair psychologists attributed their short life spans to the vicissitudes inherent in their profession and their unswerving allegiance to a code that compelled them to bottle up their emotions during moments of high drama.

Chicago O'Brien's blue-collar background made his story more interesting. Toiling as an apprentice bricklayer in the last decade of the nineteenth century, O'Brien's pay could not have amounted to much more than $30 a week. He supposedly risked only fifty cents when he made his first wager in a Chicago poolroom. But it wasn't long before he was turning heads at the Emeryville track near San Francisco, and when his long career was finally finished it was thought that he had bet more money in the aggregate than any of his fabled contemporaries. His signature bet was a wager on a big favorite to "show." This made him unique as most serious gamblers disdained bets of this nature.[9]

In reports about O'Brien's death, it was said that he was a square shooter who never resorted to shady transactions. But whenever he won an especially large bet there were rumblings that he had stacked the deck by bribing jockeys to hold back their horses. All of the big plungers were thought to be opportunists who were not above "making arrangements" when conditions were ripe. Three noted plungers—Richard "Boss" Croker, Patrick H. McCarren, and David Gideon—could not escape this innuendo because of their connections to Tammany Hall.

Before he retired to England in 1902, Croker was New York's most powerful politician. He undoubtedly was also the wealthiest. His net worth skyrocketed after he elbowed his way into the chairmanship of the Finance Committee of Tammany Hall in 1885. Within a few years of taking this post, he invested somewhat more than a half million dollars in racing stables and stud farms.[10]

McCarren, the Democratic boss of Brooklyn, served in the New York State Senate from 1888 until his death in 1909. He grew rich investing in stocks of companies that he represented as a lobbyist, notably the American Sugar Refining Company and Standard Oil. While he didn't bet as high as men like John Gates, he wagered on so many races that his volume may have exceeded them all. David Gideon, a one-term member of the New York State Senate, also embraced the grind. During the summer months, he reportedly had agents betting in poolrooms all over the country. More well-known as a horseman than a gambler, the racing stable he co-owned with gambler-businessman

John Daly (a protégé of John Morrissey) produced three winners of the Futurity Stakes.

Dishonest racing was difficult to prove, but few doubted that it was endemic. Indeed, during the racetrack-building boom of the late nineteenth century, outlaw tracks proliferated. They were called outlaw tracks because they were a law unto themselves, free from the rules of an organization such as the Jockey Club. They were also called outlaw tracks because they sheltered horsemen and bookmakers blacklisted at other tracks and because of the motley crowds they attracted. A Jersey City clergyman, visiting an outlaw track in the company of a private detective, wrote that "a more vicious and pitiable crowd cannot be seen outside the penitentiary and the idiot asylum."[11]

One of the defining features of an outlaw track was a prominent "foreign book." This was an improvised poolroom where one could wager on races run at other tracks. Since the live racing was of an inferior grade, more money was sometimes bet in the foreign book than on the live racing card.

The quirkiest of the outlaw tracks bubbled up near the waterfront in the village of Maspeth in the borough of Queens in 1894. The track opened with races scheduled in the afternoons and again at night when the half-mile track was illuminated by a row of electric lights hanging from a wire. The lighting was so poor that the horses and their riders gave the appearance of being little more than shadows. It did not auger well when the very first race run under the lights ended in controversy. The horses were bunched tight as they crossed the finish line. The judges gave the race to the horse that finished second in the eyes of most everyone else. The guiding spirit behind the track was reportedly poolroom baron Peter De Lacy. The arch-enemy of racetrack operator Michael Dwyer, with whom he had a long-running feud, De Lacy was in need of new product following a shutdown of racing in New Jersey.

A reporter visiting the track during its second week of operation noted that the only area with good lighting was the betting ring. He came to Maspeth via the free shuttle, a steam-powered boat that stopped at two pick-up points in Manhattan before crossing the East River. On board the boat, racegoers were exposed to a cornucopia of gambling games. The boat moved slower on the return voyage so as to milk more play from her passengers. The Maspeth track was here-and-gone in a hurry, the victim of legislation that prohibited night racing.[12]

Outlaw tracks, by and large, staged their meets in the colder months. This was true of the Guttenberg and Gloucester City tracks in New Jersey. Guttenberg, the most profitable of the outlaw tracks, opened in North Bergen in 1886. The more notorious Gloucester City track, situated at the opposite end of the state, near Philadelphia, opened in 1890. Both owed their existence to the political clout of major investors. Dennis McLaughlin, the Democratic boss of Hudson County, oiled the wheels for Gottfried "Dutch" Walbaum, the driving force behind Guttenberg. William J. Thompson, the Democratic boss of Camden County, ran the show at Gloucester City. At both tracks, some of the most decrepit horses were owned by bookmakers. Colored with extra-juicy odds, they were entered in races they had no hope of winning merely as a prod to more betting. Bookmakers suspected of engaging in this devious practice were dubbed undertakers.

Guttenberg was the first racetrack in the country that offered winter racing in an area where the temperature sometimes dipped below freezing. When the track was frozen, the risk of injury was high. Several horses were permanently disabled after losing their footing on the slick surface and several jockeys were seriously injured. This caught the attention of the Humane Society which joined the leading New York and Philadelphia papers in the chorus to ban winter racing.[13]

William Thompson's right-hand man at Gloucester City, Thomas Flynn, was the Speaker of the House of the New Jersey Assembly in February of 1893 when a series of bills were passed to further the interests of the profiteers running the state's disreputable racetracks. A bill that removed racetrack betting enclosures from the list of disorderly houses was broadened to make poolrooms legal if they were under the control of licensed racetrack owners.

The sponsors of the bills were leading with their chin. Their doings flew in the face of a growing hostility toward gambling that was part of a larger reform movement. Rushed through the legislature without a proper hearing, the bills sparked a backlash of such severity that racing ceased entirely in New Jersey. Men newly elected to political office on the promise that they would work to repeal the pro-betting bills were spared the trouble when a State Supreme Court justice nullified them by ruling that they violated the State Constitution.[14]

Monmouth Park, considered one of the most beautiful racetracks in the world when it opened in 1870, was caught in the web, consigned to the grave along with the outlaw tracks. Only four years earlier, the track had been completely rebuilt at a reported cost of a million dollars. Many other important racetracks would be forced out of existence in the ensuing years. Monmouth was the first casualty.

Bookmakers chased out of New Jersey were largely responsible for the appearance of two outlaw tracks near Washington, D.C. Both were situated on no man's land where legal jurisdiction was unclear—a common thread in the ecology of vice districts. The Alexandria Island racetrack sat near the shoreline of Virginia on a channel island of the Potomac River. The nearby St. Asaph track was constructed on the outskirts of the city of Alexandria, Virginia. The foreign book there, which did a landslide business, was built to accommodate heavy traffic. A long stretch of blackboard was elevated so that patrons could more easily take in the information displayed on it.

These tracks were famously known as graveyards for favorites. As a rule, favorites were over-bet, so it was usually advantageous to the bookies when the favorite "under-achieved." The simplest way to effectuate this result was to bribe the jockey. He could purposely miscalculate the pace or he could slow his mount by holding tighter to the reins, deceptions not easily detected by the stewards. Running a horse to exhaustion on the night before a race virtually guaranteed a weak showing. One might also "doctor" the horse with drowsy pills or by logging it down with a heavy meal or by withholding water and then letting the horse sate its thirst right before sending it out for the post parade.

The opposite effect—getting a horse to run faster—could be achieved with "hop-along juice," slang for any stimulant. One could also "zap" the horse with an electrical charge during the running of the race. This machination, thought to have originated in England, first turned up in the United States at Guttenburg in 1892. A rank outsider won a race with bewildering bursts of speed, after which it was discovered that the jockey had a battery strapped to his chest with wires running down his legs into his spurs through a small hole in the back of his boots. Later that year, a similar incident occurred at an outlaw track in Roby, Indiana. The jockey wasn't penalized—he broke no rule—but the stewards corrected that oversight, banning gadgets that emitted an electrical charge.[15]

Horses were sometimes entered under false names to conceal their true caliber. Sometimes this required the services of a cosmetician, a man skilled in the use of special dyes. This con could be deployed to the benefit of the bookmaker, but was more often used against him. As a rule, the imposter—the "ringer"—was far more able than the genuine article.

Crooked races were hardly confined to outlaw tracks. In 1901, a steeplechase at the Fair Grounds in New Orleans had such a bad odor about it that the stewards stepped in and canceled it, sending the patrons home early.[16] This incident happened toward the end of the meet. By and large, hanky-panky, or at least the perception of it, became more prevalent as a meet was winding down, a charge to which no racetrack was immune.

In addition to fixed races, poolroom operators had to be wary of wiretapping. This involved intercepting telegraphic information and replacing it with a bogus report. The first large-scale coup in racing dates to 1883. Somewhere in New Jersey, someone tampered with the results from Jerome Park while confederates got down bets in poolrooms as far west as St. Louis. The carnage to bookmakers nationwide was estimated to be nearly a hundred thousand dollars.[17]

A dishonest telegrapher could transmit false information direct from the track. In 1896, con men bribed a telegrapher to release the wrong winner of a race in New Orleans. Large bets were made in poolrooms in such far-flung places as Brooklyn, Pittsburgh, Louisville, and Chicago. The bettors in this well-laid plot started patronizing the poolrooms a week in advance of the coup, behaving like unsophisticated hunch bettors to avoid suspicion. In July of 1906, poolroom operators in New York, although by now sensitive to "unnatural money," were asleep at the switch and suffered massive losses when an 8/1 shot won the second race at Windsor. In actuality, the horse finished second behind the prohibitive favorite. The extent of the damage bore witness that this was something other than human error.[18]

With the advent of public telephones, a dishonest telegrapher was more likely to leave the information undisturbed, but delay its arrival. If his confederate wasn't too greedy, this might go undetected. Some poolroom keepers were charged with working a variation of this scam by holding back the result of a race until more bets were in the hopper. This was done when the poolroom keeper anticipated that more money would show on a particularly hot horse, a horse that, unbeknownst to his customers, had run out of the money.

While many rumors of crooked practices were just that, unfounded rumors, there were enough known swindles to keep the reformers in a constant state of agitation. If a man didn't come to the racing game with larceny in his heart, then it would be bred into him, or so it was postulated.

9

THE REFORMERS CRANK UP THE HEAT

In 1882, the Barclay Street pool sellers appeared to have found a safe haven in Long Island City. The authorities there were more than accommodating; they were welcoming. But the locals couldn't protect the newcomers from the wrecking ball that was Anthony Comstock. Backed by a force of twenty vigilantes, Comstock burst in on four poolrooms sitting in tight proximity. When his day's work was done, more than a dozen men were in custody and their workplaces were in shambles.[1]

A broad-shouldered man with short, thick legs, Comstock pin-balled around the vice districts of New York with all the subtlety of Attila the Hun. When he was in the mood to arrest someone, he sported his badge, an emblem that identified him as a federal lawman, specifically a U.S. postal inspector, a position granted to him by President Ulysses S. Grant at the behest of the agency that paid his salary, the New York Society for the Suppression of Vice, an organization born in a meeting room of the New York headquarters of the YMCA.

Comstock was born in New Canaan, Connecticut, the son of a farmer who owned an interest in a sawmill. He attended a Congregational church as a boy, served two years as an infantryman in the Union army, and worked briefly as a porter and then a salesman for a dry goods manufacturer before finding his calling. In time he became the most famous—nay, infamous—of all the reformers, his image defined by his dogged persistence in rooting out indecency, by which he meant anything that triggered "impure thoughts," be they French postcards, salacious literature, graphic birth control talk in medical tracts, even nude paintings by famous artists. In a career that spanned forty-three years, Comstock was responsible for nearly four thousand arrests, roughly three-fourths of which resulted in guilty pleas or convictions.[2]

Comstock believed that gambling offended the Almighty. He could not point to any specific passage in the Bible that condemned gambling, but gambling ruined lives, of that he was certain; suppressing it heeded the admonition to be "my brother's keeper," the spiritual lesson embodied in the story of Cain and Abel. (Some would say that Comstock's flights of moral indignation were manifestations of repressed envy, but that's a discussion best left to a different book.)

In an article penned for the *North American Review*, Comstock identified seven by-products of the "poolroom evil": thefts, defalcation (unpaid debts), robberies, breaches of trust, wrecked homes, heartbroken women, and beggared children.[3] This assessment was concordant with an important block of public opinion. Indeed, Comstock was the face of an organization that was championed by many of America's most distinguished citizens. Historian Allan Carlson notes that the executive officers of the New England branch of the Society for the Suppression of Vice included the presidents of Amherst College, Yale, Brown, and Dartmouth.[4]

Comstock's wars on smut overshadowed his attacks on the poolrooms, but shutting down these traps of immorality, as he called them, always ranked high on his to-do list. At various times, he carried his animus to a racetrack. In 1883, Comstock, assisted by a large posse of deputy sheriffs, walked through a jeering mob to arrest several pool sellers at Brighton Beach. In 1886, he caused the arrest of ten bet takers at Saratoga. He was there to give the keynote speech at an anti-gambling rally at the town's Baptist church.[5]

A correspondent for the *Brooklyn Eagle* judged that the organizers of the rally were on a fool's errand. By his reckoning, the great majority of Saratogans were okay with gambling. He believed that most visitors factored gambling losses into their vacation budget and were not the sort of people that indulged in illegal gambling when they were back in their home communities. As for the bookmakers that Comstock arrested, they were assigned court dates that were well beyond the final days of the racing meet. The reporter assumed that the charges against them would be disposed of quietly after things settled down.[6]

Comstock's incursion, however, was salutary in some respects. Saratoga had become tackier following the death of John Morrissey in 1877. The elegant Saratoga Club, Morrissey's former "clubhouse," still barred townsfolk and turned away tourists whose appearance didn't convey an air of prosperity, but the side streets in the downtown district sheltered swindlers running little games of chance and most of them were chased out of town in advance of Comstock's visit. Moreover, business leaders seized upon it as an opportunity to improve customer relations by placing tighter constraints on hackmen and by reining in hotel and restaurant workers who were too aggressive in hustling tips.[7] (The modern perception of Anthony Comstock is that of a loathsome character, a misogynistic, blue-nosed, totalitarian bully, but in his day he was widely admired. Editorials in mainstream papers on the occasion of his death were generally critical of his fanaticism, but otherwise eulogistic. "He served a good cause with tireless devotion, and every good citizen who really knows the nature and extent of the man's work will realize that the country has lost a benefactor and a hero," said the *New York Times*.)[8]

New York's gambling fraternity, periodically discomposed by Comstock's pestilence, suffered a more persistent drubbing after Charles H. Parkhurst assumed the presidency of the New York Society for the Prevention of Crime in 1891. Primarily a temperance society, the NYSPC broadened its scope under Parkhurst's stewardship, provoking investigations that led to reforms that had a profound effect on the political life of New York.

Parkhust was the pastor of the Madison Square Presbyterian Church. In February of 1892, he delivered a sermon that flayed Tammany Hall, accusing it of plunging the city into a cesspool of immorality. Critics demanded documentation and Parkhurst was up to the challenge. Over the next four weeks, he visited dozens of "dens of iniquity" in the company of a private detective, returning to his parish with names, addresses, and affidavits. His follow-up sermon on March 13, 1892, delivered before an overflow crowd, caused a sensation after it was reprinted in full in the *New York Times*.[9]

Parkhurst's war differed from that of Anthony Comstock in its emphasis. Parkhurst believed that purveyors of vice were less wicked than the men in positions of authority who turned a blind eye in return for a gratuity. By attacking vice as a byproduct of municipal corruption, his message appealed to a broader base. It helped that Parkhurst was far less dogmatic than Comstock. A graduate of Amherst College, he had been a high school principal before entering the ministry and had a scholarly air about him that contrasted sharply with Comstock's tough-guy aura.

As a result of Parkhurst's findings, the New York Senate launched an investigation of the New York City Police Department. The Lexow Committee, formed in 1894 and named after its chairman, a Republican from Rockland County, heard testimony that poolroom operators were paying anywhere from $50 to $300 a month for police protection. In one precinct, the assessment was five times the amount imposed on brothel-keepers.[10]

The revelations compelled the police to change their ways, but raids on "disorderly houses," to a large extent, were nothing more than public relations ploys. Part of the problem was structural. The NYPD was highly decentralized, meaning that precinct captains, even a cop walking a beat, had a great deal of discretionary power. Major reforms were anticipated when Theodore Roosevelt was appointed the president of the Board of Police Commissioners in 1895, but the ambitious Roosevelt quit the post after only two years and the reformers suffered a setback when Tammany Hall regained control of the mayor's office in 1898.

Systemic changes arrived with the election of William Travers Jerome as District Attorney. Jerome had attended Amherst College, Rev. Parkhurst's alma mater, and had served as the assistant counsel to the Lexow Committee. He took office in 1902 and served eight years.

Jerome immediately set about shrinking the city's supply of gambling houses and bordellos. Ham-fisted police raids were his calling card. In his most audacious caper, he led the charge on Richard Canfield's place. Located at 5 East Forty-Fourth Street, across from Delmonico's, Canfield's was the most exclusive gambling parlor in the city. Smashing second story windows to gain entry, Jerome's marauders were none too careful as they trampled about in search of gambling paraphernalia, damaging expensive furnishings. There was no gambling going on—Canfield had been tipped off—so he wasn't taken into custody, but the relentless district attorney got his pound of flesh, or at least a portion of it, when Canfield pleaded guilty to the charge of being a common gambler, paying a $1,000 fine. The raid, conducted late in the evening on December 2, 1902, was the capstone of a series of raids on gambling houses that was described in a front page report in the *New York Times* as "a night of tremendous excitement in the Bohemian life of the city."[11]

An aesthete who collected Whistler paintings and Chippendale furniture and listed his occupation as gentleman, Richard Canfield had so many friends in high places that he was thought to be untouchable. His Manhattan gambling emporium, which doubled as his private residence, had sister properties in Newport, Rhode Island, and Saratoga, the latter of which was none other than John Morrissey's old Clubhouse, a finely-appointed establishment that Canfield made even more posh. In the estimation of Alexander Gardiner, Canfield's biographer, the raid on his New York property was a watershed moment in the war of the reformers, the first clear indication that the tide had turned in their favor.[12]

Jerome's detractors put him down as a publicity hound. On his raids, if a photographer was present, he liked to be the man wielding the axe. After bursting through the door, he would improvise a courtroom and take depositions from witnesses. Inevitably, his critics compared him to the anti-saloon gadabout Carrie Nation. But no one questioned his guts.

In 1904, Jerome ratcheted up his attack on the poolrooms. A vast citywide sweep during the third week of May uncovered a clearinghouse for a large bookmaking syndicate that operated in a building managed by a brother-in-law of President Theodore Roosevelt. Police arrested seventy men, confiscated 152 telephones, ripping them out of their sockets, and seized fifteen telegraph instruments.[13]

Concurrent with the dragnet, more pressure was put on Western Union. The man at the forefront was F. Norton Goddard, a wealthy, Harvard-educated businessman best known as the founder of the Anti-Policy Society. (In policy, similar to keno, a man bets that a certain combination of numbers will appear in a drawing of numbers; a mutation of the game came to be associated with black urban neighborhoods where it took the name "numbers.") Using an assumed name, Goddard contacted Western Union under the guise of opening a poolroom. His dealings with the company gave evidence that Western Union's relationship with the rooms went beyond that of an information provider. Employees of the firm—technicians with special training—assisted poolroom operators in dodging the emissaries of the law. They hid wires by stringing them down chimneys and installed equipment behind partitions in secret rooms or compartments. At many poolrooms, the telegraph operator was a Western Union employee. It was joked that his training manual included a section on how to cushion his fall in the event he had to jump out a window to escape a police raid.[14]

The directors of Western Union—there were more than two dozen—included some of America's most prominent do-gooders. Prominent among them was the retired banker Morris K. Jesup. One of the founders of the New York chapter of the YMCA, Jesup was a former president of the Mission and Tract Society, America's leading publisher and disseminator of Christian literature, and had been a prime mover in the establishment of settlement houses for immigrants living in lower Manhattan. The involvement of Jesup and other civic leaders in an enterprise that fostered unlawful behavior made for an awkward coupling. While few of the directors had more than a cursory knowledge of the day-to-day operations of the company, they were held culpable for tacitly condoning a climate of hypocrisy. There were calls for a federal takeover that would turn Western Union into an adjunct of the Post Office.[15]

Western Union president Robert C. Clowry had a stock reply whenever he was asked about poolrooms. As a common carrier, he would say, the company could not discriminate and was thereby obligated to accept all dispatches, save those that were flagrantly obscene. But Clowry eventually caved in. On May 17, 1904, Western Union ceased providing information to poolrooms in New York City. Two days later, the ban was extended to every poolroom in the country.

The scrum to fill the void was the first of many upheavals in the history of the race wire, a story with a wing in the annals of American crime. In the short term, however, the impact was almost imperceptible. Western Union simply funneled their information through a third party, a disseminator masquerading as a legitimate news agency. Furnishing racing information to poolrooms in a roundabout way became a standard business practice.

WTJ (his friends called him Travers) didn't stop with the poolrooms. The feisty district attorney took his vendetta to the racetrack by drafting legislation that would overturn the Percy-Gray law and eliminate bookmaking wherever it was found. "I think it wrong," he said, "that on one side of a barbed-wire fence a man commits a felony if he does certain acts, while on the other side of the same fence the same acts are perfectly innocent and legal."[16] Among the bills that he drafted was one that made racetrack operators culpable for any illegal betting found on their premises. This bill was adopted virtually intact by lawmakers in other parts of the country.

WILLIAM TRAVERS JEROME: AN UNLIKELY CRUSADER

William Travers Jerome's anti-gambling obsession is great grist for an amateur psychoanalyst. WTJ was the son of Larry Jerome and the nephew of the fabulous Leonard Jerome. He was named for his father's best buddy, William Travers, a man whose name was synonymous with horse racing. By promoting legislation that would have assuredly killed racing as a mainstream sport, it was as if he was disinheriting his forebears.

As biographer Richard O'Connor notes, Jerome's well-known father was never a large presence in his life. An incorrigibly restless man, Larry Jerome had too many distractions to spend much time with his children. O'Connor describes the elder Jerome as a happy-go-lucky playboy who prolonged his adolescence to the point of senescence.[17]

The youngest of four boys, the future district attorney was eight years old when his father competed in the first great trans-oceanic yacht race, serving as a deckhand on the victorious *Henrietta*, a perilous undertaking (six crewmen on a rival boat were swept overboard and drowned) that made Larry Jerome and his shipmates the toast of the town on two continents. But to WTJ, this was less a proud moment than another prolonged truancy by a father that he scarcely knew. In his later years, Larry Jerome lived comfortably on the annuity he purchased after selling his seat on the New York Stock Exchange, but he was a one-generation aristocrat and his children were not raised in the lap of luxury as were most of their childhood playmates.

William Travers Jerome's mother, the former Catherine Hall of Palmyra, New York, was by nature more of a homebody than her sister (Leonard Jerome's wife) and totally unlike the man that she married. O'Connor describes her as a grim and austere woman with "a ready frown for anything that smacked of bawdy and irreverent wit."[18]

Her puritanical strain was transferred to her youngest son, but WTJ was hardly an all-out prude. A chain-smoker, he enjoyed an occasional cocktail and a friendly game of poker. Moreover, while he wasn't a womanizer, he became something of a bigamist. His relationship with his mistress, a woman considerably younger, was a long-lasting affair.

One of William Travers Jerome's brothers died an alcoholic at age twenty-three. Another went west after eloping with a servant girl and was never heard from again. According to O'Connor, his brothers' misadventures instilled within him a nagging fear that he was born with a genetic disposition to loose living. He controlled the fear by embracing the antithesis, devoting long hours to social betterment projects.

Whatever his inner motivations, WTJ was genuinely appalled at the degree of municipal corruption in New York City. He couldn't faithfully address this evil without waging war on the poolrooms, and it's a fair assumption that he eventually concluded that the only way to put the city's poolrooms out of business was to take away the leading item in their inventory, the races run at local tracks. He certainly knew that if he succeeded in eliminating on-track betting, the racing game would wither and die, and with it the pageantry that enlivened his boyhood, but perhaps he felt that reducing the incidence of gambling was a matter of such grave importance that it justified collateral damage. Prohibition was around the corner and the leaders of that movement were unmoved by collateral damage. In pursuit of their primary objective—stamping out saloons—they ruined the California wine industry. Thousands of fertile acres of agricultural land were sharply devalued in the stroke of a pen.

The chief rap against WTJ was that he was so consumed with suppressing vice that he paid little heed to crookedness in the financial district. Election betting had shifted from the poolrooms to the Broad Street curb exchange. Jerome did nothing to inhibit it, an oversight not lost on his enemies, who carped that he perverted justice by failing to apply it evenly. The brokerages that emphasized this component of their business, notably the W. L. Darnell firm, had their election odds quoted in the papers, a practice that continued into the 1920s. [19]

Jerome's immediate successor, Charles S. Whitman, and a New York City district attorney of later vintage, Thomas E. Dewey, exploited their reputations as hard-nosed crime-fighters to move up the political ladder. Jerome, by contrast, transitioned quietly back into civilian life. An early believer in the future of Technicolor, his investments in the struggling company that held the patents would eventually make him a very rich man. The "strong speculative turn," a Jerome family trait, bloomed anew.

(Jerome came out of his cocoon late in life when the scandal-plagued administration of New York mayor Jimmy Walker unleashed a new reform movement. Jerome's endorsement was useful to Fusion Party mayoral candidate Fiorello La Guardia, who swept all five boroughs in the election of 1933. An ardent foe of gambling, the flamboyant La Guardia was a two-fisted crime fighter. William Travers Jerome admired his chutzpah.)

10

RACETRACKS IN THE CROSSHAIRS

The racing game was a great money circulator. Racetrack employees and stable hands represented less than half the individuals whose economic lives were sustained by racing. Farmers and railroad workers and people in many other fields of endeavor were part of the machinery. According to one estimate, if the reformers succeeded in shutting down every racetrack in the country, upwards of forty thousand jobs would be lost. In New York, the taxes imposed on thoroughbred racing supported fifty-nine agricultural societies. In 1906, the tax amounted to $201,054, big money in 1906 dollars. Without this revenue, the New York State Fair and many smaller expositions were in danger of drying up. But the reformers were unmoved. Their counterargument was that red-light districts were important struts in the economies of New Orleans and San Francisco, but that hardly justified their continued existence.

August Belmont II, the longtime chairman of the Board of Stewards of the Jockey Club, was the leading spokesman for the horse racing lobby. A Harvard man who was left a widower with three children when his first wife died in 1898, Belmont was an apt choice to represent the industry. His tie to the Rothschilds, a legacy from his father, was a handicap, particularly after the economic downturns of 1893 and 1907 whipped up talk of an international banking conspiracy, but even those with an anti-Semitic strain were impressed by young Belmont's civic-mindedness. In 1904, he became the second president of the National Civic Federation, an organization whose membership included such notables as labor leader Samuel Gompers and social worker Jane Ad-

dams. More than a nominal Episcopalian, although his paternal forebears were Jewish, Belmont supported Episcopalian churches in New
York City; Saratoga; Hempstead; and Babylon, Long Island, where his
late father had kept a breeding farm.[1] This served him well when he sat
down with representatives of a legislative committee in March of 1906
to discuss the latest anti-racetrack-gambling bill worming its way
through the legislature. The committee, an interfaith body of church
leaders established to serve the legislature in an advisory capacity, was
persuaded to withdraw its support of the bill. In announcing the decision, Rev. Dr. Thomas R. Slicer, a Unitarian, declared that he couldn't
support legislation that would put an honorable man like Mr. Belmont
on the same plane as a poolroom keeper.[2]

As a condition to gaining the committee's support, Belmont promised that racetrack gambling would be conducted more discreetly and
that he would hold the bet takers to a higher standard. The slates
depicting the odds would come down once again and the bookies would
be enjoined to be more abstemious in refusing to take bets from minors
and those known to gamble irresponsibly. Anthony Comstock, who was
outraged by the committee's decision, considered this a hollow concession.

Within three days of the decision, Comstock and his comrade Rev.
Dr. Wilbur F. Crafts were on the offensive, counterattacking in meetings with Presbyterian, Methodist, and Baptist leaders. At the conclusion of these meetings, each of these denominations formally endorsed
the anti-racetrack-gambling initiative. The not-so-subtle message sent
to August Belmont II was that he ought to be careful about playing the
religious card as he would be wildly outgunned.

Wilbur Crafts was the superintendent of the International Reform
Bureau, an entity he founded in 1896. The objectives of the organization were set forth in a popular textbook, *Practical Christian Sociology*,
a book formed largely from lectures delivered by Crafts at Princeton
Theological Seminary. The Bureau had four key platforms: (1) temperance—it supported the efforts of the Anti-Saloon League and the
Woman's Christian Temperance Union; (2) the suppression of gambling; (3) stricter enforcement of Sunday closing laws; and (4) stricter
divorce laws. The modes of attack were legislation, lectures, and literature. The anti-gambling bill then under discussion, the Cassidy-Lansing
bill, was actually crafted by Dr. Crafts himself.

Crafts's chief lieutenant on the New York antigambling front was Albany-based Rev. O. R. Miller. Traveling the state promoting the bureau's agendas, Miller sometimes lectured as many as six times a week. At the rallies that were focused around gambling, Miller passed out a leaflet containing short clippings from New York papers telling of people whose lives were ruined as a result of racetrack betting. Attendees were goaded to come forward and take the pledge, a vow of abstinence. The pledge was a carryover from the temperance movement.[3]

In the main, Miller was preaching to the choir, but those less moralistic were increasingly warming to his message. In defending the gambling that occurred at his racetrack, Leonard Jerome had made note of how well-behaved the crowds were. The races, he said, "exercised a civilizing and ameliorating effect upon the characters of the lower order."[4] But times had changed. Judging from newspaper reports, disturbances were becoming more frequent. An unusually large gathering almost always meant a skirmish or two. These were often provoked by bookmakers' runners who were at their most abrasive in a congested environment.

There was a lingering sentiment that a woman attending the races ought to arrive on the arm of a gentleman. Many men were disquieted by the sight of an unescorted woman in an "unwholesome" place and unchaperoned women were becoming a larger branch of the racetrack demographic. The ladies were held responsible for the invasion of a parasite first seen at Monmouth Park, the racetrack pawnbroker. A reporter claimed that women attending the races there habitually went bust before all the day's races had been run. To stay in action, they put a piece of jewelry in hock. In 1905, the Bennings track in Washington, D.C., and Ascot Park in Los Angeles eliminated grandstand messengers to discourage betting by women. Racetracks in New Orleans joined the list in 1907 and the Meadows track in Seattle followed suit.[5]

Leonard Jerome and those in his social circle invited scorn with their ostentatious ways, but the press was generally kind, depicting them as amusing chaps who brightened the tone of the city. The next generation of the superrich wasn't treated as kindly. Men who made their fortunes on "The Street" were portrayed as finaglers. Among hourly wage workers—indeed anyone that performed manual labor, including farmers and craftsmen—there was always the feeling that there was something sinister about a man making money, lots of money, without producing anything tangible, and now the press was increasingly of the same mind.

In New York, a new form of journalism emerged with the arrival of Joseph Pulitzer, who acquired the *New York World* in 1883. Scandal-mongering became a staple of the paper, which acquired a daily circulation of more than one million. William Randolph Hearst entered the market in 1895, acquiring the *New York American* and the *New York Evening Journal.* The politically ambitious Hearst was the heir to a great fortune but shaped his papers to curry favor with the lunch-bucket brigade. The Hearst papers, like Pulitzer's *World*, were quick to play up shady dealings by men with large fortunes.

During the early years of the twentieth century, antipathy toward the superrich intensified. Conspicuous consumption was attacked as wasteful in Thorstein Veblen's *The Theory of the Leisure Class* (1899), an academic work that attracted considerable buzz and achieved a wide readership. The book foreshadowed a flurry of best-selling books, fiction and nonfiction, by muckraking journalists seized with moral indignation over municipal corruption and the widening gap between the rich and the poor. Frank Norris's 1901 novel *The Octopus* was a slap at railroad barons and their confederates manipulating the price of wheat. Ida Tarbell's *The History of the Standard Oil Company* (1904) skewered John D. Rockefeller and by extension every other "cold-hearted money-grubber" that ruled over an American business empire. In this environment, more people were drawn to concur with the poet and novelist Edgar Fawcett who wrote that the potentates of Wall Street played with marked cards and that admiring their ingenuity was akin to admiring the ingenuity of a man who scales a garden wall at midnight to rob a house.[6] Putting a lid on horse racing, a favorite pastime of Wall Street wheeler-dealers, was seen as just deserts.

Antigambling crusades exploited prejudicial feelings toward individuals at both ends of the economic spectrum, tapping into a growing aversion to immigrants during a period of intense immigration that reached its zenith in 1907, when more than one million immigrants swirled through the processing center at Ellis Island. Many reformers contributed to this animus with screeds that were sympathetic to society's underclass while betraying a belief in WASP superiority. Anthony Comstock and New York police commissioner Theodore A. Bingham were blunt, accusing immigrants of being the leading promoters of immorality. In January of 1907, while stumping for more resources to fight crime, Bingham cited the influx of foreigners as a special problem, declaring that many of the newcomers were of the criminal class. He would later describe the new arrivals as "the scum of Europe mostly."[7]

This opinion was powered by an anti-Semitic current that gained more steam when Bingham asserted that Jewish immigrants from Russia were responsible for half the crime in New York City. The statement appeared in the *North American Review* in an article titled "Foreign Criminals in New York." As for New York's bookmakers, Jews were an influential and growing segment, but the bookies of Bingham's day were mainly men of Irish extraction, as had been the norm from the very beginning. (The police commissioner was quick to repudiate his finding, saying he had been led astray by bad data.)[8]

Those favoring a hands-off approach to racetrack gambling worked from a short list of philosophical arguments. The recurrent refrain was that the all-out war against betting was an attack on personal liberty; government had no business criminalizing a noncoercive transaction. It was argued that the urge to speculate was human and it was foolish to waste resources suppressing behavior that was altogether normal. This viewpoint enjoyed wider currency in England. Gerald Wellesley, the headmaster of the Eton Mission Boys Club in East London, said, "The love of gambling, of excitement, of the unknown is ingrained in the British working classes, and no amount of law-making would drive it out."[9]

Racing created jobs, funded agricultural improvements through taxes, enriched the economy through tourism, and a day at the races was pictured as a healthy escape into the great outdoors for a working man who spent his days in a sooty factory and his nights in the claustrophobic confines of an overcrowded tenement. Some said the world would be a much drabber place if the reformers had their way and that any gains they achieved would only encourage them to inflict more cheerlessness. "What a nice world this would be," scoffed *New York World* sportswriter Frank W. Thorp. "No racing, no football, no boxing, no nothing, but just a peaceful existence of work six days a week and sit peacefully in church on the seventh twiddling one's thumbs."[10]

Thorp toiled for a paper that ran race results on the front page of its evening editions. In his view, the general public was largely indifferent to betting on races. He doubted that Governor Hughes would join forces with the "narrow-minded moralists" who paid the salaries of "professional agitators" like Anthony Comstock. "I do not believe that there is much danger of adverse legislation," opined Thorp as lawmakers were converging on Albany for the 1907 legislative session.[11]

Thorp was myopic. Outside New York, thoroughbred tracks were shutting down at an alarming rate. The reformers were winning.

In Illinois, thoroughbred racing staggered to a stop in 1904 when the Illinois attorney general issued an opinion that the state's antigambling law covered bettors as well as bookies. In Chicago, the sport had been under siege since 1892 when a consortium of poolroom barons opened the short-lived Garfield Park racetrack on the city's west side. The last big race in the Windy City was the 1904 edition of the prestigious American Derby at Washington Park, formerly the gathering place of Chicago's social elite. There were 216 uniformed policemen and ninety plainclothesmen on hand to inhibit betting. Three days later, the final twenty-two days of the meet were canceled.[12]

Racing ceased in Missouri in 1905 when the state supreme court ruled that the breeder's law was unconstitutional. Racetrack gambling was restored to a felony. This development was a foregone conclusion when Joseph "Holy Joe" Folk won the election for governor. Folk attacked racetrack gambling in his inauguration speech. The most notable casualty was the Delmar racetrack on the outskirts of St. Louis. A quasi-outlaw track (the foreign book always attracted a lively crowd), Delmar was a regular stop on the western racing circuit.

The Bennings track, the largest racetrack south of New York, was impoverished in 1906 by a law that forbade "setting up a gaming table." Management determined that the bookmakers could stay but that they had to keep moving. Without a distinct betting enclosure, attendance fell off immediately. Bettors were hesitant to bet for fear they would be unable to locate their man when it was time to collect.[13] The track, which opened in 1890, wobbled on through three more meets before the managers gave up the chase and threw in the towel.

As Thorpe was musing about the future of racing in New York, racetracks were folding in Arkansas and Tennessee. The handiwork of State Senator W. T. Amis, a Baptist preacher, the Arkansas anti-betting law of 1907 had a unique feature; it stipulated that a person in authority that failed to uphold the law would forfeit his office. The law completely changed the character of Hot Springs. Home to two racetracks and eight thriving poolrooms, the Ouachita Mountain resort community, with less than fifteen thousand permanent residents, was considered the most wide-open town in the country.[14]

The shutdown in Tennessee, which shuttered top-tier racetracks in Memphis and Nashville, was assailed by the pro-racing lobby as an affront to the memory of the state's most revered citizen, Andrew Jackson, whose leisure time was consumed with horse racing. "Old Hickory" kept racehorses at the White House and was involved in establishing the first track in Nashville.[15]

11

NEW YORK RACING

Feast and Famine

January of 1907 was a hectic month for William Travers Jerome. As the lead prosecutor in the sensational murder trial of Harry K. Thaw, he carried a great burden. The heir to a vast fortune, Thaw had pumped three bullets into Stanford White during the performance of a musical comedy in the rooftop theatre of Madison Square Garden, a building that White, America's most famous architect, had designed. With a great cast of characters, none more compelling than Thaw's twenty-one-year-old wife, chorus girl Evelyn Nesbit, a great beauty cast as a woman of easy virtue, the lurid trial—America's first "crime of the century"—captivated newspaper readers for months. Bookmakers in New York, Chicago, Philadelphia, Pittsburgh, Louisville, Cincinnati, Cleveland, and Denver posted odds on the outcome. (Bets were refunded, perhaps with a small service charge, when the trial ended in a hung jury. At his second trial, Thaw was found not guilty by virtue of insanity.)[1]

Despite his strenuous schedule, Jerome found time to press on with his campaign against racetrack gambling. On January 14, 1907, he made a quick trip to Albany in search of sponsors for seven bills that he had drafted, three of which addressed racetrack issues. The most caustic held racetrack operators culpable for allowing betting on their premises, subjecting them to imprisonment for one year, or a fine, or both. Another bill provided an appropriation of $210,000 for agricultural societies. This would replace the elastic stipend derived from racing receipts.[2]

Jerome had an avid supporter, very much a collaborator, in Governor Charles Evans Hughes, newly elected to a second two-year term, and an enthusiastic helpmate in first-term state senator George B. Agnew, a Republican from New York City. A staunch Presbyterian whose maternal ancestors were among the earliest English settlers to the Massachusetts Bay Colony, Agnew would introduce several anti-racetrack-gambling bills over the next few years, several cosponsored by Merwin K. Hart, a young legislator from Utica who in his later years became a leading advocate for the fervently anticommunist John Birch Society.

The bills drawn up by Jerome were presented to a Senate committee on March 20. Clergymen from every part of the state attended the hearing in a show of support, but their effort was for naught; the bills stagnated and died. Legislators from rural districts balked at the $210,000 appeasement. Some wanted assurances that the subsidy would continue into the indefinite future. Others were willing to gamble that a larger amount would accrue from maintaining the status quo. Track operators, with a big assist from the agricultural sector, were spared the shackle of repressive legislation.

The pro-racing lobby felt more secure when early returns gave evidence that 1907 would be a banner season, swelling state coffers with record receipts that would strengthen their argument that the economic benefits of racing outweighed whatever ills flowed from it. On June 20, a crowd estimated at fifty thousand turned up for the twenty-fourth running of the Suburban Handicap at Sheepshead Bay. More than seven hundred automobiles, many imported from Europe, were parked outside the park. With automobile ownership so rare (the first Model T hadn't yet rolled off the assembly line), this was a show in itself.

A reporter guessed that two world records were set that day. He calculated that women comprised half the audience, an unprecedented high, and that a record number of bookmakers were in action, approximately four hundred. Satellite betting rings appeared where none had existed before.[3]

Among other big crowds: More than thirty-five thousand were in the house for the Brighton Handicap at Brighton Beach on July 13, the largest turnout ever at Coney Island's oldest racetrack. An estimated forty thousand returned to Sheepshead Bay later that summer to see the Futurity Stakes, the richest race in the country. On November 15, Aqueduct attracted its largest crowd of the year, an estimated twenty-five thousand. The card was nothing special, but it was the final day of the metropolitan racing season. With no live racing in New York for the next five months, horseplayers were bellying up to the bar, in a manner of speaking, for one final drink before closing time.

When the racing season was finished, only Saratoga among the tracks on the New York Jockey Club circuit failed to report increased revenues. The city fathers of Saratoga were in one of their periodic "tone down the gambling" phases, a discouragement to tourism, as even the plush houses were impacted, but a larger contributing factor as to why the "Spa" failed to keep pace with her downstate cousins was the opening of Empire City, which ran races on dates that were previously exclusive to Saratoga.

The overall upsurge in the popularity of horse racing in 1907 was somewhat surprising in that it was a year of adversity on Wall Street. During the first nine months, stocks declined by 24.4 percent, and the bleakest days were yet to come. For some big plungers, the collapse of the copper market was devastating.

When the final figures were in, it would be shown that New York racegoers poured nearly $5 million directly into the coffers of racing associations, a jump of nearly 20 percent over 1906.[4] But this was a double-edged sword. From the vantage point of a racing man, the numbers proclaimed that the sport had become too big to fail; the economic fallout would be too great. But the reformers, possessed of a different mind-set, saw things differently. The numbers merely confirmed their worry that the gambling bug left unchecked would destroy society as effectively as the boll weevil destroyed the cotton crop.

THE END OF PERCY-GRAY

The success of the 1907 racing season led track operators to invest more heavily in upgrades. The expenditures reflected a positive mind-set, but the mood darkened on New Year's Day when Governor Hughes attacked racetrack gambling in his annual speech to the legislature. The Percy-Gray law must be revoked, he insisted, because its arbitrary distinctions subverted the state constitution, inviting contempt for law, and because racetrack gambling ran counter to the will of the people.[5] Five days after the speech, the legislature was presented with a new Agnew-Hart bill that incorporated the main components of the anti-racetrack-gambling bills drawn up by William Travers Jerome.

Hughes made the passage of Agnew-Hart a high priority. On Sunday afternoon, February 2, 1908, the governor held a mass meeting at the Majestic Theater, a Broadway playhouse. At the meeting, Dr. Walter Laidlaw, the executive secretary of the New York Federation of Churches, requested that every minister in the state theme his next sermon around the evils of racetrack gambling. Literature designed to aid the clergymen in the preparation of their sermons was already in the mail. The Jockey Club responded with a pamphlet that enumerated the economic benefits of horse racing and warned that the emasculation of racing in New York would drive more people to the poolrooms, where they would be seduced into making many more bets than they could at a racetrack that was under their purview.[6]

On April 8, 1908, the bill that would have repealed the Percy-Gray law in favor of a more stringent measure was defeated when the vote in the Senate ended in a 25–25 tie. Republicans favored the bill 23–8 but could not muster the required majority. A large delegation of racetrack men had descended on Albany in a last desperate attempt to scuttle the bill. When it was defeated, they were jubilant, but their mood would sour when it became known that Governor Hughes had an ace up his sleeve.

Because the vote ended in a tie, the lieutenant governor was able to table the motion for reconsideration at some future date. A legislator sympathetic to the reformers had recently died. Vacancies were normally left open until the next election cycle, but Hughes had the power to call a special election and did so, handpicking the Republican candidate who succeeded in winning the race. As he waited for these developments to play out, he revved up his crusade. Hughes took the defeat of the anti-racetrack-betting bill as a personal affront and was obsessed with rectifying the "injustice."

There were mass meetings galore in the days and weeks following the deadlock. On April 19, Hughes delivered a speech at a YMCA in Brooklyn in which he injected a new twist in his argument, framing the fight over racetrack gambling as a battle that pitted salt-of-the-earth people against mercenaries girded with "the unrighteous power of colossal wealth." His appearance filled the spacious hall to overflowing, leaving thousands of his admirers out on the street.[7]

For racetrack operators in New York and those that enjoyed wagering at New York tracks, June 11, 1908, was a dark day. On that day, in a special session of the state legislature, the Agnew-Hart anti-betting bill passed the Senate by a vote of 26–25. Governor Hughes signed the bill into law at 4:35 that afternoon. As the news spread, church bells chimed.[8]

The deciding vote was cast by newly elected senator William C. Wallace of Niagara Falls, but the man of the hour was Otto G. Foelker. Convalescing from an appendectomy, Senator Foelker (R-Brooklyn) was said to be gravely ill and he looked the part as he entered the Senate chambers braced by his physician and by his pastor, the noted reformer Canon William S. Chase. His head hung limp as speakers opposed to the Agnew-Hart bill droned on to drag out the proceedings in hopes that he would collapse before he had the opportunity to cast his vote, and when it was his turn, his voice was barely audible. Newspaper writers partial to Hughes anointed him a hero. The governor said that Foelker's performance was an act of courage as worthy of exaltation as that of a soldier who risks his life to save his comrades on the field of battle. A spokesman for the International Reform Bureau said "it was thrilling to see a man deliberately face death in order to do what he believed to be his duty."[9] (Foelker recovered quite nicely. A few months later he embarked on a successful campaign to win a seat in the U.S. House of Representatives. He lived to age seventy-seven, dying in 1943.)

THE AGNEW-HART LAW

Twenty-one years had elapsed since the Ives Pool law decriminalized on-track bookmaking. More than thirteen years had elapsed since the passage of the Percy-Gray law, which compelled the bookmakers to conduct their business more discreetly, but buffered them from serious legal repercussions by stipulating that the only penalty for accepting a wager was the forfeiture of the bet in a civil action. The Agnew-Hart Bill expunged this loophole. That meant that a man taking bets on a race course was now on the same plane as poolroom keepers, subject to arrest and imprisonment.

Governor Hughes insisted on strict enforcement. Before the ink on his signature was dry, a letter went out to every district attorney, police commissioner, and sheriff in the state requesting that they take whatever action was necessary to prevent betting. The new law went into effect on the eleventh day of the Gravesend summer meet. Two hundred policemen were on the premises to carry out Hughes's edict. Anyone seen standing in a clump of people with a marked-up program was threatened with arrest if he didn't move on. The betting ring was desolate—no bookmaker dared venture there—but the police found cause to make eight arrests. The harassment ceased when the police commissioner decided that oral bets would be tolerated if no money changed hands, but by then the meet was in its final days. [10]

The opening day of the Sheepshead summer meet with its rich Suburban Handicap was an established "happening" for high society, and 1908 was no exception. A crowd of twenty-five thousand turned up despite the constraints imposed on betting. But after that encouraging start, attendance fell off drastically. Early in the meet, the big betting shed was converted into a food court. By then, midweek crowds were down to about thirty-five hundred. This was a tough pill to swallow for the track's operators, who had spent lavishly on refurbishments and enhancements to maintain the track's reputation as the most beautiful racing plant in the country.

It appeared that the clamp would loosen when a judge ruled that the new law wasn't meant to suppress wagers between private citizens but pertained only to professional bet takers—defined as persons who framed the terms of the wager, held the stake, or recorded the transaction—but the ruling initially had the opposite effect, prompting the police to bear down harder on known bookmakers. There were numerous arrests during the Brighton Beach meet, and a key development occurred on July 21, 1908, when police arrived with arrest warrants for William Engeman Jr., William Fitzgerald, and John Cavanagh.

Engeman, the track's primary owner, Fitzgerald, the president of the Brighton Beach Racing Association, and Cavanagh, the superintendent of the betting ring, were indicted for aiding and abetting illegal gambling. The key pieces of evidence were Cavanagh's "overnight dope sheets." A bookie needed the advance information they contained—

entries, jockeys, assigned weights, and such—to get his house in order for the next day of racing. The charges were dismissed when a judge ruled that the sheets did not constitute a gambling device or apparatus, but by then Engeman had canceled his fall meet. Brighton Beach never reopened for thoroughbred racing, becoming the first casualty of the Agnew-Hart law.

The Saratoga meet, shortened from twenty-one to fifteen days, was fairly well attended. It helped that the regulars were accustomed to making their hotel reservations well in advance. It helped enormously that the Jockey Club had made peace with James Butler, who consented to splinter his Empire City meet so that there would be only one conflicting date.

The press was very sympathetic to Butler. An Irish immigrant who grew his grocery store into one of America's largest grocery chains, Butler epitomized the American dream. He had worked long and hard for the right to run a thoroughbred meet and then silenced the skeptics by running a very clean operation in his first year out of the box. Now all that effort and expense was seemingly for naught, as he had no prayer of turning a profit under current conditions. The police were out in force on opening day and shut the lid tighter as the meet progressed. Attendance declined sharply despite severely reduced admission prices.

The Empire City meet bled into the second meet of the year at Sheepshead Bay. The crowd on opening day for the Futurity Stakes was estimated at fifteen thousand, down from forty thousand the previous year. The turnout for the second day of racing was perhaps twenty-five hundred. The crowd was so thin that plainclothes detectives were easily spotted. Management kept the fall schedule intact but at considerable expense. In the final tally, receipts at Sheepshead Bay were down 80 percent from the previous year. [11]

As the 1908 New York racing season entered its final weeks, four- and five-horse fields became common. The shrinkage reached the height of absurdity on October 8 when only two horses ran in the feature race at Belmont Park. Both were owned by James R. Keene. A steward of the Jockey Club, Keene—the "Silver Fox of Wall Street"—then owned the most successful racing stable in the world.

The final meets at Aqueduct and Jamaica were cut short, amounting to eleven days in all. The five-day meet at Jamaica that marked the end of the season was expected to lose $15,000; the dent was much deeper.

When the final race was run, there were only a few hundred standing around. In summoning the horses to the post parade, the bugler strayed from his routine and played "taps."[12]

The heavy-handed enforcement of the Agnew-Hart law put the 1909 racing season in limbo. The Jockey Club was in the habit of releasing the yearly racing schedule in early January. That gave New York racing fans something to chew on until the season opened in mid-April. But in 1909, no announcement was forthcoming until April 5, and even then things were unsettled. The season, if it came off at all, was colored an experiment.

Jamaica and Aqueduct canceled their spring meets. Whether they would ever reopen was uncertain. Belmont Park, the first track to open, planned for only ten days of racing within its eighteen-day allotment. Management ultimately added one more day.

It was inevitable that short fields, endemic at the end of the previous season, would be a problem once again. Reduced purses chased many horsemen away. Most of the top horses were now in Europe. On October 16, 1908, fifty racehorses left New York harbor for England on the steamship *Minnehaha*, the most impressive gathering of equine talent ever assembled on a moving object. The stables of James R. Keene, August Belmont, and Harry Payne Whitney were well represented. Topping the list of luminaries was Keene's sensational Colin, undefeated in fifteen starts. Horses of Colin's stature were so celebrated that they were imbued with human personalities. Taking them out of circulation eroded the sport's popularity among young adults, the racegoers of tomorrow. (Colin broke down within days after arriving in England and never raced again.)

When the 1909 Belmont Park season opened, the clubhouse was missing several of its most notable members. They had already left for England to see the big races at Epsom Downs. Americans were responsible for much of the ante-post money wagered in London on Sir Martin in the Derby, forcing a sharp drop in his odds. Bred and developed by John Madden at his famous Kentucky stud farm, Sir Martin had recently been sold to American expatriate Louis Winans, formerly of Baltimore. Running on a soggy track, Sir Martin was well positioned when he stumbled and threw his rider, much to the relief of the British bookies.[13]

With the caliber of racing at a low pitch, the New York papers devoted proportionately more space to off-track developments. Several tests of the anti-bookmaking law were wending through the courts and the early returns were encouraging. On May 7, 1909, in a case involving prominent MTA members Sol Lichtenstein and Orlando Jones, a judge ruled that there could be no bookmaking without writing or recording. The result was that the police backed off in harassing bookmakers, so long as they were properly circumspect. It was estimated that three hundred arrests for gambling were made at New York thoroughbred tracks in 1908.[14] During the late spring and early summer of 1909, there were virtually none.

The promise of a less combustible environment led to the reopening of Jamaica and Aqueduct and the reinstatement of the fall meet at Sheepshead Bay. In announcing that racing would continue beyond the Saratoga season, spokesmen for the racing associations emphasized the importance of preserving the "classics." The previous year, Matt Winn, the manager of Churchill Downs in Louisville, had famously kept the Kentucky Derby intact after the newly elected City Council rammed through an ordinance prohibiting bookmaking. The wording of the new statute left open a loophole for pari-mutuel machines. They hadn't been used at Churchill Downs since 1889, and it took some doing to locate their whereabouts and then get them working properly, but Winn had them up and running on the day of the Derby.

Although track operators kept the doors open, the caliber of racing remained poor. The six-horse field for the 1909 Futurity Stakes was the weakest in years. With purses chopped to the bone, the feature races at Jamaica and Aqueduct attracted horses that would have been consigned to claiming races a few years earlier. On the final day of the 1909 New York racing season, a horse named Fitz Herbert, hailed as the best three-year-old in the country, established a new world record for the two-mile run. He accomplished the feat at Pimlico. For the moment, Maryland had overtaken New York as America's premier locale for Grade-A thoroughbred racing.

Reformers weren't satisfied with the victories they had achieved and pushed for action at the federal level. In December of 1909, the United States Senate Judiciary Committee held hearings on a bill prohibiting the transmission of racetrack odds over telegraph and telephone wires. Sponsored by Senator Elmer Burkett of Nebraska, the bill was the handiwork of the International Reform Bureau. In rebuttal to those that said that this was a matter for the states to decide, proponents cited the Louisiana Lottery. In 1890, Congress forbade lottery operators from sending lottery tickets and lottery circulars through the U.S. mail. The law even gave postal authorities the right to confiscate newspapers that carried lottery advertisements. When the law was upheld by the Supreme Court, the Louisiana Lottery, roundly decried as a giant octopus of immorality, passed into oblivion.[15]

The star of the Senate hearings was Henry Brolaski. A reformed gambler, Brolaski had worked as a racing correspondent, owned racehorses, managed poolrooms, and had booked and bet at more than a dozen tracks. He had also run a pick-selling outfit in Chicago, for which he was arrested, a piece of his bio conveniently omitted when he enumerated his credentials as an expert witness. His testimony was insightful and entertaining, bringing him so much notoriety that he was inspired to write a book. (Sample sentence: "The race track is a postule on the neck of civilization, and its owners and managers sit upon it like a bread and milk poultice on a boil, drawing the corruption of the community to a head.")[16]

Brolaski asserted that poolrooms and handbooks in New York City serviced a hundred thousand horseplayers, most of whom were men in poorly paid occupations, and that the number of poolroom patrons was growing daily. He said that the odds against the bettor were stacked so high that it was impossible to beat the game. He said that he was personally acquainted with men who became drunkards and thieves after being inoculated with the gambling germ.[17]

On the very day that the picturesque Brolaski was giving his testimony, several of New York's racing associations announced in a joint statement that they would be increasing the prize money for the big-stakes races, a calculated attempt to increase patronage by putting out a better product. Something had to give.

Reformers seeking to close the coffin on racetrack gambling were cheered when Governor Hughes underlined his commitment to their cause in his annual address to the legislature on January 5, 1910. Hughes made it known that he was deeply disturbed by the evasions of the anti-bookmaking law and recommended that violators be punished with imprisonment, rather than fines.[18]

Shortly thereafter, William Travers Jerome presented the legislature with yet another set of anti-racetrack-gambling bills. They were cosponsored by Senator Agnew and Binghamton assemblyman Harry Perkins. One of the measures prohibited newspapers from publishing racing dope, such as morning line odds, mutuel prices, and selections. This bill died in committee. Another bill allowed a policeman to make an arrest without written evidence of the wager. This bill was passed into law, as was the third bill, the Racetrack Directors' Liability law. This was the crusher.

RACETRACK DIRECTORS' LIABILITY LAW

The Percy-Gray law of 1895 exempted racetrack operators from liability for gambling so long as they posted notices that gambling was forbidden and furnished policemen to deter would-be violators. Subsequent bills attempted to quell betting by hogtieing the bookmakers but left this provision intact.

The Directors' Liability law—it came to be known as the Hughes law—eliminated this escape hatch. It made track operators criminally liable for any betting that occurred on their premises. In theory, it allowed for the arrest of the entire membership of a racing association down to the lowliest stockholder.

Al Smith, an assemblyman from the Tammany stronghold of lower Manhattan, squawked that if the bill was passed it wouldn't be safe for a man to walk around the racetrack and talk to his friends. In a desperate attempt to derail the measure, Smith offered up amendments that he knew would get shot down—that would have extended the provisions of the bill to the stock market.[19] Attorneys for the Jockey Club argued that the law was an assault on personal liberty that could be used to punish railroads, hotels, and private clubs—any establishment where card games were played for money. The solons wouldn't buy it. The Liability law passed both houses by better than a three-to-one margin.

Hughes signed the bill into law on May 27, 1910. When the law went into effect on September 1, it was lights out for New York racing. The final ten weeks of the season were canceled.

The last big race of 1910 was the Futurity Stakes. The crowning jewel of the fall meet at Sheepshead Bay, it was shifted to Saratoga,

where it ran on August 31. In the crowd were hundreds who braved bad
weather to show their loyalty to the sport. It would be several years
before they had another opportunity to witness live thoroughbred racing in New York.

12

THE GOOD-BYE YEARS

Charles Evans Hughes left office before his term expired. On October 10, 1910, not quite six weeks after the cessation of racing in New York, ex-Governor Hughes was sworn in as an associate justice of the United States Supreme Court.

Hughes's leave-taking came too late to appease those hurt by his actions. "The destruction of millions of dollars of property of other people mattered nothing to him," bristled a Kentucky reporter.[1] But his resignation was welcomed by racetrack operators in New York. The reopening of their facilities was conditional on the repeal of the Directors' Liability law and his departure was seen as a crack in the armor. However, any loosening of restrictive legislation would be going against the grain. The anti-racetrack-gambling crusade had claimed many victims.

The abolition of open gambling at racetracks in Illinois, Missouri, Arkansas, and Tennessee were big victories for the reformers, who achieved an even bigger victory in 1908 when lawmakers in Louisiana passed legislation that promised to shut down racing in famously libertine New Orleans. The first city in the country to permit racing on Sundays, the Crescent City had a rich horse racing tradition. Similar legislation was in the works in California where developments perfectly mirrored developments in New York. An exact replica of the Agnew-Hart bill found favor with legislators who tightened it with new legislation that did away with the subterfuge of oral betting.

The last thoroughbred race in California before the curtain came down was run at the Emeryville track on the outskirts of Oakland on February 15, 1911. Three notable tracks fell by the wayside before Emeryville went dark. The Ingleside track in southeast San Francisco was a casualty of the 1906 earthquake. Ascot Park, built on the outskirts of Los Angeles, ceased operations in 1907. The track's days were numbered when the strip of land on which it sat was annexed by the city, which had a municipal ordinance prohibiting pool selling. The short-lived Santa Anita track died in 1909 with the death of its founder, Lucky Baldwin. The park fell into disuse, save as a picnic ground, as Baldwin's heirs and creditors battled over his estate.

The loss of Emeryville was hard on the poolrooms. After the earthquake, the racing meet was extended and then extended again, reaching one hundred and eighty days, making it far and away the longest meet in the country. The races there were run in the colder months when live racing in New York was dormant. The situation became more critical when the Florida tracks were shut down by legislation that took effect in 1911. That dried up racing in Jacksonville, Tampa, and Pensacola. For a brief time, the only winter racing of any consequence was found in Juarez, and the political situation there was so unstable that one never knew if a day of racing would come off as planned, a dilemma compounded by frequent stoppages because of harsh weather. By then, racetrack betting was conducted openly in only six states: Maryland, Kentucky, Virginia, West Virginia, Montana, and Utah. Of these, only Maryland and Kentucky conducted the sport on a high plane. Churchill Downs was the gemstone of racing in Kentucky, but the poolroom operators wrote more business on Latonia, a track situated across the river from Cincinnati, Ohio.

The number of jobs lost as a result of the deconstruction was unknown; estimates ranged upwards of fifty thousand. Many stable hands had known no other kind of work and were too old or too small of stature to transition into manual labor. Thousands of restaurant, hotel, and boardinghouse workers were laid off. There were fewer employment opportunities for telegraphers and railroad workers. Even bootblacks suffered as every rail station had a shoeshine stand. In the peak year of 1907, the Long Island Railroad carried 780,000 passengers to the racetracks in Brooklyn and Queens, generating $400,000 in fares. That revenue stream was gone.[2]

Two places that were especially hard hit were Saratoga and the Blue-grass region of Kentucky. Unlike Coney Island, Saratoga was too far off the beaten path to subsist on the patronage of day-trippers. Some of the businessmen in the village made virtually their entire year's profit during the racing season. Many homeowners cashed in by renting out a room in their home. Some drew the same renter year after year and the annual summer visitor became almost like a member of the family. And while Saratoga remained an important destination for conventions, the conventioneers did not spend as freely as the racegoers.

The Bluegrass region suffered a deeper recession. With fewer races and smaller purses, the value of racehorses declined sharply. Breeders sold off their stock at drastically reduced prices and converted their land to crops, mainly tobacco and hemp. Between 1910 and 1912, the wholesale exodus of broodmares, stallions, and yearlings reached epidemic proportions. Some were purchased by foreign governments for military use. The best of the older horses went to breeding farms in France, England, and Argentina. The four-legged emigrants included such notables as Peter Pan and the great filly Maskette, future inductees into the National Museum of Racing and Hall of Fame.[3]

The Jockey Club remained active during the fallow years because its tentacles reached beyond the Empire State. The club set the racing dates for Pimlico and assisted the Maryland Jockey Club in supervising the meets. The partnership had deep roots. Railroad magnate Oden Bowie, the founder and first president of the Maryland Jockey Club, was a fixture at Saratoga in the days of John Morrissey and had been a major stockholder in Jerome Park. The Jockey Club developed a similar arrangement with the local operators of Jamestown Park in Norfolk, Virginia, which ran from 1910 to 1914.

The closing of racetracks in New York gave rise to new racetracks in Maryland. Laurel Park, Havre de Grace, and Bowie (originally called Prince George's Park) opened within a span of four years. The closing of racetracks in Florida led to the resumption of racing in Charleston, South Carolina, and spurred the opening of Oriental Park in Havana, a place that came to have a full-fledged gambling casino under the grandstand. As for New York's metropolitan racetracks, they were turned to other uses while awaiting an uncertain future. The Coney Island tracks were deployed for motorcycle and auto races. Belmont Park was the site of the first international aviation meet held on American soil.

BETTING ON BASEBALL

The curtailment of racing whipped baseball into a bigger betting sport. Six weeks before the start of the 1911 season, a poolroom in Newport, Kentucky, operating as the Western Commission Company, released their first "baseball prospectus." It contained a list of future book prices for teams in four leagues: the two major leagues, the International League, and the American Association. Win, place, and show odds were attached to each team. Bettors could hitch their wager to the final standings or the standings at the midpoint of the season. Teams perceived to be roughly equal were pitted head-to-head in a "most season wins" proposition. Wagers were accepted by Western Union or via private postal carriers.[4] In addition to known gamblers, the circular was sent to the sports editors of leading newspapers. The information made for a good story and the odds were widely disseminated.

The proliferation of gambling worried baseball executives. The expression that gambling killed horse racing was heard so often that it had become an aphorism and keeping baseball free of it became a large priority. The growing popularity of baseball pools made the situation more worrisome. Aimed at small players—"newsboys selling papers to help support poverty stricken families," said one critic—these pools were geared toward identifying the team or combination of teams that scored the most runs within a specified time frame. Payouts were determined on the pari-mutuel principle. In Pennsylvania, activity was especially strong in Wilkes-Barre and the nearby industrial city of Scranton. Baseball was big in these cities, which housed the only Pennsylvania clubs in the eight-team New York State Baseball League. Governor John K. Tener, a former major league player and future National League president, encouraged all of the state's municipalities to stamp out this menace, promising the assistance of state lawmen if local authorities were overwhelmed.[5]

Although the evidence is anecdotal, betting at ballparks grew more rampant. Working with local authorities, American League president Ban Johnson initiated a drive to rid the parks of the gambling element. On June 16, 1913, twenty-seven were arrested during the Philadelphia-Cleveland game at Philadelphia's Shibe Park and a large number of known gamblers were denied admission to the Yankees-Tigers game at the Polo Grounds. The Yankees were then owned by Frank J. Farrell and William "Big Bill" Devery. Farrell belonged to the Metropolitan Turf Association. Devery, an ex-bartender, was formerly New York's police commissioner.[6]

In 1915 there was a national campaign to stamp out baseball pools. Arrests were made in Philadelphia, Baltimore, Pittsburgh, Youngstown, Cincinnati, Chicago, Milwaukee, Minneapolis, New Orleans, St. Louis, Little Rock, Oakland, and other cities. In a related development, government agents seized upon the federal anti-lottery law to bring charges against the owners of a baseball weekly produced in Wilkes-Barre that was running a blind baseball pool designed as a premium to boost circulation. The paper ceased publication.[7]

Betting at ballparks remained a problem. Syndicated baseball writer Hugh Fullerton, writing in 1917, reported that well-defined betting sections were becoming more prevalent. Fullerton warned that this development, left unchecked, would morph into a scandal that would rock the sport.[8] His apprehension was prophetic.

RACING RETURNS TO NEW YORK

In laboring to repeal—or at least relax—the Directors' Liability law, the Jockey Club found supporters among higher-ups in agricultural societies and in the War Department. The centerpiece of most county fairs was the trotting races. Because these attracted gambling, many were discontinued out of fear of legal reprisal and the fairs suffered a loss of patronage. Without mentioning New York specifically, Major General Leonard Wood said that he was alarmed by the depletion of thoroughbred breeding farms. Since the best war horses were stallions with a thoroughbred strain, the needs of a strong military were being undermined. A Harvard-trained physician and Medal of Honor recipient, Major General Wood spoke with authority.[9]

The easement essential for the resumption of racing came on February 21, 1913, when the Appellate Division of the New York Supreme Court upheld the ruling of a lower court in the case of a Long Island barber arrested for taking bets at an amateur steeplechase event on the grounds of Belmont Park. The ruling, in a nutshell, absolved track operators for responsibility for private wagers of which they had no foreknowledge.[10] Later that year, racing resumed at Belmont Park with an eighteen-day meet spread across six weeks. Saratoga resumed racing later that summer. Aqueduct and Empire City came back online the following year and Jamaica reopened in 1915. Thoroughbred racing never returned to Coney Island. The three tracks were eventually chopped up into building lots. The grand hotels died out too, and an area once known for fine cuisine became identified with the lowly hot dog.

The revival of thoroughbred racing at Belmont Park on Memorial Day, May 30, 1913, was a front-page news story. The crowd was thick with members of the Social Register. A reporter noted that straw hats with plumes were in vogue for women and that some of the younger ladies accessorized their attire with a walking stick. There was no open betting. Governor William Sulzer had threatened to call out the militia if the restriction wasn't rigidly enforced.

The star-studded turnout was a testament to the pertinacity of August Belmont II. Belmont Park occupied an immense tract of land whose value had increased dramatically in just a few years as engineering advances tightened the cord between Queens and Manhattan. The Queensboro Bridge was completed in 1909. The next year saw the opening of the first railroad tunnel under the East River, a passageway connecting Queens to New York's newly completed Pennsylvania Station. When racing was under fire and the future of the sport looked grim, many of the shareholders in Belmont Park wanted to tear the place down, but Belmont persuaded them to keep the faith.

New York was back in the racing game, but restoring the sport to its former glory would take time. Track operators could not boost purses to previous levels until patronage returned to previous levels, and the prickly betting situation was a hindrance. The Kentucky Derby now ruled as the sport's marquee event, having overtaken the big New York races, and the disparity was never more apparent than in 1915. A record seven eastern horses were in the seventeen-horse Derby field, horses that in an earlier day would have stayed in New York to run in the Metropolitan Handicap. The ranks included the winner, Harry Payne Whitney's Regret, the first filly to win the Kentucky Derby.

It was helpful to Belmont's cause, however, that efforts to make race betting a federal crime had lost steam. Gambling on horse races remained an important issue for the International Reform Bureau, but less attention was paid to it as the organization's goals became more diffuse. In 1914, a more burning issue put the IRB in the forefront of a drive to establish a federal censorship board for motion pictures. Two years later, in a mild upset, Charles Evans Hughes, the great scourge of racetrack operators, lost his bid for the White House, edged out by Woodrow Wilson. Hughes went on to become the secretary of state under Warren Harding and the chief justice of the Supreme Court during the administrations of Herbert Hoover and Franklin Delano Roosevelt. He would come to be venerated as one of the shining stars in the history of American jurisprudence.

13

REANIMATION

The shuttering of racetracks in New York and then their reopening a few years later was part of a national trend. Race courses in New York, Louisiana, and California all bloomed anew after a brief period of hibernation. During the fallow, the owners of inactive racetracks were charged with finding a better method of accommodating gamblers.

In New York, the ruling that emasculated the Directors' Liability law spelled out in finer detail the essence of a bookmaker. He was a bet taker who took on all comers, evincing this disposition by displaying odds, soliciting and recording bets, and exchanging money. The statutes forbidding bookmaking, it was determined, were meant for men of this stripe, professional layers who exhibited a "continuity of practice." This interpretation put the stamp of approval on private wagers provided that there was no documentation.[1]

When the racetracks reopened, management took pains to see that the new law was followed scrupulously. The Pinkertons stopped bookmakers from forming clusters and the enumeration of odds was strictly oral. Without seeing the prices displayed on a blackboard or on a handout, bettors were less likely to take a flyer on a disfavored horse and bookmakers, with little hope of achieving a balanced book, had no recourse but to offer less generous odds. Horseplayers griped that the layers were "too greedy."

As an oral wager, by definition, was a wager made on credit, welshing became a larger concern. The bookmaker was almost always the victim, but there were cases when it was he who failed to meet his obligations. In theory the racetrack managers could do nothing about it as they took no cognizance of betting, but word got around and an untrustworthy bookmaker would soon discover that he was being watched very closely by plainclothesmen instructed to find an excuse to have him arrested and barred from the premises.

The shackles imposed on bookmakers led many to abandon the race course in favor of conducting all their business on the telephone. Outside New York, on-course bookmakers were becoming extinct, swept aside by the onslaught of the "Iron Man."

In France, where the concept originated, pari-mutuel betting acquired a legal monopoly. Bookmakers were officially expelled from the race courses in 1887, leaving the pari-mutuels the only legal option for racegoers. Germany and Austria would soon follow suit. In all of these countries, the national government took an active role in regulating race meets. In France, the chief magistrate of thoroughbred racing was the minister of agriculture. A portion of the tax assessed on pari-mutuel wagers went to agricultural prizes.

The great apostle of pari-mutuel betting in America was Matt Winn. In 1908, Winn famously dusted off six discarded machines and rushed them into service as a stopgap measure when the Louisville City Council outlawed bookmaking. The public wasn't initially receptive to them, but when the minimum bet was reduced from $5 to $2 in 1911, betting surged. When the anti-bookmaking ordinance was overturned, Winn decided against letting the bookies back in. By then, pari-mutuel wagering was the exclusive method of betting at the Lexington and Latonia tracks in Kentucky, at three of the four tracks in Maryland, and at the Ontario track in Toronto. The dominoes were falling. (An extremely popular racetrack character—Colonel Winn to the folks in Kentucky—Matt Winn was the face of Churchill Downs, but during his forty-seven-year association with the Louisville track he was all over the map. He managed tracks in New Orleans, was James Butler's right hand man at Empire City and at the Laurel track in Maryland, introduced winter racing in Juarez, Mexico, and led the charge to reopen the Hawthorne track in Chicago.)[2]

Proponents of pari-mutuels would come to accentuate the tax benefits, but during the early years other arguments were heard. At many tracks, the bookmakers were itinerants who floated from one racing meet to another. If they inflated their bankrolls during their stay, the money left town. Pari-mutuels kept the money in the community. Where bettors had a choice between pari-mutuels and bookmakers, it was observed that the crowds milling about the pari-mutuel booths were more orderly.

A big breakthrough in pari-mutuel technology occurred with the invention of the totalizator, an innovation credited to former railroad engineer George Julius, the son of the Anglican archbishop of New Zealand. Described as a massive tangle of piano wires and pulleys, Julius's machine, introduced in Auckland in 1913, transmitted electrical signals between the ticket-issuing machines, the adding machines, and a display board that was updated at frequent intervals, keeping horseplayers abreast of the money bet on each horse and the grand total in the betting pool. Julius's contraption—a precursor of the modern digital computer—was ingenious, but the first versions had serious drawbacks. Most notably, the adding machines couldn't keep up with major shifts in the odds resulting from lopsided last-minute wagering.[3]

Gamblers accustomed to betting with racetrack bookmakers were none too pleased by the transformation to pari-mutuels. It changed the dynamics of the game by diminishing the importance of shopping for the best odds. However, a big plunger could still manipulate the odds, in a fashion, by placing his money with bookmakers. His action wouldn't be reflected in the racetrack's pari-mutuel pools. The problem was that it was becoming harder to outsource a large wager. During the second decade of the twentieth century, there was a sharp decline in the number of poolrooms. More frequent police raids coupled with less "inventory" (i.e., fewer races on which to bet) drove many operators out of business.

In New York City, a large contributing factor in the decline of poolrooms was the backlash that attended the sensational murder of Herman Rosenthal. A small-time gambler who ran a little casino in the brownstone building where he made his home, Rosenthal died in a hail of bullets on the pavement in front of the Hotel Metropole shortly after 2 AM on the morning of July 16, 1912. His violent death was attributed to his refusal to pony up "ice" to the police. Five men eventually went to the electric chair, the four hired guns and the alleged mastermind, police lieutenant Charles S. Becker. The tabloids milked the story with lurid headlines for months on end.

The Metropole, where Rosenthal spent his final hours, was a favorite late-night haunt of the sporting crowd; the hotel on Forty-Third Street just off Times Square had a sports ticker in the barroom. Some of the biggest election bets were sealed and settled there. George Considine, who ran the place with two of his brothers, was a prominent bookmaker and prizefight promoter who was rumored to be the hidden owner of several poolrooms. This put all of New York's poolrooms in the cross-hairs and they went dark for two weeks following Rosenthal's murder. The mood wasn't conducive to "business as usual." The climate of fear led many to throw in the towel.[4]

Although the number of poolrooms declined, handbooks proliferated. According to a feature story in the *New York Tribune*, handbooks were found on almost every street and in almost every semipublic building in New York City that sat within five miles of a racetrack. The southwest corner of Forty-Second Street and Broadway became a clearinghouse. Men with routes in the area gravitated here after completing their rounds to share gossip and lay off bets. The land they tilled was fertile. "A large number of employees in every business house talk of racing and betting most of the day and pore over 'dope sheets' and 'past performance records' well into the night," said the *Tribune* reporter.[5]

On January 16, 1920, "dry" became the law of the land with the passage of the Volstead Act. Many saloons stayed open, adding more pool tables in hopes of compensating for lost revenue from beer and liquor sales. Pool was then very much in vogue and manufacturers of tables and cue sticks were having difficulty keeping up with the demand. By 1921, there were more than twenty-five thousand commercial pool tables in greater New York City.[6]

The upshot was that the term "poolroom" came to have an entirely different meaning. It referenced a place where the game of pool was played, not a place where people gathered to bet the ponies. The distinction, however, was somewhat blurred. Many poolrooms served a double purpose, functioning also as handbooks. That was true of Doyle's Billiard Academy, conveniently located in the heart of Times Square, although the proprietor, John "Broadway Jack" Doyle, a former sheet writer, insisted that he formulated his odds for fun, leaving the bet-taking to others. Doyle's prices on important sporting events and his World Series "future book," updated weekly, were great fodder for sportswriters. His quotations turned up in dozens of papers.[7]

The Volstead Act was bad news for struggling racetrack operators as beer sales were an important source of revenue, but the good news was that all signs pointed to a more prosperous day. The war in Europe had ended triumphantly for America and its allies, unleashing forces that hopped up the allure of spectator sports, both here and in England and France. Horsemen could sense that racing would get caught up in the swirl. The horses put up for bid in August of 1919 at the Saratoga yearling sale commanded record prices.[8]

It helped greatly that some phenomenal racehorses arrived on the scene in the immediate postwar years, a period when newspaper readership was at an all-time high and papers rushed to expand their sports coverage. Exterminator won the 1918 Kentucky Derby and got better as he got older, ultimately winning fifty races while finishing in the money in eighty-four of ninety-nine opportunities. The year 1919 marked the debut of the wonder horse Man o' War. Originally owned by August Belmont II, who disposed of his entire stable before going off to France to assist in the war effort, Man o' War was victorious in twenty of twenty-one starts in a career that spanned only sixteen months. In his final race, he defeated reigning Horse of the Year Sir Barton by seven lengths in a Columbus Day match race at Kenilworth Park in Ontario that was billed as the Race of the Century.

Three years later, on October 20, 1923, Belmont Park was the site of a heavily hyped event when Kentucky Derby winner Zev, owned by Tulsa oilman Harry Sinclair, met English Derby winner Papyrus in the first great international match race. The American entrant prevailed on a muddy track before forty-five thousand, and while the attendance was rather disappointing, the receipts, reportedly $432,000 plus $50,000 for the exclusive movie rights, were thought to be at least double the previous high for a North American racing event.[9]

Promoters elsewhere were inspired to hop on the bandwagon. In the summer of 1923, organizers launched a twenty-five-day meet at the vintage Hawthorne track in the Cicero suburb of Chicago, the most extensive program of racing in the Windy City in almost two decades. Attendance declined sharply toward the end of the meet and the organizers lost interest, but racing would continue under new ownership following a favorable court ruling on oral betting. The ruling kept intact the rule prohibiting the display of money, but racegoers were free to openly exchange marked-up slips of paper in which money was easily concealed.[10]

By 1927, there were four more tracks operating in or near Chicago. The tracks were located in Aurora (Exposition Park), Homewood (Washington Park), Crete (Lincoln Fields), and Arlington Heights (Arlington Park). The new Washington Park, built by a consortium of city, county, and state officials, was the first racetrack built in Cook County in more than a quarter century. The ubiquitous Matt Winn headed up the management team at Lincoln Fields, the grandest of the new facilities.

The inaugural meetings at Washington Park and Lincoln Fields in 1926 were conducted under the so-called modified mutuel certificate system. This was merely pari-mutuel betting clothed in language meant to keep the authorities at bay. A man making a wager, ostensibly a shareholder purchasing stock in a horse, received a ticket labeled "certificate" from a clerk working under a sign that read "broker" and his winnings, if any, were defined as dividends. This charade, which was previously deployed in Louisiana and Florida, became unnecessary when Illinois legalized pari-mutuel betting in 1927.[11]

In California, the attempt to revive thoroughbred racing proved more difficult. In the fall of 1923, racing returned to the Golden State after a twelve-year absence with a twenty-five-day meet at the refurbished Tanforan track in the San Francisco suburb of San Bruno. The next year, promoters in southern California launched a meet at a speedway in the LA County community of Culver City. Both endeavors were short-lived. California's stubborn no-betting law proved to be too big of a hindrance.[12]

Although California was a dead zone for thoroughbred racing during the Golden Era of Sports, the same wasn't true of Baja California. In 1916, an investment group headed by James W. "Sunny Jim" Coffroth opened a racetrack in Tijuana, Mexico, a dusty border town then inhabited by about fifteen thousand people. They named the track Tia Juana.

Coffroth came from San Francisco, where he had become wealthy promoting big outdoor prizefights. When California kissed goodbye to fights of national importance by restricting all bouts, amateur and professional, to four rounds, Coffroth switched to horse racing. He struggled mightily at the beginning, nearly ruined by a terrible flood, but the loosening of passport restrictions after World War I and then the Volstead Act brought about a dramatic turnaround. Tijuana became the place to go to cast off the shackles of social reform. There were no restrictions on drinking or gambling. At Tia Juana, bookmakers coexisted with pari-mutuel machines and the main bar stayed open long after the last race was run.

The races at Tia Juana conventionally ran from Thanksgiving to Easter Sunday. On special days, the card consisted of as many as fourteen races with an early starting time and a long intermission, a siesta in harmony with the culture. On these days, the Santa Fe Railroad ran excursion trains from Los Angeles to the Tijuana/San Diego trolley. The signature event, the Coffroth Handicap, became the richest race in the country and earned Sunny Jim the distinction of being the first person to promote a race with a six-figure purse. In 1929, the track gave way to a more modern plant called Agua Caliente. Coffroth was then on the outs with some of his business partners; they succeeded in reducing his influence. The Coffroth Handicap was disbanded, although management insisted that it had merely been dressed with a new name, the Agua Caliente Handicap.

As racing regained strength, off-track betting shook off the doldrums and grew in lockstep. In December of 1920, West Coast vice crusader Robert C. Barton, the founder of an organization called the Morals Efficiency Association, urged the police to clamp down on betting parlors in San Diego, the growth of which was a by-product of the lively racing scene across the border. Barton's efforts were ineffective. In 1928, there were reportedly 280 bookmakers in San Diego. The city then had a population of about one hundred forty thousand. [13]

14

A VERDANT DEPRESSION

Agua Caliente was conceived as a destination resort. The racetrack with its foreign book was the final piece of a complex that included a hotel, guest bungalows, a gambling casino (with a strict dress code), golf course, spa, airstrip, and a separate oval for greyhound racing in the summer months. The hotel gift shops stocked "only the costliest of imported perfumes, rugs, tapestries, knickknacks, and whatnot."[1] In the eyes of the developers, Agua Caliente was going to be the lever that lifted ramshackle Tijuana into a more intimate and more upscale version of naughty Havana.

The timing was clumsy. As management was preparing for the grand opening of their racetrack, things went haywire on Wall Street. In a two-day period in late October of 1929, the Dow Jones Industrial Average declined 23 percent, an ominous portent. Agua Caliente became a popular playground for Hollywood royalty during the Great Depression, but the sour economy compelled Joe Public to curtail his spending and the complex never achieved the grand vision of its founders. The racetrack was padlocked in July of 1935 by order of Lazaro Cardenas, the president of Mexico, and although the lockdown was rescinded in 1937, the track struggled without the companion attraction of the casino, which was seized by the government and converted into an industrial trade school. During the war years and beyond, thoroughbred racing in Tijuana was largely restricted to weekends. (In 1973, the grandstand was destroyed by a fire and Sunday racing was introduced at tracks in southern California. This was a double whammy. Live thoroughbred racing at Agua Caliente was doomed.)

For horsemen in general, the Great Depression was a double-edged sword. At established tracks, attendance plummeted. However, the public became more tolerant of betting, an augur of better times.

The Depression provided grist for the supposition that a society's moral backbone becomes less rigid during times of economic privation. Folks troubled by "licensing immorality," save for the hard-core, were more receptive when it was touted as a tool for reducing unemployment and lessening the burdens of hard times. A tax that would fall only on people with bad habits encountered the least resistance; indeed, some people thought it was a splendid idea.

The revitalization of thoroughbred racing during the roaring 1920s was powered by higher wages and shorter working hours and an unprecedented level of enthusiasm for spectator sports. The expansion of horse racing during the Depression was propelled by an urgent need to develop new sources of tax revenue to mend a fractured tax base. One couldn't tax horse race gambling without first legalizing it and legalization resulted in a flood of new racetracks. (A residual benefit of racetracks, said the proponents, was that it spurred an increase in gasoline consumption. Every state taxed gasoline. In the mid-1930s, the average levy was three-and-a-half cents per gallon, hardly chump change considering the rundown economy.)

The developers who opened the Hialeah Park racetrack in 1925—part of a complex that included a dog track and a jai alai fronton—were looking to establish a foothold in America's fastest-growing area. Then the real estate bubble burst, exacerbated by a terrible hurricane, and all of greater Miami fell into a rut. Local merchants, initially wary of the racetrack, came to see it as a net gain for the community and turned a blind eye when the track's operators, flouting the law, installed pari-mutuel machines in 1927. But lawmakers at the state capitol in Tallahassee, 480 miles from Hialeah, were none too pleased and the track was forced to cancel the 1928 season. The depopulation resulting from the collapse of the housing market hurt the entire state, but Floridians in the upstate "Cracker counties" had little sympathy for the folks in greater Miami, a place overrun with Northerners at a time when the term Yankee still had connotations of a carpetbagger.

When the Depression kicked in, bringing hard times to every hamlet of the state, the mood softened. On June 4, 1931, Florida lawmakers approved pari-mutuel betting on a local-option basis. In short order, thoroughbred tracks were up and running in St. Augustine (St. John's Park), Coral Gables (Tropical Park), and Pompano Beach (Pompano). Over the next four years, tracks opened or were reopened in Rhode Island, Massachusetts, New Hampshire, West Virginia, Ohio, Michigan, Texas, California, Oregon, and Washington. Pari-mutuel betting even spread to the Bahamas. The first legal racetrack in the British colony opened in Nassau in January of 1934. The government hoped that receipts from racing would cushion the loss of revenue resulting from the repeal of Prohibition. The island was a major base for American rum runners.

The dissimilar situations in Kentucky and Rhode Island offer revealing windows into the tenor of the times. In 1933, the pari-mutuel handle in the Bluegrass State amounted to barely one-fourth of what was realized in the peak year of 1928. But it wasn't as if the public had lost interest in thoroughbred racing. In August of 1934, a crowd of 37,281 turned out at the new Narragansett track in Pawtucket to welcome the sport back to Rhode Island after a twenty-nine-year absence. There was nothing special about the racing plant. Built in ten weeks on the grounds of an abandoned airport, the rickety grandstand seated only fourteen thousand. But the turnstiles kept humming and by 1936 more money was bet at Narragansett than at any track in the country. The house raked off 10 percent of the mutual handle, keeping 6.5 percent after the state of Rhode Island took its cut.[2]

Another racetrack that succeeded handsomely was Hialeah. This was to be expected when Joseph E. Widener was named CEO in 1929. A true patron of the turf (as was his brother George, who died in the sinking of the *Titanic*), Widener had succeeded the late August Belmont II as the most influential figure in American thoroughbred racing. He was the vice chairman of the Jockey Club, the president of the Westchester Racing Association that ran Belmont Park, and a member of the board of directors of several other racetracks. Partial to Australian pine trees, Widener spent more than a million and a half dollars beautifying Hialeah to please the finicky Palm Beach crowd. The finished product was extolled as a masterpiece of architectural and horticultural beauty.

Widener was born to the manor. The family home on the outskirts of Philadelphia was a 110-room mansion that housed one of the world's most valuable private art collections. But his investment in Hialeah came during a period when racetrack operators were increasingly men of humble origin branching out after making a fortune in the illicit liquor trade. William "Big Bill" Dwyer, a former longshoreman, was involved with the Coney Island track in Cincinnati, which opened in 1925; was the principal owner of Rockingham Park in Salem, New Hampshire, which reopened in 1931; and was the prime mover behind Tropical Park in Coral Gables. An associate of crime lords Owney Madden and Arthur Flegenheimer (aka Dutch Schultz), Dwyer had spent all of 1926 in a federal penitentiary for bootlegging. At his peak as an importer, he reportedly had twenty ships and a seaplane bringing contraband liquor into New York harbor.

The influence of the bootlegging crowd on the national racing scene was substantial but California managed to buck the trend and stay free of this taint. Longtime racing promoters John Marchbank and Bill Kyne were the guiding spirits behind the reopening of Tanforan and the establishment of a sister track across the bay, called Bay Meadows. Both men lobbied hard for pari-mutuel racing. Charles "Doc" Strub and Hal Roach were instrumental in putting Santa Anita back on the map. Roach was Hollywood's most prolific filmmaker. Strub, a former dentist, minor league baseball player, and active minor league team owner, had grown rich speculating in real estate in the aftermath of the great San Francisco earthquake. Constructed a stone's throw from Lucky Baldwin's old potato patch, as reporters were fond of writing, the new Santa Anita, potted against the scenic backdrop of the San Gabriel mountain range, was a point of civic pride.

America was still in the throes of the Depression when the new Santa Anita opened on Christmas Day, 1934. The national unemployment rate for the year stood at 21.7 percent. But the inaugural meet was so successful that it was extended two weeks. The mutual handle for sixty-five days of racing amounted to almost $16 million. Across the nation, racetracks were experiencing gains that betokened a brighter day. [3]

The success of Santa Anita prompted the development of two more racing plants in southern California. Del Mar opened on July 3, 1937. It was situated in the affluent beach town of the same name, approximately twenty miles north of San Diego. A far larger but less picturesque facility, Hollywood Park, opened in June of the following year. It sat on 315 acres near the Los Angeles Municipal Airport in the semi-rural community of Inglewood. Prominent Hollywood personalities were major investors in both operations. Bing Crosby, America's favorite crooner and a budding movie star, and the well-known screen actor Pat O'Brien were heavily involved in Del Mar. Jack Warner of Warner Brothers Studio owned the largest block of stock in Hollywood Park.

The racetrack building boom was accompanied by technological advances that enhanced the enjoyment of a day at the races. In 1927, race callers at Bowie and at the Fair Grounds were providing a running commentary over a public address system. Two years later, Hawthorne became the first track to use an electrical starting gate for an entire meet. Prior to the use of the gate, horses lined up behind a piece of webbing and delays at the post were endemic, sometimes resulting in injury as horses often became fractious and started kicking. Five false starts marred the 1893 American Derby, the richest of all the renewals of that Chicago turf classic. Ninety-seven minutes elapsed from the time that the horses were first brought to the barrier, a delay that despoiled a festive event. [4]

In 1932, Hialeah became the first American track with a totalizator. The ingenious contraption, imported from Australia, updated the odds every ninety seconds, a breakthrough in betting transparency. Folks with little interest in horse racing were drawn to Hialeah to see the mechanical marvel at work. The following year, an American-made version debuted at Arlington Park. The brainchild of Baltimore electrical engineer Harry Straus (aka Henry Straus), the mechanism was less bulky than the "Australian tote," enabling it to be transported more easily from track to track. The homegrown version spread rapidly and made Straus a rich man as the founding partner of the American Totalizator Company. In 1941, he and two of his top executives acquired 87 percent of the stock in Tropical Park.

The opening of Santa Anita brought an improved film processing system, the prototype of which was introduced at the 1932 Olympics. A print of the picture taken by a photo finish camera could now be developed in only three minutes. Racegoers continued to cry uncle whenever the "wrong" horse was declared the winner, but there was less bellyaching as folks came to appreciate that the camera was superior to the naked eye.[5]

A more far-reaching innovation expanded the universe of racing fans. In 1925, the first broadcast of the Kentucky Derby aired on station WHAS in Louisville. Five years later, in 1930, the race was being carried coast-to-coast by CBS and NBC affiliates and the radio audience numbered in the millions. Radio was the great leveler. It broke down the walls by popularizing thoroughbred racing in places where racing was outlawed, expanding the fan base while eroding the sway of those that opposed it.

The fifth Earl of Derby was the guest of honor at the 1930 Kentucky Derby. He was upstaged by the Earl of Sande.

Jockeys in earlier days were as prominent as the best-known baseball players and prizefighters. Edward "Snapper" Garrison, who rode from 1882 to 1897, had such an uncanny feel for pace that the term "Garrison finish" entered the language. The phrase was invoked whenever an athlete or team overcame a seemingly insurmountable deficit with a furious rally. But no jockey would be as celebrated as Earl Sande. Hailing from a small town in South Dakota, he began riding at unlicensed tracks in Idaho. The story of his ascent to the top of his profession was a true-life Horatio Alger tale. His recovery from a terrible spill in 1924 made the story more compelling. Sande's injuries were so severe that he wasn't expected to ride again, but he was back the next year and went on to claim his third riding title in 1927.

People rooted for Sande in the spirit of rooting for the underdog, and it made no difference if his horse was heavily favored. He rode Gallant Fox in the 1930 Kentucky Derby, and while the horse performed as expected, outclassing the field, the outcome was good for racing because it buttressed the legend of Earl Sande. "This boy Sande has become something of a Babe Ruth," marveled Westbrook Pegler, one of America's most widely read sportswriters.[6]

Damon Runyon celebrated Sande in several poems. Runyon's 1930 rendition became an iconic specimen of Jazz Age sports journalism:

> Say, have they turned back the page,
> Back to the past once more?
> Back to the racin' ages,
> An a Derby out of yore?
> Say, don't tell me I'm Daffy,

Ain't that the same ol' grin?
Why it's that handy guy named Sande
Bootin a winner in

The heightened competition that attended the flurry of new race-tracks encouraged longer meets where the sport was already estab-lished. Longer meets intensified worries about oversaturation.

Track operators in New York were especially vocal in expressing this concern. On the pari-mutuel front, they were behind the curve. Betting was still done with bookmakers, and done covertly in accordance with the law. If New York was going to keep pace with national develop-ments and stay relevant, then betting had to be unshackled from the charade that forced bettors and bet takers to conduct their business as if they were schoolboys sneaking a smoke behind the teacher's back dur-ing recess.

The Depression exerted a terrible toll on thoroughbred racing in New York. Between 1929 and 1933, receipts dropped more than 60 percent. The 1933 tally was barely 20 percent of what was needed to meet the annual payrolls of the racing associations and the horsemen.[7] Thousands of people were thrown out of work and thousands more were at risk of losing their jobs. But help was on the way. Senator James J. Crawford and Assemblyman William Breitenbach, Brooklyn Demo-crats, were carving out legislation intended to remediate the situation.

The racetrack bill that they sponsored passed both houses of the legislature by comfortable margins and was passed into law by Govern-or Herbert Lehman on April 19, 1934. The new law did indeed open up betting, but not in a manner consistent with the national trend. To the contrary, it rolled back the clock, unfettering the bookmakers and reani-mating the hubbub of the betting ring!

Two days after the Crawford-Breitenbach bill was passed into law, the New York racing season opened at Jamaica where the track's operators were girded for action. John Cavanagh, now seventy-three years old, was back at his old superintendent's stand in the big betting shed. Photographers were on hand to record the first bet, the first overt cash transaction in twenty-six years. The ceremonial wager was placed with Timothy J. Mara. A protégé of Chicago O'Brien, Mara, a former news-boy who had dropped out of school at age thirteen to help support his widowed mother, was involved in other sporting ventures besides the racing game, as was true of many other big bookmakers, and in 1934 was arguably the most popular sportsman in the city. The football team that Tim Mara built from scratch, the New York Giants, was coming off a successful season and would do even better in the fall, winning the NFL title.

"As the crowds streamed through the entrance gates," noted a reporter, "the question on every tongue was 'where is the betting ring?'" The racegoers swarmed the enclosure in such numbers that many had difficulty placing their bets. Hats were knocked askew as bettors were jostled about, but the crowd remained in a good humor. The bookmakers, seventy-one in all, did their part to keep the mood festive by offering attractive prices. (In the old days, it was common for bookmakers to offer more liberal odds on the opening day of a racing meet.) The only discordant note was struck by a few bold women who openly competed for the best odds in the same high-spirited fashion as the men. Pressured to restore the old order, management subsequently bowed to tradition, banning women from the betting pavilion. Women wishing to bet were gently remanded to the areas serviced by messenger bettors. [8]

Heeded by the situation at Jamaica, metropolitan tracks proactively enlarged their betting enclosures. In the final tally, attendance at New York racetracks rose nearly 80 percent. Some of the increase was artificial. Bookmakers paid for the privilege of conducting business inside the track by purchasing a stipulated number of admission tickets. However, gross receipts more than doubled and a 15 percent state tax on gate receipts, a component of the new betting law, generated almost $300,000 for the state treasury. [9]

The return of bookmaking as it had been practiced in the good old days failed to generate a new crop of men hailed as big plungers, save for Arthur Rooney, a Pittsburgh man whose fabulous run at Saratoga in 1937 galvanized turf writers and gossip columnists. It would be written that Rooney, the son of an Irish immigrant saloonkeeper, arrived at Saratoga in a broken-down jalopy and that, having failed to make advance arrangements, he and his driver, an ex-journeyman boxer, were reduced to spending their first two nights at the Spa in a fleabag motel. Propelled by a six-figure score on opening day, he purportedly won $300,000 during the course of his stay. [10]

Newspaper writers portrayed the thirty-six-year-old Rooney as a regular guy, the sort of fellow that would stop to help a stranded motorist fix a flat tire. An amiable man with an Irish glint in his eye like his great friend Tim Mara, Rooney had the demeanor of a blue-collar worker, but beneath the surface he was a sharp businessman with a keen mathematical mind who was schooled in the vicissitudes of gambling at an early age. He went on to forge companies that managed harness and greyhound tracks and in his dotage became a hero in his hometown, venerated as the benevolent owner of the Pittsburgh Steelers football team.

The reintroduction of bookmaking was generally understood to be a stopgap measure. New York couldn't institute pari-mutuel betting without amending the state constitution and that required legislative approval in two consecutive sessions and then a vote of the people. But the bookmakers were not about to surrender their turf without a fight.

A bill to make pari-mutuel betting the exclusive form of wagering at New York racetracks passed muster with the legislature in 1934, but was shot down when it was reintroduced in 1935 and 1936. Some of those that voted for it in 1934—including the very sponsor—switched sides. The switch-overs sparked talk of a slush fund. The fund, it was tacitly understood, originated in the rooms of the Turf and Gridiron Club. An entity born from the ashes of the Metropolitan Turf Association, the club was founded by Tim Mara.

For all their influence, the bookmakers couldn't keep the Iron Man at bay indefinitely. Pari-mutuel betting was spreading across the land and the politicians that promoted it were lauded for their good sense. In New York, the pari-mutuel drive was spearheaded by State Senator John J. Dunnigan, a Bronx Democrat. While it was true that attendance shot up dramatically with the reintroduction of open betting, Dunnigan believed that most of the increase was the reflection of an improved economy and that the increase would have been even greater with pari-mutuels. Because New York derived no tax benefit from bookmaking, the state, said Dunnigan, was leaving an awful lot of money on the table.

Few challenged this assessment, but navigating a pari-mutuel bill to the finish line was a tricky process and the second period of open bookmaking at New York tracks would last six years. The bill authorizing pari-mutuel betting—the death knell for the on-track bookmakers—finally got to the voters in November of 1939 and was approved by a large majority. (Dunnigan left politics in 1944 for a cushy job at the

Hamburg harness track outside Buffalo. The principal owner of the new track was his son, James Dunnigan.)

The "yes" vote was a foregone conclusion after pari-mutuels were approved in New Jersey in a special election in June of that year. Threatened with a state income tax if the measure didn't pass, Garden State voters approved the bill that revived thoroughbred racing in New Jersey after a freeze lasting more than four decades. The bill prohibited Sunday racing and racing after dark and specified a 10 percent takeout with 3.5 percent going to the state. In the circular produced by the sponsors of the bill, it was asserted that the pari-mutuel tax would enrich the New Jersey treasury by $2 million annually and that pari-mutuel wagering would wipe out illicit gambling in New Jersey and neighboring states.[11]

The ratification of pari-mutuels in New York didn't automatically dictate the end of fixed-odds betting. Herbert Bayard Swope, the head of the reconstituted state racing commission, favored the dual system found in England whereby patrons had both options at their disposal. There was a precedent for it in the United States. In 1934, the Crescent City Jockey Club in New Orleans allowed a handful of bookmakers to set up shop in the clubhouse at the Fair Grounds.[12]

The New Orleans experiment was a flop. The dual system was abandoned before economic conditions improved. But that didn't deter a cabal of New York bookmakers from pursuing a similar setup. They proposed a compromise whereby they would restrict their dealings to the clubhouse and accept no wager smaller than $100, the maximum that one could send through a pari-mutuel machine in a single transaction. It was argued that this would bring more well-heeled tourists to New York while simultaneously benefiting the ordinary racegoer. Wagers made by big plungers, men better equipped to make shrewd selections, would be kept out of the pools, theoretically putting more money into the hands of everyone else. But track operators were unmoved by this logic and decided that the bookies had to go.[13]

The final year of bookmaking was a record-setting year. Attendance at New York tracks surpassed 1.5 million and the state derived $616,872 in tax revenue. The figures for the first year of pari-mutuel betting blew the doors off those numbers. Attendance soared to over 2 million and the state raked in almost $6 million, 86.4 percent from the pari-mutuel tax.[14]

Senator Dunnigan and his allies were all smiles, but pari-mutuels changed the culture and others rued the passing of an era. The *New York Times* reporter, commenting on the opening day of the 1940 racing season, noted that the occasion had lost some of its charm. Although there were well-known entertainers in attendance, they didn't circulate as they had before.[15]

The betting ring, notwithstanding all the tumult, was always something more than a marketplace. It was a place where men, many of whom lived alone, found kindred souls to slake their need for social interaction. Many of the regulars had night jobs. They were waiters, bartenders, musicians, stagehands, and so on. Vaudeville entertainers, particularly comedians, had a well-deserved reputation for being exuberant horseplayers. One could always count on seeing a few of these individuals in the ring and their vibrant personalities brightened the scene. With the advent of pari-mutuels, they did not mingle as freely and there was less laughter.

15

A SIDE TRIP TO THE WINDY CITY

A tipster arrested in 1935 asserted in his prospectus that his skill at beating the races had caused him to be blacklisted by the Chicago Board of Pool Room Proprietors. There was no such body. However, Chicago likely had more poolrooms and handbooks than any city in the country and the men at the top of the pyramid and their information providers were important cogs in the national apparatus. Moreover, Chicago was the first city to mount a serious push for legalized off-track betting in privately owned establishments.

An 1871 editorial in the *Chicago Tribune* asserted that Chicago had become the nation's dumping ground for professional gamblers: "Whenever a professional has met ill-luck or persecution from the authorities in other cities, he can come here and ply his trade with immunity."[1] The city was so wide open and competition so keen during the decade of the 1870s that a poolroom operator brazenly put up a sign proclaiming that his establishment was chartered by the state of Illinois.[2]

Michael C. McDonald was then growing his fiefdom. Born in Niagara Falls in 1839, McDonald entered the wholesale liquor business after arriving in Chicago in his early twenties. Although he never ran for political office, historians would credit him with being the first boss of Chicago's Democratic machine. It would be written that one didn't open a poolroom in the Windy City without taking on Mike McDonald as a consultant.

James Patrick "Big Jim" O'Leary, whose family cow reputedly kick-started the Great Chicago Fire by knocking over a lantern (Jim was then a toddler), got his start in the McDonald organization. At the turn of the century, O'Leary owned a big gambling saloon opposite the stockyards, a resort advertised as "the most complete establishment of its kind in the world." Patronized by stockyards workers and wealthy cattlemen in town on business, the saloon boasted a Turkish bath, bowling alley, billiard room, cigar store, barber shop, and newsstand. The poolroom was in a separate building out back.

It was useful to O'Leary that he was married to the daughter of a police captain, but that didn't immunize him from periodic crackdowns on his operation. When times were tough, he did what inner city "vice lords" always do: he decentralized. Working in close concert with rail-way companies, he established a provisional poolroom in wide-open Roby, Indiana, a hamlet on the south shore of Lake Michigan roughly twenty miles from the stockyards, and at Byrneville, Illinois, a whistle-stop on the fringe of Chicago in DuPage County. O'Leary was also connected with John Condon in the Harlem Racetrack in the Chicago suburb that took the name Forest Park. A former barber and faro dealer from Logansport, Indiana, Condon was a stockholder in multiple racing associations and a silent partner in dozens of poolrooms.[3]

Nationally known because of his widely quoted future books on im-portant horse races and political elections, Big Jim O'Leary was at vari-ous times an accomplice and a rival of Bud White; loyalties were fran-gible. White was the driving force behind America's first floating pool-room, a daring enterprise that attracted national attention. White's syn-dicate acquired a steamship at a foreclosure auction. Registered under the name *City of Traverse*, the boat took horseplayers several miles out into Lake Michigan, rotating in slow circles when it reached safe water. Race results and related information arrived via the newfangled tech-nology of wireless telegraphy.

The poolroom made its maiden voyage on June 29, 1905, and oper-ated on and off for the next two years. The caper goaded the Chicago City Council into passing an ordinance that allowed the police to appre-hend "habitual loafers"—the ordinance specifically named steamboat docks as a place where men of this description would be subject to arrest. Anti-loafing laws would become commonplace during World War I, giving the police another tool to impair poolroom activities, but the Chicago ordinance, although yielding a few dockside arrests, was ineffectual. In exasperation, the authorities turned to the federal government. The bookmakers retired the vessel when the Department of Commerce and Labor threatened to confiscate the ship.[4]

Attempts to incapacitate the poolroom were often comical. In August of 1906, a tugboat pulled up beside the *City of Traverse* and began blowing its foghorn. The idea was to disrupt the betting by obscuring the telegraph messages. The incessant blare was interpreted as an SOS signal and the water was soon overrun with rescue boats. Mont Tennes was fingered as the perpetrator. Tennes was then outfitting a boat to compete with the *City of Traverse*. He ultimately shelved the project, reasoning that Lake Michigan couldn't support a second poolroom.[5]

Mont Tennes was a polarizing figure. A great organizer, he was also a relentlessly avaricious man who made many enemies. His incentive for challenging the aquatic poolroom was simply spite. "This band of men," he said, referencing unnamed business rivals, "decided to put me out of business, but I was hard to kill and I have begun to get square with them."[6] This shrill declamation, rendered on June 30, 1906, foreshadowed a turf war among poolroom operators that foreshadowed the bloodier turf wars that roiled Chicago during Prohibition. Over the next three years, more than thirty dynamite bombings were attributed to men allied with or against Mont Tennes. Five hundred buildings were damaged, but there were no confirmed fatalities. The perpetrators were careful to set off their bombs late at night when few people were on the street. There were some arrests but no convictions.

Tennes emerged from the tumult stronger than ever. He did it by seizing the lion's share of the national wire service.

When Western Union stopped serving poolrooms directly, a number of individuals rushed to repair the rent. John Payne, a former Western Union telegrapher turned poolroom keeper, built the largest network. The main office was in Covington, Kentucky, a few furlongs from Latonia. In 1907, Mont Tennes acquired the Chicago franchise of the Payne News Bureau. After renaming his agency General News Bureau, Tennes squeezed Payne out of the Chicago market and then expanded the operation to where he had subscribers in every region of the country. Outside Chicago, his prime enclaves, in descending order of profitability, were New York, San Francisco, St. Louis, Albany, Buffalo, Louisville, and Pittsburgh.[7]

In building up his business, Tennes acquired an ownership stake in some of the rooms that he serviced. In 1913, it was revealed that he owned a big piece of a poolroom in faraway Salt Lake City. As for Chicago, it was claimed that he controlled one hundred fifty poolrooms and handbooks and that he fixed it so that these establishments were left alone whenever there was a police sweep. Tennes sold his business in 1927 to concentrate on his real estate investments. When he died in 1941, he left an estate valued at $5 million, a portion of which was dedicated to the establishment and maintenance of a "character home" for wayward boys.[8]

No large city was hammered harder by the Great Depression than Chicago. The unemployment rate reached 40 percent, far above the national high. The downside to be being America's rail center was that the city became the leading port of call for America's hobos. In March of 1934, there were 90,785 families on the relief roles of Cook County and reportedly twenty-five thousand homeless transients. The public school system was a mess, flogged by mass layoffs, increased teacher workloads, and the elimination of programs. The schoolteachers were owed eight month's salary when the federal government came to the rescue with a loan from the Reconstruction Finance Corporation. It was in this climate that Mayor Edward J. Kelly proposed a bill that authorized municipalities to license, tax, and regulate off-track betting, a bill that would be amended to apply specifically to Chicago. Half the proceeds would go into the city's general fund. The remainder was earmarked for the Board of Education.[9]

Kelly's proposal wasn't unique; maverick politicians were forever introducing bills to legalize off-track betting. Some of the proposals were guilefully crafted. In 1935, the mayor of Atlantic City hoped to surmount opposition by hitting the bookmakers with a weekly fine, a license fee clothed in a different name.[10] What all these bills had in common was that they had scant chance of making much headway. Kelly's bill was the exception.

Kelly found unexpected allies in H. B. Chamberlin, the founder and operating director of the Chicago Crime Commission, and Ernest W. Burgess, a sociology professor at the University of Chicago. Burgess asserted that antigambling campaigns were doomed to failure—no Western society had ever succeeded in suppressing gambling for a long period of time—and that it made sense to divert the spoils from crooked politicians and gangsters into meeting the expenses of government. He also believed that legalization would actually reduce gambling as it would strip away the allure of a forbidden fruit. An authority on juvenile delinquency, Burgess was a giant in his field. His viewpoints—he also favored a municipal lottery as an alternative to a sales tax—were noteworthy because they ran counter to the prevailing sentiment of the Protestant reformers, a catechism with which sociology was then closely identified.[11]

Kelly's bill advanced to the governor's desk. The experts, the so-called wiseguys, were of the opinion that it would pass. The governor, Henry Horner, was a Chicago man. As a member of the Jewish faith, Horner figured to be more open to the idea of legalization. Moreover, defying Mayor Kelly was seen as a bad political move as Kelly, the son of a fireman, was enormously popular. In the 1935 general election, he blew away the opposition, outdistancing his Republican rival by a nearly 5-to-1 margin while becoming the first mayoral candidate in the history of Chicago to carry all fifty wards.

The experts guessed wrong. In explaining his decision to veto the measure, Governor Horner said he didn't want to be remembered as the man who gave his blessing to a bill that flew in the face of a time-honored perspective. Horner conceded that there may have been "only occasional instances" where individuals were ruined as a result of their dealings with bookmakers, but said that society had an obligation to protect its weaker members.[12]

Kelly didn't control the police. They took their orders from Thomas Courtney, the state attorney for Cook County. In 1937, Chicago police raided 5,194 alleged handbooks and betting parlors.[13] Some of these places were quite large. A parlor on the second floor of a building in the Loop had eighteen employees and 354 so-called inmates (horseplayers) on the premises when the police burst in. Only one of the workers arrested, a cashier earning $8 a shift, had his case brought before a jury. It was truly a jury of his peers and he was acquitted. Eleven of the twelve jurors acknowledged that they had made bets on horse races.[14] If Chicago were a nation, one could fairly say that playing the ponies was its national sport.

The assault on bookmakers occurred while Mayor Kelly was preparing a new plan for legal off-track betting. In December of 1937, the Chicago City Council approved by a 43-4 margin a proposal to license "pari-mutuel brokers." For a 5 percent commission, a broker would telegraph a wager directly to the track. The plan never got out of the starting blocks, scuttled by a ruling that it violated the state constitution. By now, the relationship between Kelly and State Attorney Courtney had become more than chilly. Courtney continued his harassment of bookmakers, but with greater zeal than before. Policemen wielding firemen's axes destroyed the furnishings of the bookie joints they entered, leaving behind a mess of twisted rubble.[15] Courtney challenged Kelly in the 1939 Democratic primary for mayor. Kelly won in a landslide.

During the early years of Edward Kelly's mayoral reign, a Chicago man, Moses "Moe" Annenberg, cemented his status as the most powerful person in the constellation of bookies. The fall of Annenberg was a big news story with bad repercussions for poolroom operators nationwide.

Born in 1877 in a little village in East Prussia near the border of Poland, Moses Annenberg arrived in the United States at the age of eight. As a boy growing up in Chicago, where his father was a junk dealer, Annenberg and his older brother Max were gang leaders in the city's violent newspaper circulation wars. Both went on to head the circulation department of papers in the Hearst newspaper chain.

Beginning with a half-interest in Mont Tennes's General News Bureau, Annenberg grew his holdings into a multifaceted empire that supplied bookie joints with all of their sundry needs, even blackboard chalk. At the height of his power, he controlled both horseplayers' "Bibles"—the *Daily Racing Form*, founded in Chicago in 1894, and the *New York Morning Telegraph*, the offspring of a weekly paper born in 1839—and had his fingers in several racing tip sheets, one of which was co-owned by an Illinois state senator.[16] Most of these sheets were published daily, but some were published weekly. The weekly sheets were organs of a telephone service. Each horse listed in the sheet was assigned a corresponding code name. Purchasing the sheet entitled the buyer to call the service for "best bets." The picks were dispensed in code, shutting out the freeloaders.

The glue of Annenberg's racing empire was the wire service. Rechristened Nationwide News Service, it had subscribers in the United States, Canada, Mexico, and Cuba. In Chicago, where there were reportedly a thousand poolrooms and handbooks in the metropolitan area, six hundred fifty inside the Chicago city limits, the service purportedly had more than two hundred clients paying an average of $80 a week. A subsidiary, "Teleflash," was the audio component.

Nationwide News Service had numerous branches, each having the outward appearance of an independent company. Annenberg formed so many corporations and subsidiaries that his operations were likened to an enormous marionette show. His legitimate holdings came to include newspapers in Milwaukee, Miami, Philadelphia, and Massillon, Ohio. His jewel was the *Philadelphia Inquirer*, purchased in 1936 for a reported $10.5 million in cash. One of America's oldest daily papers, the *Inquirer* was the newspaper of choice for the region's old guard. Under Annenberg, the paper's editorial stance became more rigidly conservative. Annenberg attacked FDR's New Deal programs as costly boondoggles. Articles in the paper were credited with restoring the primacy of the Republican Party in Pennsylvania in the elections of 1938.

Annenberg's actions ruffled the feathers of higher-ups in Washington. The Department of Justice struck back by dredging up the law created for the purpose of squashing the Louisiana Lottery. Largely the handiwork of Anthony Comstock, the law prohibited newspapers from carrying lottery advertisements and made it illegal to send lottery circulars through the mail. Annenberg was acquitted of this charge—a federal judge rejected the outlandish argument that mutuel prices constituted "a list of prizes awarded by means of a lottery"—but he couldn't outmaneuver the IRS.

Sixty-six revenue agents were assigned to the Annenberg case. Hundreds of poolroom operators were interviewed in an effort to determine Annenberg's true income. Some were happy to assist in the inquiry. They thought Annenberg's prices were out of line and welcomed the opportunity to hit back at the man that was gouging them. A side effect was that the federal tax bureau developed a clearer picture of off-track betting. It was determined that a fair assessment on a man operating a full-fledged horse parlor was 6 percent of his gross.[17] (This finding fell through the cracks. Magazine writers, by and large, and some government officials, continued to wildly exaggerate the take, blurring the line between gross and net receipts.)

Among the arguments offered up by Annenberg's legal team was that errors on his tax returns were honest mistakes born from a lack of formal schooling; he quit school at age twelve. The revelation that he billed a daughter's wedding expenses to the *Daily Racing Form* complicated this argument. He would eventually accept a plea deal that resulted in a $9,500,000 settlement—the largest tax lien since the tax-collecting agency was created in 1913—and a three-year prison term. Paroled after twenty-three months after being diagnosed with a brain tumor, Moses Annenberg died on July 20, 1942. [18]

The vendetta against Annenberg was undoubtedly hatched at the White House. President Roosevelt would be scolded, even by writers partial to him, for using the Bureau of Internal Revenue and the Justice Department to flay his enemies. However, Annenberg was an unsympathetic figure. With growing concerns that the United States would soon be drawn into another war, there was little sympathy for tax evaders. Men of wealth that resisted paying their "fair share" were rebuked as unpatriotic. Westbrook Pegler, one of America's most widely read columnists, wrote that Annenberg's sharp dealings were particularly abhorrent because he was an immigrant. "All Americans suffered from the greedy rascality of this ruthless master-ingrate," wrote Pegler. [19]

During his ordeal, Annenberg acquiesced to pressure to shut down his race wire. He dissolved the operation, which reportedly had five hundred employees, after the final race was run on Wednesday, November 15, 1939. The next day, according to the Associated Press, off-track wagering dropped by as much as 90 percent in some locales. Demobilizing the wire muted Teleflash and the excitement that it created, dulling the allure of a horse parlor. A bigger issue was that information dribbled in at a snail's pace. Post times arrived before bettors knew the fate of their previous bet, depressing the "churn." However, bookmakers had been forewarned and many were able to establish arrangements that minimized the fallout. In Dade County, Florida, returns arrived via shortwave radio from Cuba and it was business as usual. Bookmakers in Southern California received race results by code from XELO, a border-blaster radio station in Tijuana. [20]

Bookmakers and those that nourished their operations were a hardy breed, as stubborn as yucca trees on a sun-parched desert. Four days after Annenberg's race wire went dark, his longtime circulation manager, James S. Ragen, founded a new wire service, Continental Press. Joining him in the venture were his trusted lieutenant Tom Kelly, and Kelly's brother-in-law, Arthur "Mickey" McBride. A former Chicago newsboy who went on to own several lucrative taxicab franchises, including the largest fleet in Cleveland, McBride would be remembered as the founding father of the Cleveland Browns football team.

The main office of Continental Press was initially located in the same building in the Chicago Loop that once housed Mont Tennes's General News Bureau. The company encountered immediate competition and what ensued was another war between racing news suppliers, a war that harked to the days of Tennes, but splattered considerably more blood on the streets of Chicago. The bombs that disrupted Tennes's operations weren't intended to maim or kill him, but to intimidate him. James Ragen's enemies were more ruthless.

On June 24, 1946, the sixty-five-year-old Ragen was the focal point of a gun battle. Driving home at rush hour, he stopped at a red light. A dilapidated fruit truck, the contents of its bed concealed by a tarpaulin, pulled up alongside. Two would-be assassins wielding sawed-off shotguns emerged from underneath the tarpaulin and sprayed him with bullets. Ragen's two bodyguards, trailing him in a separate vehicle, returned fire. Remarkably, no bystanders were hurt.[21]

Ragen anticipated that he would die a violent death. Two months before this encounter, he eluded suspicious characters in a high-speed auto chase that ended with him seeking asylum inside a police station. In his statement to the police, he asserted that he was fending off a takeover by members of the old Capone mob. Ragen died in the hospital while recuperating from his injuries. It was widely thought that he was poisoned. His travails were large news stories in a tempestuous decade that began with the final eradications of fixed-odds betting at American racetracks and ended with a little-known senator from Tennessee leading a movement that fomented the extinction of privately owned horse betting parlors across most of the nation.

16

MID-CENTURY REFORMERS

La Guardia, Kefauver, and Kennedy

On Monday, April 15, 1940, a crowd estimated at twenty-five thousand, undeterred by frigid weather, turned up at Jamaica to welcome in the opening of the racing season and the inauguration of pari-mutuel betting in New York. The grandstand was dotted with many more women than had been the norm. At the pari-mutuel windows, the ladies were as welcome as the men. The betting ring, and the code that kept women out of it, were shards of a bygone day.

There were 316 pari-mutuel clerks on duty when the bell rang to signal the start of betting. "The horseplayers charged the mutuel windows as if behind them lay the secret of eternal youth," said Joe Williams, the sports editor for the *New York World-Telegram*. The turf correspondent for the *Brooklyn Eagle* likened the scene to a frantic mob scrambling into a bomb shelter. The day's handle exceeded the most optimistic expectations. Williams called it the greatest betting day in the history of modern New York racing.[1]

LA GUARDIA

There were many politicians in attendance. Fiorello La Guardia wasn't among them, but he was in the neighborhood. By coincidence, La Guardia, New York's first three-term mayor (1934–1945), was in Jamaica, Queens, roughly fifteen furlongs from the racetrack, when the first legal pari-mutuel wagers were made in New York. After laying the cornerstone at a federally funded housing project, he gave a short speech. Low-cost housing, said the mayor, represented human progress, whereas legal gambling represented a step backward. "I don't believe the people should be encouraged to spend money needed for food, clothing, and housing," he added.[2]

The son of Italian immigrants—a lapsed Catholic father and a Jewish mother—Fiorello La Guardia, an Episcopalian married to a woman descended from a line of German Lutherans, was a curious amalgam of his constituencies. He was, said the wags, a balanced ticket all by himself.

Born in New York City in 1882, La Guardia spent his formative years in Prescott, Arizona Territory, where his father was the bandmaster at the Fort Whipple army post. Typical of western frontier towns, Prescott was then chockablock with gambling saloons. La Guardia claimed that he knew of men who were ruined in these establishments, instilling within him a burning hostility toward gambling of all kinds. As noted by his biographers, although the peppery, five-foot-two La Guardia came to be seen as the quintessential New Yorker, his sense of right and wrong was forged in a distant place where integrity was less ambiguous and justice was swift.

During his first term in office, one of La Guardia's top priorities was ridding New York of slot machines. A famous newsreel clip, filmed in 1934 aboard a municipal tugboat, showed him smashing slot machines with a sledgehammer before they were dumped into the ocean. During his third term, he rammed through a municipal ordinance outlawing pinball machines and then had them confiscated and destroyed, more than three thousand, the legs of which were made into police billy clubs. He viewed the pinball machine as a cousin to the slot machine. While they weren't gambling instruments per se, he felt that they unleashed the gambling instinct and started young boys on the road to juvenile delinquency.

Late in his first term, La Guardia feuded with Brooklyn district attorney William F. X. Geoghan. Bookmaker Frank Erickson was at the center of the storm. In 1936, when a grand jury was convened to decide whether Geoghan should be removed from office, the outgrowth of a botched murder investigation, it was learned that the district attorney

and the bookmaker, whose central office was outside Geoghan's jurisdiction in New Jersey, were the closest of friends. They often sat together at important prizefights and testimonial dinners. To La Guardia,
this was an outrage. He called Erickson a tinhorn punk, his pet name
for big gamblers, and recommended that the Manhattan district attorney's purview be expanded to include all five boroughs, thereby eliminating Geoghan's office. In return, Geoghan advocated that Brooklyn
secede from the rest of New York City.[3]

A fourth-grade dropout, born in Finland, or Norway, or Brooklyn
(accounts vary), Erickson was raised by an aunt in Brooklyn after spending time in an orphanage. He got his start as a bookmaker while bussing
tables in a Coney Island restaurant. Serving as the runner when a patron or coworker felt the urge to place a bet with the handbook down
the block, Erickson took to holding these wagers whenever he had
sufficient coin in his pocket to cover the bet. From this humble beginning, he rose to the top of the bookmaking pyramid, overseeing the
largest operation in the country with clients in all forty-eight states.
There were always whispers that he was merely the front man for his
good friend Frank Costello, the slot machine czar, but Erickson was
very much his own man.

Erickson controlled his jeopardy by funneling some of his bets into
pari-mutuel pools. Some tracks refused comeback money, but others
welcomed the action and even offered a rebate. In some instances,
Erickson overcame the opposition of track owners to comeback money
by buying into their operations. At various times, he reportedly had
direct lines into the mutuel rooms at Santa Anita, Pimlico, Hialeah, and
several smaller tracks where agents equipped with ready cash stood by
to fill an order at a moment's notice. One of the original backers of
Tropical Park, he held a 20 percent stake in the Miami racing plant
when he was forced out by state racing authorities in 1941.[4]

A man with a quiet demeanor, Erickson ran his operation like a Wall
Street brokerage. Customers received monthly statements. At Christ-
mastime, he thanked his clients—he called them consumers—with a
holiday gift or by wiping a debt off the books. For his best customers, he
chose gifts from the Tiffany catalog. He accepted the fact that he would
be skinned now and then by a dishonest race, but bore the perpetrators
no malice provided that they were steady customers. He schooled his
employees in the importance of hospitality and paid them well.[5]

In January of 1942, La Guardia began a series of Sunday talks on New York's municipal radio station. During one of these broadcasts, he encouraged boys to tattle on their fathers if their fathers frequented a bookie joint.

"A little fellow named George," said the mayor, "wrote to me about a store where gambling is going on, where bets are taken on horses and how his father goes there to bet and then comes home without his weekly pay and how that makes the family unhappy.

"George," continued the mayor, "I'm going to put a policeman in that store. You just keep me informed, and (let me know of) other little boys who see the family happiness destroyed because some thieving tinhorn is robbing his daddy of money on horse races or gambling . . . I won't tell anybody."[6]

The Little Flower, as he was dubbed in the tabloid press, talked tough, but was also a man of action. On September 27, 1942, a Friday, in a meeting with two hundred police officials, La Guardia avowed that he would shake up the department if gambling persisted. "If you don't clean up the situation, I will clean you up," he said. Over the ensuing weekend, police arrested 645 men on gambling-related charges, 27 of whom were arrested for obstructing the sidewalk while reading a scratch sheet. In related developments, La Guardia urged citizens to sue for the recovery of gambling losses and ordered racing publications withdrawn from sidewalk newsstands. The ban was overturned by the courts.[7]

La Guardia never had the satisfaction of seeing Frank Erickson packed off to prison. Trumped-up charges—vagrancy, disorderly conduct, perjury—never stuck. But Frank Hogan, Manhattan's legendary nine-term district attorney, who took office in 1941, turned the trick, filing charges that sent Erickson to Rikers Island, New York City's main jail complex, where he served sixteen months of a two-year term. Fifty-four years old when he spent his first day behind bars, Erickson subsequently served ten months in a New Jersey prison for gambling and six months in a federal penitentiary for tax evasion. His tax problems arose when it was discovered that he was receiving 5 percent of the profits from the Colonial Inn, a nightclub and gambling house in Hallandale, Florida, near Gulfstream Park.

Erickson was a free man during the war years, but these were difficult times for men in his line of work. In the aftermath of Pearl Harbor, every racetrack in California was shut down with the exception of Bay Meadows, which purchased an exemption by agreeing to give virtually all of its profits to the war effort. Hollywood Park and Golden Gate Fields were deployed as processing centers for Japanese internment camps and were then converted to other military uses. Del Mar became a Marine base and then a manufacturing and storage plant for warplane equipment. During the war, shortages of gasoline and rubber led federal authorities to clamp down on unnecessary driving. Racetracks lacking good public transportation suspended operations or shifted their meets to a sister track that was more centrally located. In 1943, all of New York's major harness meets were conducted in Yonkers. From 1942 through 1944, there was no racing in Saratoga; its meets were conducted at Belmont Park. In Maryland, racing was restricted to Pimlico.

It wasn't only horse racing that was crippled. In the aftermath of Pearl Harbor, many colleges discontinued football. The Indianapolis 500 and the U.S. Open golf tournament were shut down in 1942 for the duration of the war. With titles frozen, boxing waned as a betting attraction despite an increase in the number of neighborhood fight clubs. The heavyweight division, which drove the sport, languished following Joe Louis's demolition of Max Schmeling in 1938. Louis stayed busy until he was inducted into the army, but his opponents, other than Billy Conn, were of such inferior quality that the public wasn't turned on and bookmakers wrote little business. The lull persisted until Louis's rematch with Conn in 1946.

The entire horse racing industry in America came to a complete standstill on January 3, 1945, by order of War Mobilization director James F. Byrnes. The reasons given for the blackout, which was attached to a midnight curfew on places of amusement, were to alleviate a manpower shortage in critical industries by freeing up racetrack workers, breeding farm workers, and individuals engaged in the illegal bookmaking trade for work in defense plants and to spur the sale of war bonds by diverting money from pari-mutuel pools. Reports of heavy absenteeism in war plants located near racetracks when a racing meet was in progress were a large contributing factor.

During the ban, which was lifted on May 9, 1945, desperate horseplayers were left to rummage in races run in Havana, Mexico City, and Tijuana, the latter of which then held races only on Sundays and holidays. More than half the bookie joints in America's major cities report-

edly suspended operations. A by-product was an uptick in college basketball betting. College athletic directors reported a big upsurge in
requests for "dope" and instructed their coworkers in the publicity department to stop providing information to anonymous callers.[8]

Bookmakers were cheered by Harry Truman's shocking upset of
Thomas Dewey in the presidential election of 1948. Proud of his small-
town values—he was born and raised in Owosso, Michigan—Dewey
had a caustic opinion of off-track betting, viewing it in the same light as
the policy game, which he had smashed while serving as Manhattan's
district attorney. Truman was perceived to be indifferent. Harry's earliest political triumphs owed to the machinations of his great friend Tom
Pendergast, the late Kansas City political boss. In his heyday running
one of America's most wide-open cities, Pendergast, a degenerate
horseplayer, was on a first-name basis with America's biggest bookmakers.

KEFAUVER

Any thoughts that Truman would take a benign approach to off-track
betting were quickly dispelled. Thirteen months after the election,
Estes Kefauver, a forty-five-year-old freshman senator from Tennessee,
proposed legislation that would fund an investigation into interstate
gambling by the Senate Judiciary Committee. Congress appropriated
more money than he requested, enjoining him to broaden the scope of
his investigation to include organized crime in general, identified as
"prostitution, narcotics, loan shark rackets, swindling schemes, organized murder, and extortion rackets, preying upon legitimate business
and labor in many different fields."[9] Kefauver took the role of chairman
on the five-member panel that would steer the investigation.

In June of 1950, the month following the birth of the Kefauver
Commission—more formally the U.S. Senate Special Committee to Investigate Organized Crime in Interstate Commerce—President Truman provided the body with a sharp new tool. Exercising a rarely used
presidential prerogative, he allowed the committee to access confiden-
tial tax records. Westbrook Pegler, ever the cynic, characterized Truman's action as a hypocritical ruse designed to divert attention from his
past associations with members of the Kansas City underworld.[10]

The antecedents to the Kefauver hearings were a series of reports by state and municipal crime commissions, a rich source of juicy material for tabloids and popular magazines. Political gossip columnist Drew Pearson, a muckraker of the Westbrook Pegler stripe, painted a lurid picture of illegal bookmaking in various installments of Washington Merry-Go-Round, a column that ran in more than eight hundred papers. *Life* magazine, America's top-selling weekly, published several long articles on the subject before providing readers with the "definitive" skinny on "the nation's biggest racket" in a special report that consumed parts of twenty-three pages.[11]

These pieces drew heavily on the findings of Virgil W. Peterson. A former FBI agent who was raised in a small farming community in Iowa, Peterson was appointed the managing director of the Chicago Crime Commission in 1942, filling the vacancy caused by the death of H. B. Chamberlin. Peterson was an admirer of Fiorello La Guardia and a tenacious watchdog whose work was guided by the premise that illegal gambling in America was run by the same big-city gangs that conducted reigns of terror during the bootlegging wars of the Roaring Twenties. In his keynote speech to a national conference of mayors in 1949, Peterson said it was important for cities to pool their resources to eradicate gambling syndicates. His remarks were interpreted as a call for federal assistance.[12]

The grandson of a Baptist preacher, Estes Kefauver hailed from the eastern hill country of Tennessee. He attended the University of Tennessee, where he lettered two years as a tackle on the football team, and returned to his native state, setting up a practice in Chattanooga, after earning a law degree from Yale. A lanky man with a laconic demeanor that invited comparisons with movie actor Gary Cooper, Kefauver appeared in publicity photos wearing a coonskin cap, an accouterment that paid homage to Daniel Boone and Davy Crockett, iconic frontiersmen with Tennessee ties. A grown-up man in a coonskin cap conveyed the picture of a backcountry Bubba, but beneath that façade lurked one of America's craftiest politicians, a man who was a trailblazer in harnessing the power of television to build an army of supporters.

The Kefauver Commission held hearings in fourteen cities, stopping twice in New York. The second visit, consisting of eight days of hearings in March of 1951, caused a sensation. Aired live by TV stations in twenty-one cities, and in their gavel-to-gavel entirety by WPIX in New

York, the hearings riveted the nation. In New York, where 51 percent of the homes had televisions (the national high), the interrogations were so compelling that the number of TV sets in use was twenty times higher than normal for daytime programming.[13]

The marquee deponents during the second round of New York hearings were the city's former mayor, William O'Dwyer, and a man with whom he was acquainted, Frank Costello. A politically powerful man with legitimate business holdings in liquor distributorships, nightclubs, and commercial real estate, Costello was characterized as the "prime minister of the underworld."

An immigrant from Ireland who arrived in the United States as a teenager, William O'Dwyer was a former policeman who advanced to the post of King's County (Brooklyn) district attorney after earning a law degree from Fordham. After serving in World War II, where he was accorded the rank of brigadier general in the Army Reserve, he reentered the political arena and was elected mayor in 1945, succeeding Fiorello La Guardia. He left in the ninth month of his second term upon being named ambassador to Mexico. His sudden departure came as his enemies were loading their muskets with fresh ammunition.

During his early days as a district attorney, O'Dwyer was known as a racket-buster. Seven members of the cabal dubbed Murder, Inc. were sent to the electric chair during his tenure. It was alleged, however, that he was highly selective in pursuing mobsters, an opinion that gained traction when a great scandal erupted as he was about to begin his second term as mayor, a scandal born from a series of articles in the *Brooklyn Eagle* newspaper. The man at the center of the scandal was Harry Gross, a thirty-four-year-old bookmaker with more than two dozen offices scattered around the boroughs of New York, Nassau County, and northern New Jersey. Gross allegedly spent a million dollars a year on police protection. The allegation sparked an investigation into police corruption that led to the most massive shakeup of the force since the Herman Rosenthal scandal.

Although the interrogation focused mainly on his days as a district attorney, Kefauver concluded that O'Dwyer fostered organized crime during his tenure as mayor by taking no effective action against the city's uppermost racketeers. But Kefauver stopped short of saying that O'Dwyer's passivity betrayed an ulterior motive. "I believe, and always have believed, that William O'Dwyer is an honest man," Kefauver told Drew Pearson in 1958.[14]

The dapper, sixty-year-old Costello—born Francesco Castiglia in Calabria, Italy—agreed to testify on the condition that his face wouldn't appear on camera. TV viewers were left with the image of his fidgety, well-manicured hands which, conjoined with his raspy voice , formed an indelible picture of an aging mob boss.

Costello ended his interview abruptly, complaining of a sore throat. Summoned back the next day, he then left again before his interrogators were finished with him. He provided little useful information, dodging the tough questions with terse replies or by invoking the Fifth Amendment. He acknowledged that he had been a bootlegger and a bookmaker, but claimed to have abandoned those pursuits to concentrate on his real estate investments. As for gambling, he allowed that he enjoyed making an occasional wager with his friend Ed Curd, a Lexington, Kentucky, bookmaker.

Costello's vacuous testimony, perceived as insolence, resulted in an indictment for contempt. He was convicted and served fourteen months in a federal prison. He subsequently served time for tax evasion and was stripped of his citizenship despite having lived in the United States since the age of four.

Some journalists judged the investigation to be an expensive waste of time, an opinion that grew when Congress adjourned without adopting any of the committee's recommendations. However, the hearings certainly redounded well to Estes Kefauver. Virtually unknown outside his home state when he entered the Senate in 1949, the Tennessean was transformed into a serious presidential candidate. He won the popular vote in the 1952 Democratic primaries only to be passed over at the convention in favor of Adlai Stevenson II, and became Stevenson's running mate in the 1956 race, a resounding triumph for incumbent Dwight D. Eisenhower.

While the hearings were ongoing, Kefauver, a father of four, was named "Father of the Year" by the National Father's Day Committee. At the conclusion of the hearings, the Tennessean was fairly described as the most admired man in the country, notwithstanding vocal detractors who charged him with hijacking the chairmanship of the committee to promote a self-serving agenda.

Kefauver fueled this opinion during the New York portion of the hearings by turning up as the mystery guest on the popular TV show *What's My Line?* A ghostwritten series of four articles, subtitled "What I Found in the Underworld," ran in the *Saturday Evening Post* before his committee's final report was submitted to Congress. Looking back, syndicated columnist Robert Ruark dismissed the proceedings as "old-fashioned hokum" and spoke charitably of Frank Costello. "Costello may be guilty of everything from assault to horse-stealing," said Ruark, "but in my book they railroaded him. The only charge of which he is actually guilty is refusal to be an unpaid actor in a professional sideshow dignified slightly by a congressional stamp."[15]

The main thrust of the committee's conclusions, which parroted that of several state crime commissions, was that gambling was the bedrock of organized crime. On April 1, 1951, in an appearance on the popular NBC Sunday morning program *Meet the Press*, Kefauver declared that Continental Press was public enemy number one and said that putting the wire service out of business was his top priority. This declaration stamped bookmaking the red light district of gambling.[16]

On March 12, 1952, Mickey McBride yielded to government pressure and closed Continental Press. The company was then held in the name of his son, a law student at the University of Miami in Coral Gables, a community where the elder McBride was reputedly the largest property owner. Other agencies kept the service alive, but in hindsight the race wire industry was slowly dying as handicappers were increasingly drawn to sports betting. Moreover, the actions of state racing commissions and the Kefauver Committee may have unwittingly encouraged this transposition. As David G. Schwartz notes, the focus on stamping out illegal horse betting enabled sports betting to fly under the radar.[17]

Inspired by the Kefauver hearings, the Federal Communications Commission threatened to not renew the licenses of TV and radio stations that carried horse racing information as part of their regular daytime programming.[18] In Florida, radio stations and other carriers were prohibited from reporting the results of a horse race until thirty minutes after it was run. A far more sweeping mandate, the Federal Excise Wagering Tax, emerged from the halls of the United States Congress.

Designed to suppress bookmakers, but expanded to include those that ran lottery-type games for profit, the Federal Excise Wagering Tax, which took effect on November 1, 1951, imposed a 10 percent tax on gross receipts, payable monthly, and required the operators and their employees to purchase an occupational stamp with an annual fee of $50 and to register with the Internal Revenue Service. The stamp was not to be construed as a permit, but merely as a tax. The names of purchasers were passed along to local police departments and provided to news organizations on request. Many gambler-businessmen leading a double life were "outed" when they were identified as a tax stamp purchaser in their local paper. In Illinois, state lawmakers prohibited "any person, establishment, partnership or corporation" with a gambling tax stamp from obtaining or renewing a liquor license.[19]

Bookmakers derided the legislation as the "Heads You Win, Tails I Lose Law" and were overwhelmingly noncompliant. Punchboard operators acquiesced in greater numbers than bookmakers, as did agents for lottery games. A congressional committee estimated that the taxes would enrich the U.S. Treasury by $400 million annually. During the first four years, the total yield was only $33.2 million. IRS commissioner T. Coleman Andrews attributed the poor returns to the fact that the law applied to individuals who were tax evaders by nature. In 1961, Andrews's successor, Mortimer Caplin, estimated that 98 percent of all gambling transactions in the United States escaped federal taxation.[20]

Ironically, Kefauver was opposed to this legislation—the only federal law dealing with gambling that emerged in the immediate aftermath of his hearings. The man from Tennessee felt that taxing gamblers sanctioned immorality and predicted that it would open a Pandora's Box, encouraging an ever-greater dependence on gambling to fund public needs.[21]

As would be true years later with cigarettes, proponents of the tax maintained that it would lead to a reduction in the incidence of the activity being taxed, a net benefit to society. And while the evidence is admittedly sketchy, the federal tax did accomplish this purpose, reducing illegal betting *in the short term*. In New York City, sales of racing sheets declined by 90 percent at some newsstands.[22] Across the nation, old-fashioned bookie joints, places where a few hundred people might gather on a Saturday afternoon, faded from the scene. A man could still get down a bet by merely picking up the telephone, but man is a social animal and for many individuals this convenience was an inadequate substitute for whiling away an afternoon in a horse parlor with fellow "hobbyists."

KENNEDY

Ten years after the release of the Kefauver Report, bookmakers had another plague visited on their house. The man wielding the toxin was Attorney General Robert F. "Bobby" Kennedy. Appointed to his post as a reward for running his brother's presidential campaign, Kennedy had previously served as the chief counsel of the Senate Labor Rackets Committee, a post he held from 1957 to 1959.

In 1960, the year the voters sent JFK to the White House, *Newsweek* ran a cover story on the upsurge in sports betting. "The cash that Joe Waldorf loses betting may help provide the down payment on a brothel or start a narcotics salesman on a new route," said the author.[23] Bobby Kennedy's public pronouncements on the subject of bookmaking were concordant. In his first news conference as attorney general, he proposed broadening the federal law by banning the use of interstate telephone or telegraph wires for betting and by prohibiting the interstate shipment of gambling paraphernalia. Congress granted him the tools that he requested in the form of three interrelated bills that were signed into law by his brother on September 13, 1961, at a ceremony at the White House with FBI director J. Edgar Hoover and other dignitaries in attendance.[24]

Violators of the Federal Interstate Wire Act, commonly called just the Wire Act, risked a $10,000 fine and a five-year prison sentence. The law put the kibosh on the few remaining, privately operated non-Nevada bookie parlors. In Minneapolis, sixty-four-year-old Leo Hirschfield shut his doors for good. Hirschfield ran a publishing house, but the cornerstone of his business was his line service, the industry leader in originating the national sports betting line.

Raids orchestrated by Attorney General Kennedy and his lieutenants were more wide-ranging than anything seen before. On April 9, 1963, an army of three hundred federal agents from Illinois, Michigan, and Wisconsin swooped down on thirty-nine suspected bookmaking establishments in Chicago. The raids, reportedly six months in the planning, were hailed as the most sweeping in the history of federal gambling enforcement. Three weeks later, on the day of the Kentucky Derby, federal lawmen raided eighty-eight suspected gambling establishments in forty-three cities spread across thirteen states. An estimated four hundred federal agents were involved in this caper. Operation Big Squeeze, as it was dubbed, continued after Kennedy vacated his post. In September of 1964 he resigned to pursue a seat in the U.S. Senate.[25]

Operation Big Squeeze put a dent in illegal sports and race gambling, but to what degree and to what long-lasting effect, if any, are questions without easy answers. However, the Wire Act would come to be cast as RFK's great legacy. More than four decades after his death at age forty-four, the Wire Act still had non-Nevada bookmakers walking on eggshells.

17

THE TAX MAN COMETH

By 1938, twenty-two states had approved pari-mutuel betting. They all taxed it in some fashion—for example, license fees or a tax on admission tickets—but only ten states taxed pari-mutuel pools directly. By 1948, when pari-mutuel betting was conducted in twenty-five states, every state with pari-mutuel racing with the exception of Nebraska was taxing pari-mutuel pools.[1] Revenues for state treasuries grew dramatically in the aftermath of World War II as the popularity of racing reached new heights, but that only served to whet the appetite for a bigger piece of the pie.

On Memorial Day, 1945, twenty-two days after the United States and its allies rejoiced in the formal surrender of Nazi Germany, betting marks were set at eight American thoroughbred tracks. Topping the list were Jamaica, where 64,537 wagered $3,564,151, and Santa Anita, where 76,640 wagered $3,051,776. Later that year on September 22, a new world betting record was set when $5,016,745 was wagered on the eight races at Belmont Park, the first $5 million handle in the history of the American turf.[2]

New records were set in 1946. On March 9 of that year, 80,200 witnessed the races at Santa Anita. The main attraction was the Santa Anita Handicap, which drew a twenty-three-horse field. Eight weeks later, over a hundred thousand crammed into Churchill Downs for the Kentucky Derby, the first six-figure crowd at a horse race in the United States in more than a hundred years.

As racetracks across the country were becoming bigger cash cows, New York fell backward. In 1946, attendance at New York tracks declined nearly 15 percent and the average daily betting handle fell 27.54 percent.[3] The erosion continued through the end of the decade. By 1949, pari-mutuel receipts from thoroughbred racing were down a staggering 34 percent from the peak year of 1945 despite an expansion of the racing calendar that delivered forty-two more days of racing.[4]

The resumption of thoroughbred racing in New Jersey oiled the drop-off, but a larger factor was a 50 percent jump in the takeout, the result of a 5 percent municipal and county surcharge levied on bets made at New York racetracks. Championed by Mayor O'Dwyer but reputedly the handiwork of powerful parks commissioner Robert Moses, the surcharge, approved by the legislature in 1946, was a hard pill for horseplayers to swallow. It raised the takeout from 10 percent to 15 percent in one fell swoop. The only good news was that the O'Dwyer bite, as it was dubbed, had an expiration date. It was designed to fade away after a three-year run, by which time New York City, the main beneficiary, would supposedly have repaired the holes in its budget.

Turf writers had warned that a higher tax would cause horseplayers to rebel, kicking in the law of diminishing returns. This sentiment was echoed by the members of the New York Racing Commission. Their surveys showed that the biggest drop-off was at the $100 windows, a development that suggested that the smart money had abandoned the sport. But the legislature rejected their pleas for tax relief, extending the 5 percent surcharge beyond the expiration date and then stabilizing the takeout at 15 percent where it remained until 1968.

The O'Dwyer bite encouraged other states to raise their levies. New Jersey was able to dig deeper into the pockets of racetrack patrons while yet maintaining a competitive edge. In 1948, the pari-mutuel tax in New Jersey was raised from 10 to 12 percent with the state commanding the larger share of it if the volume of betting reached certain benchmarks. At the high water mark, the state would get 10 percent of the handle, leaving only 2 percent to the racetrack owners. Simultaneously, the breakage was inflated from a nickel to a dime with the state receiving all of the odd pennies, whereas previously the split was 50/50. (Breakage refers to the odd pennies left over after payouts are rounded off. When breakage was first introduced, the rationale was to speed up the lines at the cashiers' windows by obviating the need to count pennies. Save in the infrequent case of minus pools when there is so much money bet on a particular entry that the track must make up the difference to meet the stipulated minimum payout, the pennies are *always rounded down.*)

The unrelenting pressure to boost the pari-mutuel tax, a national trend, infuriated racetrack owners. Industry spokesmen warned that over-taxation would kill the golden goose. The most vocal among them likened the tax collector to a gangster extorting protection money from a shopkeeper.

Speaking at the 1953 convention of the National Association of State Racing Commissioners, NASRC chairman Harry Millar said, "It is indeed unfortunate that because of his love for excitement, glamour and the great outdoor theatre that is racing, he (the racing fan) must pay, pay and pay until his recreation budget dies a lingering and painful death on the rack of excessive and unfair taxation. It is difficult to justify the attitude of our lawmakers toward the individual who likes to smoke, drive a car, drink an occasional glass of beer, and perhaps go to the races. Woe to him who, after working hard all year to support his family and pay his just income taxes, that he dare allow himself a few of life's fast diminishing pleasures."[5]

Millar's complaint went nowhere. The politicians could turn a deaf ear because the sport as a whole was booming, even in New York, which shook off the doldrums without a reduction in the pari-mutuel tax. Pronouncements that the beleaguered horseplayer was at the end of his rope clashed with the facts.

A NEW GOLDEN AGE?

In 1951, attendance nationally was up 6 percent over the previous year and wagering was up 17 percent.[6] In 1952, the upswing continued. Attendance increased 11.9 percent, wagering 19.8 percent, and the national pari-mutuel handle exceeded the $2 billion mark for the first time.

Nearly forty-six million people attended thoroughbred and harness races at seventy-seven U.S. and Canadian tracks in 1952, roughly five million more than witnessed professional baseball games at 332 major league and minor league parks. On Memorial Day, fourteen thoroughbred tracks reported an aggregate attendance of 364,855. Record crowds were reported at Hawthorne and at Detroit and a near-record crowd at Garden State Park.[7]

"Racing Now Virtual King of Sports," barked the front page headline in the *New York Times*. The accompanying story noted that attendance at major league ballparks declined by roughly 1.5 million from 1951 to 1952 whereas horse racing experienced a 2.1 million jump. During the first month of the 1953 baseball season, there were several days in which the races at the musty Jamaica track outdrew the combined total of two major league baseball games played that same day in New York. That same year, the seating capacity at Garden State was boosted by 44 percent.[8]

The surge, accompanied in many places by a rise in the takeout, had pundits scratching their heads. It was theorized that many new fans were converts from baseball, a sport whose leisurely pace was said to be better suited to a more agrarian age. Larger turnouts at racetracks, in particular night races at harness tracks, were held largely responsible for the shift of Boston's National League franchise, the Braves, to Milwaukee—the first relocation of a major league baseball club since 1903—and for hastening the migration of New York's National League teams to greener pastures in California. Track operators cited more sophisticated anti-doping measures and other actions that addressed concerns about skullduggery. The race-going experience was enhanced as track operators made good on long-delayed modernization plans, installing elevators, escalators, and air-conditioned dining areas. Advances in electronic tote boards supplied racegoers with more information updated at more frequent intervals. The new board at Ak-Sar-Ben in Omaha, installed in 1953, was described as "a genius capable of doing everything except marking the program and buying the racing fan a bag of peanuts."[9] By then, watching the board was an entrenched component of a day at the races. In a sense, the toteboard was America's first jumbotron.

Another theory pointed to the crackdowns spawned by the Kefauver hearings. In March of 1952, following the conclusion of the Fair Grounds meet, the head of the Louisiana State Racing Commission formally thanked government crime-fighters for rubbing out off-track betting in and around New Orleans. In his view, this was the key that opened the door to the most spectacular meet in the seventy-seven-year history of that storied racetrack. The betting handle was up 43.8 percent.[10]

The commendation betrayed a shifting mindset. The first opponents of off-track betting were men like Anthony Comstock. Their opposition flowed from the belief that gambling was an evil that aggravated a host of social problems. As society drifted away from this doctrine—a doctrine fueled by intemperate sermons and screeds—men like Estes Kefauver provided the good citizens of the Republic with another reason to clamp down on bookies. Their very name now conjured up a vast criminal network, a shadow government with a growing concentration of wealth. But a cynic would say Kefauver's conclusions provided a smokescreen for crackdowns that were ostensibly designed to make society less corrupt but were actually propelled by financial considerations. Bookies were bad because they siphoned money away from parimutuel pools, thereby robbing the public till of tax receipts that would have been used in service of the common good.

Bookie-busters were reluctant to emphasize this aspect. Florida governor Fuller Warren was an exception. In 1949, Warren ordered the arrest of every bookie in the state, an action that brought results, paralyzing a major industry in Dade and Broward counties, home to Miami Beach and other communities rife with professional gamblers. Fuller said the action was necessary to spare law-abiding citizens from the burden of additional taxes.[11] Florida then took eight cents from each dollar placed in a pari-mutuel pool, one of the highest levies in the country. The money was divided among the counties.

Bookies of earlier eras were also seen as parasites, but the incentive to thin their ranks took on a larger dimension when state governments seized an ownership stake in the racing game.

18

MULTIPLE-HORSE WAGERING TAKES FLIGHT

The boom in thoroughbred racing that characterized the early years of the 1950s was no flash in the pan. The growth in subsequent years wasn't as dramatic, but the upward trend continued. From 1950 to 1959, attendance nationwide at thoroughbred tracks increased 39.5 percent, the pari-mutuel handle increased 76.0 percent, and the pari-mutuel tax paid to the states that sanctioned pari-mutuel racing more than doubled, increasing by 115.3 percent. In the constellation of America's top growth industries, racing was a bright star.[1]

There seemed to be no end in sight. Records were smashed again in 1960. A crowd numbering 70,922 turned out on Memorial Day at refurbished Aqueduct, setting an attendance record for a racing program in the Empire State. On the day after Christmas, an even larger crowd, 71,017, turned up in Arcadia, California, for the opening day of the Santa Anita winter meet. In a throwback to an earlier era, the crew from the *LA Times* included the editor of the society page. Her report, which opened on the front page, reeled off so many names that it read like a phone book. Among other tidbits, her readers learned that the garnet sports jacket of a certain dignitary was the same color as a society woman's fur hat.[2]

The big numbers obfuscated a crack in the armor. On closer inspection, the growth was fueled largely by longer racing meets. More people were being ushered through the turnstiles, but average daily attendance was actually declining and the betting wasn't keeping pace with inflation. Moreover, track operators were faced with ever-increasing operating expenses. In New York in 1956, the net profit of the four major thoroughbred tracks was the lowest in sixteen years. This was the first full year in which the tracks were consolidated under the umbrella of the Greater New York Association, a nonprofit agency that would be renamed the New York Racing Association (NYRA). Reapportioning the pari-mutuel tax—somewhat less for the state, somewhat more for the racetracks—was seen as the simple solution. Across the country, racetrack operators petitioned for a larger share of the take.[3]

Periods of slack were prods to newfangled types of bets. In North America, the "daily double" was a Depression-era contrivance. By most accounts it first appeared in the United States at Aurora Downs in Illinois in 1932. Shortly thereafter, *quinella* betting and *exacta* betting diffused into horse racing from the game of jai alai. Both required bettors to pick the first two finishers in a race, the difference being that in an exacta one had to have the correct order. A wider menu of exotic bets was impractical because the technology wasn't there. Accumulator bets, as they were called in England, were labor intensive because they had to be hand graded. A totalizator with the capability of registering daily double combinations didn't appear in the United States until 1940. The mechanism, imported from Australia, was first put to use at Bay Meadows.

The daily double, which involved picking the winners of the first two races, was designed to lure customers to the track early so they would spend more money on concessions. It proved to be highly effective, but many racetrack operators were uncomfortable with it; they worried that the racing game would come to resemble a lottery. In New York, the daily double was discontinued at thoroughbred tracks following the 1945 season after a five-year trial. Defending the ban, a state racing commissioner asserted that the daily double attracted the wrong crowd, drawing in mugs that made no effort to ascertain the form of the horses before making their selections. "The history and the background of this form of wagering have not proven conducive to the best interests of the sport . . . it has assumed the proportions of a gigantic numbers game" he said.[4] The daily double continued on at harness tracks and was restored at New York's thoroughbred tracks in 1949.

When stagnation set in during the 1960s, track operators pushed the envelope and multiple-horse wagering spread like wildfire. High risk/

high reward propositions were promoted under such names as the Big Bonanza and the Gold Rush. Their allure was the chance to "win a lumberyard with a toothpick."

The first "pick six" in North America was introduced at Agua Caliente in April of 1956. The exotic wager, which took the name "5-10," was the brainchild of track manager John Alessio, a wealthy San Diego businessman. The Tijuana racing facility was then in difficulty, as had been true for most of its choppy history. The foreign book was profitable and the dog races, run five nights a week on a portable track, were almost breaking even, but the thoroughbred cards, presented on weekends, sometimes Sunday only, were a big cash drain. The "5-10" was the perfect elixir. Two years after its introduction, business was up 80 percent.[5]

During the spring and summer of 1960, there were several five-figure jackpots on $2 "pick six" wagers at Rockingham Park in New Hampshire, Lincoln Downs in Rhode Island, and Shenandoah Downs in West Virginia. And for the first time, the federal government took cognizance of pari-mutuel payouts.

A windfall involving a lucky bettor at Lincoln Downs captured the attention of the bureau chief of the Providence branch of the Internal Revenue Service. He dispatched an agent to the track with orders to find out who that man was. The agent interviewed dozens of people but came up empty. This incident would be credited with provoking the IRS into commanding racetracks to obtain the names, addresses, and Social Security numbers of bettors cashing tickets paying off at odds greater than 300 to 1—that is, payouts in excess of $600 on a $2 wager. Racetrack operators were none too pleased. The paperwork was a nuisance and conformity was bound to result in lost patronage. The cash grab was consistent with a long-standing IRS policy that gambling winnings counted as ordinary income for tax purposes. (In time, racetracks, in addition to filing the requisite IRS form, would be required to withhold money directly. Initially a flat 20 percent was deducted from payouts totaling more than $1,000.)[6]

The first application of the IRS edict in New York came on October 3, 1960, at Belmont when the daily double returned $693.70. At the payout windows, scenes of jubilation irrigated into scenes of outrage. A common complaint was that providing identification constituted an assault on personal liberty. Of 206 winning tickets, 63 remained uncashed at the close of business. (The deadline for collecting winning wagers was the day preceding the opening of a new racing season, in this particular instance, March 24, 1961.)[7]

Those that held off collecting their winnings likely returned with a phony ID or found a proxy to cash the ticket. The common stipend for a proxy was 10 percent of the winnings. A 1966 investigation of tax fraud at Yonkers Raceway estimated that 75 percent of all winning tickets on high-paying exotics were cashed by "10 percenters." Many of the surrogates were racetrack employees or individuals working in cahoots with racetrack employees.[8]

Yonkers Raceway was Empire City reincarnated as a harness track. It opened in 1950, catching the wave of a harness racing boom that was even more meteoric than the contiguous boom in thoroughbred racing. At the forefront was Roosevelt Raceway in Westbury, Long Island, where George Morton Levy ruled the roost. A former criminal defense attorney—his clients included alleged mafia chieftains—Levy came to be seen as the father of the modern era of harness racing, the man most responsible for transforming a sport previously identified with dusty back roads and agricultural fairs into a nighttime diversion for suburbanites and city folk.

The new generation of harness track operators, unlike many of their counterparts on the thoroughbred side, had no inhibitions when it came to salting the wagering menu with bets of the get-rich-quick variety. Harness tracks powered the trend toward exotic wagering. The downside was that harness tracks were caught up in far more betting scandals than thoroughbred tracks. Damage control was complicated by frequent revelations of shady deals between harness track operators and men with political clout. As had been true of the outlaw tracks of the late nineteenth century, Democratic machine politicians were heavily involved in the harness racing boom. When the sport's popularity waned, a loss of trust in the integrity of the game was cited as a contributing cause.

Horseplayers in New York, irked that the IRS had taken an interest in their affairs, had one more reason to bellyache when New York introduced a new formula for calculating breakage in 1965. Under the old system, payouts were rounded down to a nickel. Thus, a bet calculated to pay off at odds of 3.48 to 1, for example, would return $6.90 on a $2 wager. The new system rounded bets down to a dime. The same bet now returned only $6.80 (keep in mind that the skim-off is on each dollar). To a serious player striving to exploit a small edge over a large number of trials, this wasn't chump change. And in the aggregate, the odd pennies amounted to a lot of loot for the state treasury.

The pari-mutuel tax was then 15 percent. Factoring in the new formula for breakage, the true bite was 16.2 percent. For a significant number of racetrack gamblers, this was the last straw. Attendance declined 2.5 percent and betting went down 3.6 percent over the course of the next fiscal year despite eighty-nine more racing dates.[9]

For many people, horse racing served as a gateway into the world of financial speculation. Those that abandoned horse racing when the take-out became too severe may have turned to stocks or commodities or some other legitimate form of gambling. Others switched over to team sports. This development had been ongoing for some time.

19

PRO FOOTBALL CORRODES
THE RACING GAME

In 1936, according to a survey by the *Chicago Tribune*, bets on horse races accounted for more than two-thirds of all the money that changed hands in gambling. Approximately 85 percent was bet away from the racetracks.[1]

The findings were derived from interviews with gamblers, employees of gambling houses, attorneys, nightclub owners, and policemen in "nearly a score" of major cities. While this was a poorly designed survey, the general conclusion—that horse racing transcended team sports as a magnet for betting, and by a substantial margin—was likely true.

Subsequent reports told a different tale. By 1949, according to an article in the *New York Times*, bookmakers were handling more money on sporting events than on horse races, with baseball accounting for the lion's share of the sports action.[2] Ten years later, records seized during a coordinated series of raids on the offices of a bookmaking ring operating in five upstate New York cities—Albany, Syracuse, Rochester, Utica, and Buffalo—presented a similar picture. Baseball, basketball, and football accounted for 57 percent of the handle.[3] Baseball, by virtue of its long season, was tops; football came in third. While no breakdown was provided between college and pro football, the college version of the game was then decidedly more popular. Ivy League games in particular attracted heavy play, especially in Eastern precincts.

A major catalyst in the transition from horse racing to team sports was the point spread, an innovation that was slow to catch on, but—

when it did—spread like wildfire, achieving nationwide acceptance as the preferred way of structuring a straight wager on a football or basketball game.

The point spread is a simple construct. The team rated superior is assigned a point handicap and must win by more than that margin to be judged the winner for betting purposes. For example, if a team is established a ten-point favorite, it must win by at least eleven points to reward its backers. Those "taking the points" would win their wager if the underdog loses by nine points or less or wins outright. If the favorite wins by exactly ten points the bet is a tie, in gambling parlance a "push." Prior to the adoption of the point spread, the margin of victory was superfluous. The greater the perceived disparity between the opposing teams, the higher the odds on the favorite.

In gambling lore, the point spread was invented circa 1940 at the Gym Club, a bookie joint at 617 North Halstead Street in Chicago. The inventor, Charles K. McNeil, wasn't the owner but had the run of the place.

An eccentric who collected recordings of college fight songs—on Friday nights at the Gym Club, he would play the songs of the teams that he had bet on over the loudspeaker—Charles K. McNeil taught math at Denison College in Ohio and at Lehigh in Pennsylvania and then worked as a security analyst for a Chicago bank before becoming immersed in the world of sports gambling. His personal bets purportedly ranged in size from the price of a hotdog on the outcome of the next pitch while sitting in the bleachers at Wrigley Field to a high-five-figure wager on a college football game. His opinion and his honesty were so respected that bookmakers turned to him whenever a quirky happenstance complicated the resolution of a bet. Like John Cavanagh of an earlier era, McNeil was a one-man Supreme Court. [4]

McNeil would also be credited with inventing "teasers," a type of parlay that allows players to adjust the spread in either direction in return for a lower payout. This attribution is more credible as he certainly didn't invent the point spread.

Rummaging through old newspapers, one stumbles upon references to point spreads dating back to Ivy League football games in the early 1890s. These were man-to-man wagers transacted through an intermediary, the stakes-holder. Point spreads also turned up on parlay cards before McNeil arrived on the scene.

Football parlay cards, called pool cards when they achieved wide currency in the 1930s, required players to make multiple selections from a list of games, typically a minimum of four picks and a maximum of ten. The games that appeared on the cards were hair-line games— that is, matchups in which both teams were accorded an equal or near-equal chance of winning. There were proportionately more of them in those days, when low-scoring games were the norm and scores of 7–7, even 0–0, weren't that unusual. And therein lay the rub. All of the selections had to win for the player to collect and a game that ended in a tie was counted as a loss.

Late in the season when many of the teams had completed their schedule there weren't enough hair-line games to make up a good list. The easy solution—in lieu of discontinuing the operation while there were still games to be played—was to improvise hair-line games by the application of a point spread. If a game happened "to fall"—that is, if the spread was congruent with the final score, nailing the favored team's margin of victory—this was the same as if the game ended in a tie. The player lost his wager, no matter if all of his other picks were good.

In December of 1938, a Los Angeles operator tailored a pool card to the forthcoming New Year's Day bowl games. A syndicated sportswriter shared the particulars with his readers, an early example of the point spread insurgency.[5]

Orange Bowl	Tennessee -8	Oklahoma
Sugar Bowl	TCU -7	Carnegie Tech
Cotton Bowl	Texas Tech even	St. Mary's
Rose Bowl	Southern Cal -6	Duke

In many places, the parlay card business had no connection with local bookie parlors. The parlay card people weren't interested in taking wagers on individual games. As a rule, the cards were printed outside the area in which they circulated. By using agents to distribute the cards, an operator was better able to conceal his identity. The cards were especially popular in factory towns where they typically materialized on Friday (payday). They also surfaced in college dormitories.

Judging from newspaper reports, the big public universities affiliated with the Big Ten Athletic Conference were the busiest hives.

The payout table varied from place to place. The men behind the cards were far more conservative than their modern counterparts, offering odds that in today's marketplace would induce yelps of highway robbery. A pool card that circulated in the financial district of New York in the mid-1930s had payouts ranging from 6 to 1 on a four-teamer to 85 to 1 on a perfect 10-spot. A card distributed in Salem, Oregon, had payouts that ranged from 7 to 5 on a two-teamer to 1,000 to 1 for sixteen correct selections. The maximum wager was $25.[6]

Although pool cards were intended for small-fry bettors, the aggregate weekly play nationwide during the years of the Great Depression was thought to be many times higher than what was handled in straight wagers. Vilified for running a sucker's game, the pool card purveyors yet stood to lose big on those Saturdays when there were no ties and the outcomes jibed with the consensus of the experts. The history of parlay cards is replete with tales of bettors left holding the bag as the men behind them vanished into the night.

That Chicago would take the lead in adapting point spreads to straight wagers was undoubtedly influenced by the accomplishments of the Bears, the city's preeminent professional football team. The 1940 Bears routed the Redskins 73–0 in the league championship game and lost only three games over the next three seasons. Under the established way of framing a football proposition, it would have been hard to attract business on their games. Bettors in the main were averse to laying heavy odds, as the rate of return was so low. The reward didn't justify the risk.

When point spreads crossed over from pool cards to straight bets, many bookies retained the "ties lose" feature by dealing a *split line*. A line of "6-8," for example, meant that the favorite had to win by more than eight points whereas the underdog, to be graded the winner for betting purposes, could not lose by more than five points. Since all bets were even money, the bookie stood to profit only if the game landed "6," "7," or "8":

> If the favorite won by exactly 6 points, those backing the favorite *lost* and those backing the underdog *"pushed"* (had their bet refunded).
>
> If the favorite won by exactly 8 points, those backing the underdog *lost* and those backing the favorite *pushed*. As in the first exam-

ple, there were no winners save for the bookmaker who in theory bagged 50 percent of the money staked with him.

If the favorite won by exactly 7 points, this was a "perfect middle." The bookmaker broke out the champagne; he won every bet.[7]

When the Bears met the seemingly overmatched Redskins in the 1942 NFL title game, some bookmakers dealt a line of "19-22." They stood to win all the bets if the game fell "20" and "21." In a sense this was fair, as a lopsided competition has less chance of landing on any particular number, but players' squealed that this wasn't kosher and went looking for a better deal. (For the record, the Redskins scored a monumental upset, winning 14–6.)[8]

During the 1940s and 1950s, the leading disseminator of point spreads was the Minneapolis firm that operated under the name Athletic Publications, Inc. The day-to-day operations were run by Leo Hirschfield, a World War I veteran who renamed the company that was formerly called Gorham Press after acquiring it from a local businessman, Billy Hecht.

Athletic Publications was a small company with eighteen year-round employees. The firm published sports annuals and weekly football and basketball newsletters, but the main source of the company's income was the line service. During football season, subscribers called in on Monday to get the opening line and called in again at intervals for updates.

Four employees had input into the opening football line. Working independently, they weighed each game and then met as a group on Monday morning to hash over their differences and form a consensus. Asked to provide a job description, Hirschfield said "I pay these guys to sit around all day reading the paper." He reportedly subscribed to fifty-nine daily and Sunday papers and about a hundred college newspapers. In 1957, Hirschfield made plans to relocate the major part of his operation to Davenport, Iowa. Although there were undoubtedly more salient considerations, Hirschfield cited the advantage of being closer to the center of the country's population where many of the papers would arrive one day earlier. The move was scuttled when the papers caught wind of it. The news prompted some of the locals to tell Hirschfield that he wasn't welcome in their neighborhood.[9]

A common question posed to Hirschfield was whether he had locker room spies on his payroll. He did not. However, many of the firm's clients had close ties to their local team and were privy to information they willingly shared. The comp list for the weekly newsletters included many sportswriters who could be called upon to check out a suspicious rumor. Mort Olshan, briefly a member of Hirschfield's oddsmaking panel, recalled that the firm routinely beat the national newswires to sports news stories of national import.[10]

Bookmakers referred to the numbers dispensed by Hirschfield's firm as the Minneapolis Line. The name bore witness that there were other companies offering the same service. The number two company of the industry was the Angel-Kaplan firm in Chicago run by Don Angelini and Bill Kaplan. Some bookmakers used both services and supplemented them with consultants that specialized in a minor sport or games of regional interest. Akin to the situation that prevailed at racetracks before the pari-mutuel takeover, the bigger a bookmaker's handle, the more money he spent on information providers.

Bookmakers that accepted football wagers ahead of the herd customarily tweaked the opening line to reflect the perceived biases of their best customers. Some tested the line by letting handicappers with respected opinions bet into it for modest amounts before opening the line to the general public. A betting line made available to a select few came to be called an "outlaw line." Beyond this point—barring late breaking developments certain to impact the betting, such as an injury to a star player—adjustments resulted from an unbalanced book. Point spreads were concocted with an eye toward bringing in an equal amount of money on each team, but a 50–50 split was elusive. Moving a point spread off the original number—increasing or decreasing the degree of favoritism, depending on the circumstance—was designed to make the disfavored team more attractive and thereby even up the betting. Line services kept abreast of fluctuations by monitoring the activity of bookmakers that booked high.

Bettors liked the point spread because of its simplicity. It was easier to process the hodgepodge of information displayed on a wagering board or conveyed over the telephone. Bookmakers found it easier to keep track of their jeopardy. But there was one fly in the ointment. It was now possible to manipulate the outcome of a game without transposing the winner and loser; merely by shaving down the margin of victory. Connivers zeroed in on college basketball games with double-digit betting lines. Each new scandal rekindled the debate over the propriety of printing point spreads in newspapers. Sports editors found that the most vocal opposition came from college athletic organizations rather than the religious groups that spearheaded earlier campaigns to censor racing news.[11]

When bookies abandoned the "split line," they attached odds of 6 to 5 on straight wagers in football and basketball. This was a carryover from baseball where bettors were customarily required to risk $6 for each $5 they hoped to win on a matchup that the linemaker rated a toss-up. At 6/5 odds, a bookmaker stood to keep 8.33 percent of what he handled *assuming balanced action.* In the lingo of a modern corporate bookmaker, this was his "theoretical hold percentage." It is figured by dividing the handle into what the bookmaker gets to keep after distributing the winnings. (For illustrative purposes, let's assume that a bookmaker's handle on a football game consists entirely of two $120 wagers, one on each side. The winner gets back $220, of which $100 is profit, leaving the bookmaker $20 for his trouble, the equivalent of 8.33 percent.) Then some bookmakers took to dealing football and basketball at odds of 11/10, a practice eventually adopted by virtually all of their cohorts. The spearhead of this innovation was Ed Curd, the Lexington, Kentucky, bookmaker who achieved sudden notoriety during the Kefauver hearings when the notorious Frank Costello mentioned his name.

At 11/10, a bookmaker keeps one dollar for each $22 that is bet *assuming balanced action.* That reduces the hold percentage from 8.33 to 4.545 percent, an enormous difference in a game where winning to a professional means exploiting a tiny edge over a large number of trials. Ed Curd did nothing more than reduce his prices, but he revolutionized the game in a way that attracted hordes of new bettors, many defectors from horse racing who were fed up with the incessant push to raise the pari-mutuel tax.[12]

The National Football League was founded in 1922. During the early years, annual battles such as Army-Navy overshadowed anything that the league had to offer, a situation that persisted beyond the midpoint of the century. The East-West Shrine Game, a college all-star game played in San Francisco, attracted more buzz than an NFL title game.

The 1958 title game between the New York Giants and Baltimore Colts, played at Yankee Stadium on December 28, would come to be seen as the turning point. Televised nationally on CBS but blacked out in the New York area, the game was laced with drama. Baltimore rallied to draw even after squandering an eleven-point lead and then won the game in the first-ever sudden-death overtime, 23–17. In their recap, *Sports Illustrated* branded the contest the greatest game ever played. Dozens of retrospectives would play off that theme, but in reality the public's interest in pro football was well whetted before this allegorical big bang.

In those days, the lords of college football looked upon the medium of television as a gorilla that had to be kept on a short leash. As late as 1958, only eleven college football games were nationally televised across the entire spectrum of the regular season. Regional telecasts were restricted to four Saturdays and no team was permitted more than two exposures unless they were invited to a bowl game. In their public proclamations, NCAA honchos emphasized the importance of keeping the college game from becoming overcommercialized. A more compelling reason was to protect the gate.

Bert Bell, the commissioner of the National Football League from 1946 until his death in 1959, was dead set against teams televising their home games within their regional market and succeeded in imposing his will on recalcitrant owners but otherwise took the opposite tack, embracing television as an elixir rather than a toxin. During his tenure, the number of TV sets in use soared from a few thousand to roughly fifty million. By 1960, there were twenty-one professional teams, eight in a newly formed expansion league called the American Football League, and virtually every game was televised somewhere. In time, the Monday Night game on ABC became the biggest game in any town, attracting more betting than any other sporting event during the week that it ran.

Two years prior to the Colts-Giants title game, a reporter opined that watching the NFL Sunday afternoon double-header from the comfort of one's living room was America's new national pastime. To a betting man, the one-eyed monster, as detractors called it, functioned much like the wire that piped in race results to an old-fashioned horse parlor. One learned the fate of his bet in real time and formed new opinions from the circumstances that affected the outcome.

The 1958 NFL title game was a fitting climax to an entertaining season. According to Commissioner Bell's own figures, underdogs were victorious in thirty-eight of the seventy-two regular-season games. The strides made by the weaker teams—that is, parity—were cited as a big reason why the league set an attendance record for the seventh straight year.

In the days leading up to the big game, bookmakers across the country were showered with bets. "This game," said a New York bookie, "will be the biggest betting event of the year—bigger than the World Series, bigger than any fight and, as a matter of fact, perhaps bigger than any betting event we've had in any year. It's stupendous." Looking back, a West Coast bookmaker of long standing, quoted in *Newsweek*, said the Colts-Giants game attracted far more action than any event in his memory.[13]

No matter how the game played out—even if it had been a snoozer—it wasn't going to arrest the momentum.

20

NEW YORK WELCOMES OTB

Campaigns to suppress off-track betting never had the full support of the public. Whatever the social benefits, said the opponents, that didn't justify the heavy cost incurred in stamping it out, especially as repressive measures rarely had long-term effects.

In 1937, as Mayor Kelly was stumping for off-track betting in Chicago, maverick lawmakers in Ohio, Maryland, and California introduced similar bills. The Ohio bill, first introduced in 1935, was shot down by the Ohio General Assembly. The Maryland bill, which exempted nineteen of the state's twenty-four counties, passed the House of Delegates but was vetoed by the governor. The California proposal passed the Public Morals Committee of the State Assembly, but went no further.[1]

Lawmakers in other states and municipalities also weighed bills to legalize off-track betting. There was a flurry after the Kefauver hearings. The evidence suggested that the scope of illegal gambling had broadened to where it couldn't be extinguished without a massive infusion of money and manpower; it made more sense to regulate it. St. Louis bookmaker James J. Carroll, a Kefauver Commission deponent, expressed an opinion that resonated with many law-makers: "Gambling is a biological necessity for certain types . . . the quality that gives substance to their daydreams," said Carroll.[2]

New York City finally broke the ice but it was a long, drawn-out process. In 1947, grand juries impaneled to investigate gambling in Brooklyn and Queens issued separate reports favoring off-track betting under state supervision. State senator James J. Crawford, the cosponsor of the legislation that brought back the bookies, picked up the torch, authoring bills that would allow for citywide bookmaking stands staffed by licensed agents of New York's various racetracks.

Crawford had an ally in Mayor O'Dwyer. In January of 1950, nine months before his sudden resignation, O'Dwyer came out publicly in favor of legalized sports betting—not just horse racing, but all sports, amateur and professional—at betting shops that would be manned by employees of the state. "After 40 years in this city," said O'Dwyer, "I am satisfied that the public is interested in sports, not only from the standpoint of sports themselves but also from the pleasure they get from betting on sports." Up in Albany, Governor Dewey said that O'Dwyer's outlook was indicative of New York's morally bankrupt Democratic leadership.[3]

Others voicing approval of off-track betting on horse races included the powerful parks commissioner, Robert Moses; Pulitzer Prize–winning reporter Herbert Bayard Swope, formerly the head of the New York Racing Commission; twenty-one of the twenty-five members of the New York City Council; and the majority of the state's registered voters. In a 1951 survey, 67 percent of the respondents said they would vote "yes" on a measure to legalize off-track betting. The degree of favoritism ranged from 69 percent in New York City to 56 percent in rural areas.[4]

The loudest opponents of Senator Crawford's bills were state and national racing authorities and Protestant clergymen. A spokesperson for the New York State Council of Churches said that legalized gambling violated the principal of Christian stewardship. Herbert Swope's rejoinder was that his feelings were in accord with Anglican Church leaders in England and with the findings of the American Catholic Philosophical Association.[5]

The push for off-track betting picked up steam again in 1958 during the second term of three-term mayor Robert Wagner. When Wagner came to Albany in 1959 to plead for off-track betting he came armed with a more detailed proposal than had ever been submitted. The betting shops would be located a reasonable distance from saloons, schools, churches, welfare centers, and unemployment offices. They would be uniform in appearance and bare-bones to inhibit loitering. No one under twenty-one, whether alone or accompanied by an adult, would be allowed to enter.[6]

With both houses of the legislature controlled by Republicans, Wagner's proposal was doomed, but his efforts advanced the cause and in 1970 the long campaign bore fruit when the legislature gave the city the green light to establish a corporation for the purpose of administering off-track betting. New York City would keep 80 percent of the annual net proceeds on any amount below $200 million, beyond which the split between the city and state would be 50–50. Governor Nelson Rockefeller, a longtime foe of off-track betting, reluctantly signed the bill into law. With New York City teetering toward bankruptcy, the city's tax base eroded by a white flight to the suburbs, Rockefeller was persuaded to go with the flow.

The covenant wasn't girdled exclusively to New York City—the law allowed for other OTB districts—but this was a victory for the Big Apple, whose representatives did all the heavy lifting. The verdict feathered the cap of Wagner's successor, John V. Lindsay. An ally of Governor Rockefeller, with whom he later had a falling-out, Lindsay began his political career as a Republican and won the race for mayor on a Fusion ticket. An Episcopalian, he was the first New York mayor born into the Protestant faith in fifty-six years, a useful chit when cultivating support for off-track betting in Albany.

Lindsay selected wealthy Rochester businessman Howard Samuels to head the city's OTB operation. Samuels envisioned OTB diversifying into sports like football and basketball, accommodating bettors of many persuasions.

Setting up America's first computerized off-track betting network was a complicated undertaking. A full year elapsed before the first bets were taken. The launching pad was Grand Central Station, where the OTB Corporation had installed ten betting terminals at windows formerly assigned to the New Haven Railroad. Later that same day, April 8, 1971, a second outlet opened in Forest Hills, an affluent community in the borough of Queens. OTB also offered telephone wagering to in-state residents. The minimum deposit for opening an account was $25. A flurry of sign-ups in the days preceding the opening of the Belmont meet boosted the number of subscribers to six thousand.[7]

Despite numerous glitches that challenged the patience of bettors, the "New Game in Town" opened with a big splash. On Day One with the menu consisting solely of the harness races at Roosevelt, more than $100,000 was wagered at Grand Central Station on the daily double alone. Most of the bettors were couriers getting down bets for friends, neighbors, and coworkers. As the first post time approached, tickets were rationed five to a customer to speed up the lines. Four weeks later, with six sites up and running, New Yorkers wagered a shade over $1 million on the Kentucky Derby during three-and-a-half days of selling. OTB honchos elected to take bets on the nationally televised race without the consent of the management of Churchill Downs, which threatened legal action.[8]

Fourteen months after the first bets were taken, at the end of the first full fiscal year, New York had eighty OTB parlors—they were called branch offices—and the corporation was handling an average of more than $1.5 million in wagers each day.[9] At its peak, OTB, with 156 branches and 2,600 employees, was New York City's largest retailer. Five more OTB chains—two on Long Island and three upstate—eventually dotted the Empire State map. These were independent entities.

Howard Samuels and his advertising consultants conceptualized the opening of each new branch as a socially progressive event. The theme was hammered home in an advertising slogan: "Money to the People. Bet OTB." Later campaigns had a get-rich-quick theme. A banner reading "Winners Ride in Limousines—OTB" was plastered on the sides of city buses.

Some found the advertising repugnant. It was one thing to tax a vice, quite another to encourage it. What next? Would government encourage people to take up smoking to derive more revenue from the tax on tobacco? And while many merchants welcomed betting parlors for the added foot traffic, others were hostile. When OTB proposed to open a branch on Fifth Avenue a few steps from the luxury department store Bergdorf Goodman, the shopkeepers on the block raised a fuss. "We surveyed the other OTB offices and found . . . they were filthy and a disgrace to the neighborhood," said a spokesperson for the shopkeepers association.[10]

The OTB shops were set up in accordance with the recommendations set forth by Mayor Wagner's advisors. They were sparsely furnished to discourage loitering. Selling snacks was taboo, even from a vending machine, and the restrooms were for employees only. The stop-and-go model, a concession to the obstructionists, would eventually be liberalized, but most locations remained Spartan.

A survey commissioned by OTB in 1971 determined that the typical OTB client was a white, middle-class, middle-aged, unmarried male "with more brains and money than his neighbors." This conclusion, derived from interviews with 11,000 bettors at twelve OTB shops, was contradicted, in a fashion, by a 1973 study that showed that players betting off-track lost proportionately more than those attending the races. This was attributed to a higher propensity for multiple-horse wagers.[11]

Appearing at the ribbon-cutting ceremony at the OTB headquarters in Times Square, CBS sports personality Jimmy "the Greek" Snyder vouched that legal betting would produce legions of new fans for the Sport of Kings and that this would redound to the benefit of the race-tracks, driving up attendance. The Greek could not have been more wrong. In the first year of OTB, attendance at New York's four metro-politan tracks (Belmont, Aqueduct, Roosevelt, and Yonkers) declined by 1.2 million. Of those tracks, all but Roosevelt experienced a sharp dip in wagering activity. Reduced patronage prompted lay-offs that ex-acerbated labor unrest. The first strike by mutuel clerks wiped out seventeen racing days at Aqueduct in 1972.[12]

The following year, state legislators were persuaded that a reduction in the takeout would stem the bleeding, bringing long-term benefits that would overcome an initial drop-off in taxes for the state treasury. The takeout for the sixty-five-day Aqueduct fall meet was reduced from 17 to 14 percent. The reduction carried over to the summer meet at Belmont Park. But the experiment wasn't continued, notwithstanding the fact that it resulted in a significant jump in attendance. And then, in 1974, as part of an effort to abate New York City's worsening budget problems, the O'Dwyer bite was resurrected, in a fashion, when the city slapped a 5 percent surcharge on winning off-track wagers. What this meant was that a man betting $2 on a 10/1 shot at Aqueduct or Belmont stood to get back $22, whereas the same wager at an OTB shop would have returned only $20.90.

The OTB brass felt betrayed. The surcharge was bound to result in a loss of patronage. Some OTB regulars would simply quit and others would join the vast horde of those that bet with illegal bookmakers. Howard Samuels, who had just stepped down to give his full attention to an ultimately unsuccessful bid for the Democratic gubernatorial nomination, called the surcharge a government-issued gift to organized crime. When OTB was just getting started, Samuels said that making money for the city and the state was secondary to incapacitating the illegal bookies whose activities burdened and corrupted the police and the courts.[13]

Five percent was misleading. With breakage, a man betting on a heavy favorite to show might surrender as much as 50 percent of his winnings. When Ruffian met Foolish Pleasure in a celebrated match race at Belmont Park, an OTB bettor lost 11 to 25 percent of the payout at the racetrack, no matter the outcome. When the surtax took effect on July 1, 1974, the number of individuals with telephone accounts had soared to 34,000. These individuals tended to bet more than those that made their wagers in person and they were relatively more turned-off by the new levy. In the first three months of the surtax, bets of $1,000 or more declined by 70 percent.[14]

The initial bump in racetrack patronage that resulted from the OTB surcharge was unsustainable. Attendance slumped once again. Periodic work stoppages by unionized workers exacerbated the problem. And in 1976 another threat emerged when a new track opened at the Meadowlands complex in New Jersey. Operated by a new state agency, the New Jersey Sports and Exposition Authority, the new facility was less than nine miles by car from the heart of Times Square. Used primarily for harness racing, the one-mile oval morphed into a thoroughbred track in the autumn. Both kinds of races were held at night. On the first night of thoroughbred racing, a Tuesday, the attendance was 25,158, compared with 14,546 for the afternoon races at Belmont Park, where racing was of a higher quality.[15]

By all indications, the population of bookies tapered off in the years preceding the advent of OTB. Legal off-track betting was going to deplete their ranks even further, but perversely the exact opposite occurred. In January of 1974, a privately circulated paper said that OTB created a climate that was a godsend for outlaw bookmakers. "Thousands of people who never in the world would have thought of betting on football or basketball or baseball are now betting with bookies," said Chief of Police Paul F. Delise.[16]

The document pegged the rise in illegal gambling at 62 percent. While the figure was little more than an educated guess, the general conclusion was supported by other studies. According to America's leading gambling authority, Eugene Christiansen, wagering in the New

York metropolitan area more than doubled between 1974 and 1983 and during this period horse racing's share plummeted from 50 to 18 percent. After the surtax went into effect, bookies became more brazen. Agents were spotted soliciting business openly on sidewalks near OTB parlors.[17]

POSTSCRIPT

New York City's OTB operation received a shot in the arm in 1995 when a city-run cable station chartered to provide programming of an educational and governmental nature began airing horse races from local tracks. Because the city owned NYOTB and derived tax revenue from the shops, the races were deemed to be in the public interest. The first telecast, with pre-race commentary and frequent views of the tote board, showed the harness races at Yonkers. The convenience of watching the races in the comfort of one's home spurred 12,000 new OTB telephone accounts.[18] But this infusion of new money failed to steady the listing ship.

The corporation declared bankruptcy in December of 2009. Twelve months later, an era died in New York City when the fifty-four parlors still standing after a decade of downsizing were padlocked. Roughly thirteen hundred employees were thrown out of work, and nine hundred retirees lost their health insurance.

The collapse was foreseeable. When the corporation was born, horse racing had a monopoly on legal gambling in New York. Then the lottery and other games were legalized and the competition got immensely tougher. Like all aging corporations, obligations to retirees became an ever larger burden. However, a poor business model and reckless spending were large contributing factors. From the very beginning, NYC-OTB was a vessel for political patronage. For some of the higher-ups, the job was nothing more than a sinecure. On the day the plug was pulled, the corporation had a fleet of eighty-seven cars, roughly four for each executive.[19]

The shift from horse racing to team sports, as previously noted, was well under way before OTB arrived on the scene. The last big multistate roundup of the 1960s netted twenty-two of America's top bookmakers, men characterized as layoff commissioners. They reportedly accepted sports wagers only, no horses.[20]

Off-track betting was an important source of tax revenue for most of its existence, but early estimates of profitability were shown to be wildly exaggerated. New York's official horse bookie was swimming upstream from the very beginning.

21

A SIDE TRIP TO OLD NEVADA

Nevada was granted statehood in 1864. Five years later, the state legalized gambling with a minimum age of seventeen. A saloon-keeper offering games of chance paid a quarterly license fee and was assessed an additional tax on each type of game that he provided. The fees were earmarked for public schools.

In 1910, Nevada fell in line with the rest of the nation, becoming the last of the extant forty-six states to outlaw gambling. By one estimate, the ban erased a thousand jobs, roughly 2.5 percent of Nevada's workforce. Reno, in particular, suffered a sharp increase in unemployment. The little city on the Truckee River was America's last great hive of unmolested gambling.

In 1913, amendments to the bill exempted card games where the deal rotated among the players and approved nickel slot machines that issued prizes, the value of which could not exceed $2. In 1915, the law was amended again to allow on-course pari-mutuel betting. The takeout at the upcoming meet at the Reno Fairgrounds was set at 10 percent. The state took one-sixth for the highway fund.[1]

In 1931, to the horror of much of the nation and the shame of many of its citizens, Nevada backtracked, liberating games of chance from the back rooms and cellars where they were conducted with little interference. During the first nine months of "wide-open" gambling, thirty licenses were granted in Reno alone. Some were for a single slot machine, craps table, or keno setup, and many of the licenses were relinquished the next year when the Depression scarred Reno's economy in lockstep with the nation at large. Bookmakers weren't part of the first wave, but this quickly changed. A UPI correspondent visiting Reno in 1932 reported that the betting parlors in the bigger clubs were doing a landslide business on the November elections.[2]

The Reno bookmakers were bending the law. Nevada didn't officially authorize bets on out-of-state races until 1941. Governor E. P. Carville disapproved, but the legislature overrode his veto. Carville was worried that the authorization would redound into Nevada becoming "the headquarters and very heart and center of a nationwide racket." With Moe Annenberg in jail, the national racing wire was thought to be vulnerable to a takeover by the hoodlum element. Earlier that year, the Washoe Publishing Company of Reno, a Continental Press subsidiary, was shut down in a joint raid by Nevada and California authorities. The agency's tentacles reached horse parlors in parts of Arizona and California with the highest concentration in Bakersfield.[3]

When Nevada legalized gambling, there were fewer than 100,000 inhabitants in the entire state (91,058 according to the 1930 U.S. Census). Over the next twenty years, the population more than doubled. Mirroring the pattern in neighboring California, most of the growth was in the south. By 1951, the year that bookmakers were hit with the 10 percent federal excise tax, Las Vegas was as large as Reno. The population of Clark County—home to Las Vegas, North Las Vegas, and incorporated areas that included a stretch of road that came to be called the Las Vegas Strip—reached 50,000 that year, a ten-fold increase over 1930. Clark County then housed thirteen of Nevada's twenty-four race and sports books. Eight were clustered in downtown Las Vegas, either in one of the hotels where the operation was leased to an independent contractor or in a store that from a distance looked like any other store on the block.

It wasn't easy being a bookmaker in Nevada in the years straddling the midpoint of the twentieth century. Horse and sports betting were in such disrepute that the licensed bookmakers existed in something of a leper colony.

In January of 1945, the college basketball world was rocked by a point-shaving scandal involving players at Brooklyn College, an event that proved to be the tip of an iceberg. The scandal lent credence to rumors that many of the games played at Madison Square Garden were crooked. Two years later, a known bookmaker, Jerome Zarowitz, and three other individuals were convicted of conspiracy in a failed attempt to sway the outcome of the 1946 Giants-Bears NFL title game. In 1948, the whiff of scandal touched down at the state university in Reno when a writer for *Sports Week*, a scruffy New York tabloid, asserted that Reno bookmakers and "a few dozen" Nevada football players connived to rig the November 6 Nevada-Santa Clara game, a 14–0 defeat for the heavily favored Nevada squad. When attorneys for the school demanded a retraction it became a national story.[4]

The sensational murder of Flamingo Hotel builder Benjamin "Bugsy" Siegel on June 21, 1947, redounded into a flurry of news articles critical of Las Vegas. The forty-one-year-old Siegel was killed by a machine gun-wielding assassin shooting through an open window into the palatial Beverly Hills home leased by his girlfriend, wealthy divorcee Virginia Hill.

The first theory about the murder to gain wide currency evoked the specter of another Chicago-style turf war. Siegel was the West Coast representative of Trans-America, a fledgling racing wire service that was muscling in on the established provider, Continental Press. The assassination of James Ragen in June of the previous year was such an audacious caper that the story was still vivid. Las Vegas and Beverly Hills were a long way from Ragen's Chicago, but it was widely assumed that the ambushes were connected.

Fears that gangland violence could spread to Nevada were intensified when it was discovered that a Las Vegas horse parlor on the outs with Continental Press because of a billing dispute was pirating race information from a rival book. The information was received via a hidden wire planted after drilling a hole in the roof. The duplicitous book and two other books thought to be lightning rods for gangland strife were shut down.[5] The regulators considered rescinding all of the bookmaking licenses in Las Vegas but backed off in favor of heightened scrutiny and tighter regulations. A bookmaker wishing to renew his license had to reapply quarterly, whereas previously renewals were a once-a-year thing.[6]

Bookmaking was the only form of legalized gambling in Nevada that had a direct tie-in with illegal gambling in other states. This point was hammered home during the one-day stopover of the Kefauver Commission in Las Vegas on November 15, 1950. Testifying before the panel, William Moore, the executive vice president of the Last Frontier Hotel, acknowledged that bets made in the book at the Last Frontier were laid off to bookmakers all over the country. Moore was then a member of the State Tax Commission, the agency that regulated gambling in Nevada, licensing operators and supervising their operations.[7]

In May of the following year, the regulators prohibited lay-off betting. All wagers had to be processed face-to-face at the counter. Later that month, a brazen robbery at the Flamingo Hotel provided the anti-bookmaking faction with more ammunition. Bypassing the casino cage, four stick-up men proceeded directly to the race book and made off with $3,800. Through fingerprints left on a paper sack, lawmen were able to identify one of the masked gunmen. He was Anthony Brancato, a hoodlum who had been questioned about several California gangland killings, including that of Bugsy Siegel. The FBI placed him on the "ten most wanted" list. He didn't stay there long. Six weeks after the robbery, Brancato and a male companion were found dead in the front seat of a car parked in front of a Hollywood, California, apartment house. They had been shot in the back of the head.[8]

The federal excise tax, which went into effect on November 1, 1951, was devastating. It wasn't only that a bookmaker could ill-afford to give 10 percent of his volume to Uncle Sam—his profit margin was too slim—but he couldn't pass the levy on to his customers without losing a big chunk of his business. A horseplayer would balk if required to pony up an extra dollar for the privilege of making a $10 bet. A losing football or basketball wager structured to win $100 now cost $121, rather than $110, and a serious player accustomed to laying 11/10 odds would simply say "no." There were plenty of curbstone bookmakers around to fade his action. The licensed bookmakers, facing a $10,000 fine and/or five years in prison if they failed to pay the tax, were in a quandary.

When the excise tax became law, there were twenty-four licensed bookmaking establishments in Nevada; thirteen in Las Vegas, nine in Reno, and two in the isolated ranching and mining community of Elko. In taxes and fees, the bookies produced about 13 percent of Nevada's revenue from legal gambling. Two months after the law took effect, only four were still open to walk-in traffic. Three books in Reno and one in Elko were all that was left.[9] Moreover, under current conditions there was scant chance of a turnaround.

The regulators understood that a bookmaker would struggle to make a go of it without fudging on his taxes. If one or more of Nevada's bookmakers was prosecuted for tax fraud in a case that attracted national attention, this could potentially put the entire gambling industry in jeopardy. The authorities, in the main, thought that bookmaking should be stopped altogether. "The tax commission has been doing considerable thinking about the bookmaking situation," said the political writer for the *Nevada State Journal*. "In fact, the members of the commission are agreed among themselves it would be an excellent thing for Nevada gambling—present and future—if all bookmaking activity were to cease immediately."[10] Governor Charles H. Russell, who chaired the commission's monthly meetings, felt this way too. Scrubbing away the remaining bookie parlors, however, was an act that required legislative approval.

Deterred from outlawing race and sports betting, the commissioners succeeded in imposing new constraints. In April of 1952, it was decided that the bookmakers had to conduct their business in a building separate from one that offered other forms of gambling. No food or drink was allowed, an exclusion that would stay in effect for the next fifteen years.[11]

Two bills to outlaw bookmaking were presented to the legislature in 1953. They likely would have passed if not for the opposition of Elko Democrat John Robbins. The longest serving member of the Nevada State Senate, Robbins had helped write the seminal open-gambling law for which Nevada was famous. "If race betting is outlawed," he said, "it would lead some longhairs to decide next that craps was not in the public interest. It would be a wedge which might be used to try to run gambling out of the state."[12]

The legislature considered three more bills to ban bookmaking in 1955, but these too were waylaid before reaching the governor's desk. The legislators that voted against the bills were satisfied that the practices of the bookmakers would be more thoroughly scrutinized. Early in the legislative session, the solons established a new regulatory body, the Gaming Control Board, which usurped many of the powers delegated to the overstretched Tax Commission (a sister agency, the Nevada Gaming Commission, was created in 1959).

The 1955 squabble would be the last serious threat to legal sports and race betting arising internally. Subsequent attacks were promoted by lawmakers in Washington. But bookmakers were continually under the microscope, and there was more aggravation in 1960 when the regulators dredged up an obscure law from 1911 to halt betting on the presidential election. After two dead election cycles—Republican standard-bearer Dwight D. Eisenhower was an overwhelming favorite, depressing the betting—the 1960 race between Kennedy and Nixon was a doozy with strong two-way action, a hot item for Nevada bookies until the regulators stepped in, with less than a week remaining until the polls closed, and halted the betting. Some of the bookies paid off on the bets they were holding whereas others refunded all wagers. They were damned if they did and damned if they didn't. [13]

Despite all the impediments, as the 1950s wore on there was a revivification of bookie joints. The new licensees were transplants, bookmakers drawn to Nevada because conditions were less onerous than in their home communities. They came from such places as Los Angeles, St. Louis, Omaha, Chicago, and Detroit. Professional sports and race bettors swelled the migration. Cleveland and Toledo were big exporters

The operators survived by keeping two sets of books. A stranger walking in off the street paid full fare, but a preferred customer was spared the burden of paying the tax. A $500 wager might be recorded as a $50 wager on the handwritten receipt. A tiny mark was penciled on the betting slip to indicate the deception. "To compete, we must cheat," was the silent mantra of the bookmakers, legal and illegal.

In 1968, bookmakers and their employees were freed from the burden of purchasing an annual tax stamp when the U.S. Supreme Court, in a suit brought by a Connecticut man, effectively nullified the requirement by ruling that a person could not be criminally prosecuted for failing to comply. For this welcome development, bookmakers could thank the Communist Party.

In 1950, at the height of the Red Scare, Congress passed the Subversive Activities Control Act, the handiwork of Nevada senator Pat McCarran. The act required members of the Communist Party to register with the United States attorney general. In 1965, the court ruled that this was unconstitutional, as it violated the Fifth Amendment privilege against self-incrimination. This set the precedent by which gambler-businessmen were free to ignore the tax stamp law without fear of legal reprisal. (The lone dissenting voice on the court in the tax stamp matter was that of Chief Justice Earl Warren. This was entirely in character. The son of Scandinavian immigrants, Warren was known for his anti-gambling initiatives during his tenure as governor of California. He was in many ways the reincarnation of Charles Evans Hughes. Warren shared Hughes's visceral hostility toward bookmakers and his career as a public servant followed a strikingly similar course.)

Six years after the tax stamp was declared unconstitutional, the federal tax imposed on Nevada's bookmakers was reduced to 2 percent. Senator Howard W. Cannon, the leader of Nevada's congressional delegation, spearheaded the campaign to lower the tariff.

On January 1, 1975, when the reduction took effect, there were seven bookie joints open in greater Las Vegas, three of which accepted horse wagers only. The top performer, by most accounts, was Sammy Cohen's Santa Anita, a book that sat on a choice piece of real estate in the center of the Las Vegas Strip. (Cohen's lasting contribution was the "house quiniela." A wager separate from pari-mutuel pools, the payout is figured by multiplying the "win" price by half the "place" price.) Statewide, four times as much was bet on horses than on sports according to information provided to state gaming authorities, but this ratio perverted the truth. Horseplayers exhibited less resistance to paying the tax. Sports bettors' wagered larger sums and the bulk of it went unrecorded.[14]

The reduction in the federal tax led casino operators to take a fresh look at sports and race betting. In a competitive market it made sense to have this amenity, if only to discourage hotel guests from straying off to rival properties. This sentiment wasn't unanimous. Howard Hughes, owner of six Las Vegas casinos and another in Reno, thought it prudent to preserve the status quo. Testifying before the gaming commission, a representative of Hughes's Summa Corporation said that allowing bookmaking inside a posh casino-hotel was bad idea; a potential can of worms that would open Nevada to more intense federal scrutiny.[15]

Had Hughes been there in person, his petition would have likely been granted. As Nevada's largest employer, Hughes had considerable clout. But the famously reclusive millionaire conducted all of his Nevada business dealings through emissaries and it was easier to say "no" to a surrogate. This was one argument that he didn't win. On May 23, 1975, the law was amended to allow bookmaking to once again coexist with other forms of gambling under the same roof. Within a few months, sports and race books were up and running inside Harrah's Club in Reno and the Union Plaza Hotel in downtown Las Vegas.

The Union Plaza, the first of the new Las Vegas books, became identified with its congenial in-house odds consultant, Bob Martin. Born in 1918 in the Brownsville section of Brooklyn, Martin was involved in a bookmaking operation in Washington, D.C., from the early 1950s to the early 1960s and had previously hung his hat at Churchill Downs—not the famous racetrack, but a book on the Las Vegas Strip— where he emerged as the most influential oddsmaker of his generation. As a young handicapper, Martin attracted notice for his facility in handicapping prizefights, but after serving in World War II, pro football became his main focus. His NFL lines were considered the gold standard. When they were chalked on the wagering board on Monday morning, the scene had the trappings of a formal press conference at the White House. When the ritual was finished, correspondents for out-of-state bookies dashed to the nearest pay phone, beginning the process by which Martin's numbers would ripple through the sports betting subculture. Sportswriters increasingly turned to him to get the skinny straight from the horse's mouth. His affiliation with the Union Plaza gave the new book instant cachet.

The next coupling of a bookmaking operation with a Las Vegas resort hotel was more noteworthy. On July 26, 1976, the Stardust—ballyhooed as the largest resort hotel in the world when it opened in 1958— unveiled its new book. Consuming almost nine thousand square feet, the book was far more impressive than the book at the Union Plaza and stood in stark contrast to the austere bookie joints of previous decades. Those places were designed to be functional and they weren't friendly; their clientele was clannish. The Stardust book, in an open area with heavy foot traffic, drew mostly locals but was designed to capture the tourist trade; individuals intent on sampling all of the gambling games as part of their Las Vegas experience.

The book was built to the specifications of Stardust overseer Frank "Lefty" Rosenthal. The model for Ace Rothstein, the character portrayed by Robert De Niro in the movie *Casino*, Rosenthal came by his interest in sports betting naturally; as a young man in his native Chicago he was the glue of the oddsmaking team at the Angel-Kaplan service. A man with a checkered past, Rosenthal had been ruled off race courses in Florida for bookmaking, had been accused of attempting to fix a college basketball game (he pleaded "no contest" and was fined $5,000), and was indicted by a Los Angeles grand jury for illegal interstate gambling, a charge that would be dropped. [16] Other properties, notably Caesars Palace and the Las Vegas Hilton, would open books that were more spacious, more high-tech, and better equipped than the book that Lefty commissioned at the Stardust, but his book would be recognized as the prototype, the book that foreshadowed a new era. And Rosenthal would come to be seen as a visionary; the man who dressed up the common bookie joint in a new suit of clothes, an important first step in taking sports betting out of the closet and into the mainstream.

The second and third books to open inside hotels on the Las Vegas Strip, although far less lavish, also left large footprints. The Hole-in-the-Wall book at the Castaways, which opened in 1977, introduced season-long NFL handicapping contests. The book, which accepted sports wagers only, was run by Julius "Sonny" Reizner, an affable and impish man in his mid-fifties who appeared in TV ads that captured his personality, bringing the vibe of a good neighbor to an industry in need of a facelift. The book at the Barbary Coast, which opened in 1979, became the prime incubator of sports book managers. Many of those that earned their spurs at the Barbary Coast, notably Pittsburgh-area natives Jimmy Vaccaro, Art Manteris, and Chris Andrews, were lured away when other properties came on line. Andrews settled in at the Cal-Neva in Reno and built it into the dominant book in northern Nevada.

Michael "Roxy" Roxborough figured prominently in the development of the corporate era of bookmaking. In 1982, at age thirty-one, Roxborough founded Las Vegas Sports Consultants, a company whose primary mission was the dissemination of odds. His timing was impeccable. Oddsmaker-deluxe Bob Martin was about to leave the scene, his departure hastened by an arrest for interstate bookmaking that led to a thirteen-month stay in a federal prison. The new era demanded an oddsmaker with a wider sphere of expertise, accomplished by assembling a team of oddsmakers, and without the conflicts of interest that made Martin unsuited to be an industry spokesperson, a role for which the articulate Roxborough, a native of Vancouver, British Columbia, was ideally suited.

During most of his tenure—he sold his company in 1999 and retired to Thailand—Roxborough was joined at the hip, in a fashion, with Scott Schettler, the director of the Stardust Race and Sports Book. By virtue of being the first legal book to accept large wagers into virgin betting lines, the Stardust became the most closely watched book in the sports betting cosmos.

A 2 percent tax on the wagering handle was tolerable but it was still a deep bite. More relief was forthcoming when the tax for legal bookmakers in Nevada—but not their illegal counterparts—was reduced to one-fourth of one percent (0.25), effective January 1, 1983. The machinations that led to this modification remain a mystery, but there was little doubt that President Ronald Reagan would rubber-stamp the bill when it got to his desk. Reagan's closest friend in Washington was Nevada's Republican senator Paul Laxalt. Their friendship was born when they were the governors of their respective states. Both were very fond of Lake Tahoe, the meeting-up place for business and pleasure.

This second abatement in the federal tax caused a stampede. By the end of 1984, there were seventeen books in Las Vegas hotel-casinos and five more on the verge of opening. Some were cubbyholes like the Castaways that offered only sports betting. The book at Caesars Palace stood at the opposite end of the spectrum. With twenty-five oversized video screens displaying live sporting events and computer-generated betting information, the Olympiad Race and Sports Book drew comparisons to the mission control room of the NASA Space Center.

The sudden surge was a great boon to the consumer. Hard-core players formed crews to canvas the city for the best odds. Recreational players were courted with various kinds of promotions. A larger and more diverse betting menu and higher odds on parlay cards were conspicuous manifestations of the scrum for increased market share. The hold-percentage in sports declined to where it was razor-thin, but the books made substantially more money because of the increase in volume. In 1974, the statewide handle in Nevada was $8 million and the hold-percentage 7.5. The figures for 1984 were $929 million and 2.3 percent.[17]

The variance in betting lines was bound to flatten out. The first great leveler was a ruling in 1983 that gave license holders the green light to operate more than one book. Two years later, in a related development, the authorities mandated computerized betting terminals. As the start-up costs were high, the books were given until June of 1988 to make the changeover.

The rulings were advantageous to Vic Salerno who gave up a lucrative dental practice in Marina Del Rey, California, to join his father-in-law in running a seedy downtown bookie joint called Leroy's.

The computerized betting systems that were available back then were inadequate for the industry's needs, so Salerno hired a young computer whiz named Javed Buttar and charged him with building a better mousetrap. The result was a product that not only met his needs but could be customized to meet the needs of his competitors and, more importantly, could be configured so that multiple books could interface with a central computer.

The pioneers of the race wire—men like John Payne and Mont Tennes—priced their product beyond the means of some of the poolrooms they serviced and wound up taking an ownership stake in lieu of their standard fee. Salerno followed a similar path and his little Leroy's book became the hub of a betting chain. By 1992, one-third of all the books in Nevada, including four in Las Vegas Strip hotels, were controlled by Leroy's parent company American Wagering, Inc. As Salerno booked conservatively and stayed with the basics, eschewing exotic propositions and other frills, the creeping homogenization caused considerable grumbling.[18]

Another important technological advance was *simulcasting*, which was introduced in Nevada in 1983. A term that first appeared during the early days of television, referencing a program aired simultaneously on radio and on the new medium, simulcasting in horse racing denotes a satellite video feed executed for the purpose of wagering at a site other than where the races are held. Simulcasting simulates the racetrack experience. Patrons at a race book receive the same picture seen on the monitors at the track. For racetrack operators, the beauty of it was that viewership could be restricted to parlors in faraway places so as not to hurt on-track attendance. The fee charged for originating the closed-circuit telecast was newfound money.

Nevada's casino operators were excited about the prospects of simulcasting, which was expected to pump new life into aging properties. Warren Nelson, the owner of Reno's Cal-Neva Club, anticipated that betting the races would eventually overtake dollar slot machines in popularity.[19]

In 1984, the first full year of simulcasting in Nevada, the horse racing handle jumped 22 percent. However, sports betting jumped 44 percent.[20] As a betting attraction, racing was moving ahead while falling further behind.

22

SIMULCASTING

Racetrack operators, particularly those at smaller tracks, looked upon simulcasting as a lifeline. Their rush to embrace it was a tacit admission that it was time to let go of the notion that the solution to horse racing's ills lay in finding the right recipe to rekindle the allure of a day at the races. Simulcasting initiatives attested that horse racing was less a sport than an enticement to gamble. The pioneers—Belmont, Jerome, Travers, et al.—knew that horse racing would wither and die without gambling, but were reluctant to acknowledge it.

The seeds of simulcasting were sown when New York's OTB parlors began taking bets on the Kentucky Derby. Those that staged the event—the horsemen and racing association—received nothing and were none too happy about it.

The upshot was the Interstate Horseracing Act. Signed into law in the fall of 1978, the law legalized interstate simulcast wagering provided that four entities granted their consent: (1) the association representing the horsemen at the originating track, (2) the management of the originating track, and (3,4) the state racing commissions at both ends of the continuum, sender and receiver. Negotiations invariably bogged down on the fairest way to divvy the spoils. The Kentucky Derby wasn't piped into simulcast venues until 1984. Horsemen at Churchill Downs were the stumbling block.

The federal bill, which progressed into law very quietly, disentangled interstate horse betting from the web of the Wire Act. Around the country, promoters rushed to knock down whatever hurdles remained at the state level. Simulcasting encouraged the development of complexes where a horseplayer could relax in comfort, enjoy a nice meal, and have a few cocktails, if he or she so desired, a far cry from New York's austere OTB parlors where hospitality was objectified as an efficient transaction. Connecticut took the lead.

Connecticut approved pari-mutuel betting and off-track betting in 1971. The first OTB parlors, eleven in all, opened simultaneously on April 29, 1976. They were then restricted to carrying races from New York tracks. The shops were owned by the state, but leased to AmTote (the American Totalizator Company). In 1979, barely a year after the Interstate Horseracing Act was signed into law, America's first racing theatre, called Teletrack, opened in the harbor district of New Haven, seventy-five miles from New York City. In the theatre, a twenty-three-hundred-seat auditorium, races were simulcast on a movie theatre–sized screen and on smaller monitors disbursed throughout the building. AmTote envisioned that the concept—an indoor racetrack with everything but live horses—would eventually sweep the country. The potential for sports betting animated the developers. "The probability of sports betting being legalized in the next five years is excellent," said Frank J. Hickey, the chairman of AmTote's parent company.[1]

There were copycats, albeit built on a smaller scale, but inter-track wagering became the focal point of off-track betting. With inter-track wagering (ITW), a racing plant could stay open during periods when it would normally be closed. Between meets, the track would import racing from other tracks via a closed-loop video feed. The importing and exporting of races opened two previously untapped income streams.

Interstate simulcasting caught on big in the 1990s, propelled by a technological breakthrough that allowed for the commingling of pari-mutuel pools. Initially, each individual satellite track and OTB confederation had a separate pool. For example, when Swale won the Kentucky Derby in 1984, he paid $8.80 to win at Churchill Downs. At other venues, the payout ranged from $8.00 to $12.20. By then, nearly three-quarters of the money wagered legally on the Kentucky Derby was placed off-track.[2]

The commingling of wagers tended to level out the betting and was especially advantageous to big players at smaller tracks where a single bet could seriously disturb the odds. In Nevada, simulcasting made the work of a race book supervisor more mundane by scrubbing away the risk-management aspect. The books previously paid track odds, subject to certain limitations. The operators managed their jeopardy by curtailing suspiciously large bets and by turning away or restricting wagers on overplayed horses. As one didn't wish to alienate regular customers, this required a delicate balance. When the bets were integrated with those at the track, this was no longer necessary. All bets were "go"—the bigger the better.

When simulcasting first took flight, the emphasis was on expanding the reach of horse racing's premier events. This flowered into full-card simulcasting where patrons could wager on the entire card at one or more tracks. Many racetracks now stayed open year round, showing races from other tracks during periods when they would otherwise be dark. In the next phase, racing plants began running simulcasts concurrently with live racing. Because there were political and legal issues, the progression wasn't seamless and the timeline varied by state.

Full-card simulcasting breathed new life into doddering racetracks and spurred the resurrection of others. Suffolk Downs reopened in 1992 after sitting fallow for two years. Within a few short years, the Boston track had more than two dozen simulcast partners, including a handful of greyhound tracks. On a particularly busy day, patrons at Suffolk Downs could wager on several hundred events. For some workers, a twelve-hour shift became standard.

At tracks where the quality of racing wasn't quite major league, simulcasting became the main draw. Serious players were partial to races with good horses on the theory that these were less susceptible to random factors and thus easier to handicap. The situation echoed that of the outlaw tracks of the late nineteenth century with their large foreign books.

As Andrew Beyer noted, the physical layout of racetracks was incompatible with the new dynamic. On live racing days, one would typically find large swaths of empty seats in the grandstand whereas the simulcast areas would be packed. In close quarters, loutish customers were a greater nuisance. Upgrading and expanding simulcasting areas became a high priority, funneling money away from other infrastructure needs.[3]

As live racing became less important in the overall scheme of things, meets were shortened. In some cases, simulcast licenses were conditional on live racing and mini-meets were contrived to satisfy this requirement. The annual meet at Horsemen's Park in Omaha, typically a three-day affair, bubbled into a festive occasion but the original purpose was simply to fulfill the state requirement for operating a simulcast theatre. Fifty miles away in Lincoln, the 2013 live racing season began and ended with a single race on a straight track on the second Tuesday of January.

Off-track betting quickly superseded on-track betting in pari-mutuel receipts, but simulcast theatres rarely measured up to their expectations. The first OTB parlor in Illinois, called Winner's Circle, opened in Peoria in 1987. The five-hundred-seat facility, owned by a consortium of Illinois racetracks, broke quickly from the blocks, but business fell off sharply with the opening of a nearby riverboat casino. The place closed in 1995, reopened five years later under a different name, and then shut down again in 2009.[4]

A somewhat similar scenario played out in Connecticut. The state eventually privatized its floundering OTB system. Teletrack, hailed as the prototype of a new era, proved to be a white elephant. The building sat empty for two and a half years before reopening in early 1995. Now called Winners Sports Haven, the facility is owned by Sportstech, which purchased Connecticut's OTB system lock, stock, and barrel in 2010. A British company whose core business is soccer pools betting, Sportstech acquired the operation under the assumption that legal sports betting wasn't far down the road. The thirst for it intensified with the planned opening of a mega-casino in Springfield, Massachusetts, roughly ten miles from the Connecticut border.

The commingling of wagers on horse races accelerated the trend toward multitiered bets with big jackpots. This mirrored the narrative in state lotteries

23

LOTTERIES, CASINOS, AND RACINOS

LOTTERIES

When New Hampshire introduced the Granite State Sweepstakes in 1964—America's first state-sanctioned lottery in sixty-nine years—the horse racing industry was unconcerned. Rockingham Park, then a thoroughbred track, and Hinsdale Raceway, a lower-level harness track, stood to benefit, as they were authorized to sell lottery tickets, the only exceptions to the stipulation that restricted sales to state-run liquor stores. The lottery, based loosely on the Irish Sweepstake, was wrapped around horse racing and the first semiannual drawings, conducted with great fanfare, were held at Rockingham Park.

The vote to establish the lottery was a resounding defeat for the Puritan ethic. The measure was approved in 237 of 248 voting precincts. This was inconsistent with the stereotype of New Hampshire as a stronghold of old-fashioned Yankee Protestant piety, but this image was out of date. The Catholic faith now claimed two out of every five residents and while the state was still home to the *Old Farmer's Almanac*, 15 percent of the population worked in manufacturing, the second-highest ratio behind Connecticut.[1]

New Hampshire had no state sales tax or state income tax. A good chunk of the state's revenue came from taxes on cigarettes and liquor, commodities priced cheaper than in neighboring states, translating into heavy sales to out-of-state residents. Most of the revenue from the lottery was likewise expected to come from out-of-state, a big selling point for lottery boosters. Rockingham Park in the town of Salem, part of the greater Boston metropolitan area, was New Hampshire's top tourist attraction. The Hinsdale harness track was situated in the south-west tip of the state where New Hampshire abuts Massachusetts and Vermont.

The reopening of Rockingham Park in 1933 had a domino effect, hastening the arrival of pari-mutuel betting in Massachusetts and other nearby states. The lottery had the same effect. Indeed, the history of legal gambling in the United States can be seen as a history of border wars. Gambling establishments and lotteries suck money from neighboring states, inducing those states to launch their own games to stanch the cash drain. In 1971, the Massachusetts legislature, overriding the governor's veto, established a lottery that put the Bay State on equal footing with New Hampshire, New York (1967), and New Jersey (1970). By the end of 1974, nine more dominos had fallen. By 1986, the number of states with lotteries had swelled to twenty-two and eventually that number would double. (The holdouts, as of 2015: Alabama, Alaska, Hawaii, Mississippi, Nevada, and Utah.)

Similar to OTB in New York, the lotteries were swamped with bets during their infancy. However, the operators discovered that new games were needed to sustain the attraction. In Delaware in 1976, the refreshment yielded "Football Bonus" and "Touchdown," offerings with weekly cash prizes linked to the outcome of NFL games.

The Delaware Sports Betting Debacle

"Football Bonus" was comprised of two separate pools, one for each conference. In a normal week, each pool consisted of seven games. There were no point spreads; one merely picked the winners. The pay-outs could not be determined in advance because these were pari-mutuel pools. If the games ran according to form, there would be many winners and correspondingly lower payouts. The maximum bet was $20, but there was no restriction on the number of contest cards that one could purchase. The cards, delivered on Wednesdays, were sold at an odd assortment of business establishments, e.g., newsstands, delicatessens, hardware stores, pharmacies, and barber shops. The dealers received a 5 percent commission.

"Touchdown," the other NFL-linked lottery game, required players to select three, four, or five teams and then refine the selections by placing them within the parameters of three point-spread ranges: "0" to "7," "8" to "14," or "15" and over. Incorporating margins of victory into the framework made for a more cerebral game, but the rules were confusing and the response was poor. For some odd reason, the maximum bet per card was $10, half the maximum for "Football Bonus."

Delaware scrapped the ill-conceived "Touchdown" late in the season, substituting a new parlay card listing twelve games, each with a point spread, using a half-point line to eliminate ties. Players selected four or more teams. The payouts were fixed, graduating up from 10/1 for a four-teamer. A perfect card, 12 for 12, paid 1,200/1. Payouts in the higher ranges were considerably higher than what the illegals offered, but the men that formulated the game were confident that when all the cards were graded the "hold" would approach 55 percent, the take riveted to Delaware's established lottery offerings.

The lines for the games were supplied by a firm founded by Princeton University mathematicians, a developer of instant lottery games. Their line-making methodology was proprietary, but from all appearances the data they weaved into the tapestry was entirely statistical, omitting such factors as injuries, public perception, and incentive to win, the latter a variable that comes to the fore late in a season when some teams are jockeying for post-season eligibility or for a more advantageous slot in the playoffs. Inevitably, there were deviations between the Delaware Sports Lottery lines and those found in Nevada. The mathematicians entrusted with making the lines were exposed as a bunch of amateurs.

On the final week of the NFL regular season there were two extreme discrepancies. In Las Vegas, the Saints and Falcons were favored by three points. On the Delaware contest cards, they were six-and-a-half-point *underdogs*! These discrepancies became a hot topic of conversation with the result that the contest drew hordes of first-time players, attracting three times as much action as the previous week. The Saints and Falcons were wildly over-bet.

On the Friday before the games, Peter Simmons, the lottery director, stopped the contest and declared all bets void. Formerly a building materials salesman for a gypsum company, Simmons defended the action on the grounds that illegal gambling elements were lousing up his game to restore their monopoly. "What happened here," said Simmons, "was that the bookies were advising people to get in on the action and rip off the state." The decision was overturned by the Delaware attorney general, who ruled that the state was obligated to pay off all winning bets, but by then the pundits had had a field day barbing Delaware with the saw of a welsher.[2]

The gods of fate were kind to the Delaware Lottery Commission. A big loss was averted when the New Orleans Saints, the most popular selection, failed to cover the contest line. The card produced a $28,599 profit. Over the course of the fourteen-week season, the sports lottery game in its various manifestations handled $722,000 in wagers, less than what was needed to cover operating expenses and a far cry from the initial projection of $6 million.[3]

The NFL attempted to stop the sports lottery before it got started and kept up the fight after failing to obtain a restraining order. In November, with the season winding down, the NFL brought heavy guns into a Wilmington, Delaware, courtroom for a hearing expected to last seven days. Baseball commissioner Bowie Kuhn and Congressman Jack Kemp (R-NY), a former pro quarterback, conjured up the age-old argument that legal betting would destroy the integrity of sports. The general manager of the Philadelphia Eagles said that he feared for the safety of the players if legal gambling became widespread. In many games, one player stands out as the goat. This individual, he believed, would be tracked down and punished by irate gamblers. League attorneys argued that the games violated NFL trademark and property rights.[4]

The league failed to win the permanent injunction it sought, but it became a moot point when the sports lottery wasn't renewed.

Multistate Lotteries

Second-generation lottery games tended to be geared to faster returns. The scratch-off ticket debuted in Massachusetts in 1974. The next year, New Jersey introduced a "pick your own digits" daily lottery game that replicated the numbers game associated with inner-city neighborhoods. Bets could be made in multiples of fifty cents up to $5. The game proved to be extremely popular. It spread quickly and variations of it would soon account for a large share of lottery revenues in states with high urban concentrations.

A third phase began in 1985 when Maine, New Hampshire, and Vermont established the first multi-jurisdictional lottery game. Two years later, six states—Iowa, Kansas, Missouri, Oregon, Rhode Island, and West Virginia—and Washington, D.C. joined forces in a multi-jurisdictional alliance. Initially called Lotto America, it was renamed Powerball in 1992. Four years later, a third multi-jurisdictional game was started in Georgia. Called The Big Game, it would be renamed Mega Millions. Virtually all of the lottery states would eventually offer both games. Each had a bi-weekly drawing.

California was late to the party. The Golden State adopted Mega Millions in 2005 and Powerball in 2013. By then, betting into lotteries with mega-jackpots swollen by enormous carryover pools had become something of a national obsession. In May of 2013, when the annuity value of the next Powerball drawing swelled to almost $600 million, the wait in line at California's biggest ticket seller reached nine hours. This property was a convenience store that sat on the California side of the Nevada-California line off Interstate 15, the main artery to Las Vegas.

The advertised value of a Powerball mega-jackpot assumes that there will be only one winner and that he or she will choose to collect the prize in annual installments. Taking all of the money in one lump sum reduces a $600 million jackpot to about $375 million. Federal and state taxes will eat away another 40 percent or so, leaving the lucky winner with roughly $225 million, a life-changing amount of money, but a chop of such severity from the advertised payout as to cause the lottery to be disparaged as a tax-gathering machine designed especially for people who are bad at math. This snarky put-down is consistent with a 1999 study that found that lottery participation varied inversely with educational attainment. High school dropouts spent an average of $334 a year compared to $86 by college graduates.[5]

CASINOS

In 1976, Nevada's monopoly was broken when voters in New Jersey approved full-blown casino gambling for Atlantic City. Two years earlier, the electorate had roundly defeated a broader bill that would have

amended the State Constitution to allow casino gambling in any munici-
pality that voted for it. The narrower version, specific to Atlantic City,
passed with flying colors. The bill imposed an 8 percent tax on the gross
win with receipts to be channeled to programs for senior citizens and
the disabled.

Known for the Miss America pageant and saltwater taffy and for
inspiring the board game Monopoly, Atlantic City with its Steel Pier
and miles of boardwalk had suffered a steep decline, both as a vacation
destination and as a residential community. Dilapidated buildings lit-
tered the landscape and roughly half the working age population was
jobless for at least part of the year. Conditions were so bad that a
coalition of priests, nuns, and rabbis advocated in favor of casino gambling, renouncing the position set forth by the New Jersey Council of
Churches. Arresting unemployment and urban decay, they argued,
trumped whatever evils flowed from casino gambling.[6]

Atlantic City's casino era began on Memorial Day weekend, 1978,
with the opening of the Resorts International Hotel, a property named
for the parent company, a Miami-based firm with casino holdings in the
Bahamas. The law required a casino to have a minimum of four hundred hotel rooms, a restriction that slowed the pace of development,
but within a decade there were a dozen Las Vegas-style casinos up and
running sixteen hours a day and eventually 24/7. Atlantic City surpassed
Las Vegas in gross casino revenues in 1985, a position it would hold for
the next thirteen years.

When gambling came to Atlantic City, there were four pari-mutuel
tracks in New Jersey: Atlantic City Race Course; Monmouth Park;
Freehold Raceway, a historic harness track; and the new kid on the
block, the Meadowlands. A fifth track, Garden State Park, situated in
the Philadelphia suburb of Cherry Hill, lay fallow, the victim of a devastating fire. The park reopened in 1985, a rebirth inspired by flamboyant
penny stock promoter Robert E. Brennan, and it would briefly rank
among the most prominent tracks in the country, but it closed for good
in 2001, the same year that Brennan was sentenced to nine years and
two months in prison for money laundering and bankruptcy fraud.

Brennan spent lavishly to make Garden State a first-rate facility, but
he entered an oversaturated market. There were twenty-seven tracks
within a two-hundred-mile radius, many of which were then hanging on
by a thread. He looked upon Atlantic City as a potential ally, a natural

cohort for cross-marketing promotions, but the synergy that he apperceived was a mirage. A study directed by University of Louisville equine economics professor Richard Thalheimer concluded that during the first ten years Atlantic City casinos were responsible for a 33.9 percent drop in betting at Garden State racetracks, roughly twice the drop-off caused by the lottery.[7]

The strain on racing intensified when Atlantic City casinos were allowed to open race books. Simulcasting was introduced at the Showboat in 1993 and spread to six other properties. The casinos that adopted it were compelled to establish a fund that provided subsidies to the racetracks. This was a trade-off. In return, track operators agreed to stop lobbying the legislature for video slot machines.

In the summer of 2001, New Jersey approved an expansion of off-track betting that allowed up to fourteen freestanding betting parlors. These were parceled out to the racing associations, the bulk going to the New Jersey Sports and Exposition Authority which now ran Monmouth Park as well as the Meadowlands. After a lengthy squabble over the apportionment of the pari-mutuel receipts, an OTB parlor opened in the South Jersey community of Vineland. With high-definition televisions, a fully equipped kitchen, and a party room, New Jersey's first off-track betting parlor had the feel of an upscale sports bar. The integration of pari-mutuel betting into a sports bar environment was deemed essential to cultivating a new generation of horseplayers.

South Dakota became the third state to harbor a casino district in 1989 when poker, blackjack, and slot machines were allowed in virtually every commercial building in the historic Wild West town of Deadwood. The concept diffused to neighboring Colorado. In 1991, casino gambling arrived in Central City, Blackhawk, and Cripple Creek, rough-and-tumble mining towns in their evanescent heydays. These places, where bet limits were initially $5, were too remote to become major gambling centers, serving primarily as symbols of a shift in the national mood. Two years after legal gambling penetrated Colorado, the state's leading thoroughbred track, Pikes Peak Meadows, a facility with a checkered history, shut down for good.

During the 1990s, three major casino districts emerged in Mississippi. The largest cluster was centered in Biloxi, a seaside community with a rich gambling tradition, and the others in the Natchez/Vicksburg area and upstate in impoverished Tunica, a town roughly thirty miles from

Memphis. The impetus was the Mississippi Gaming Control Act of 1990 which authorized waterway gambling on a local option basis in counties along the Mississippi River and the Gulf of Mexico. It was modeled on legislation formulated in Iowa, but with one major exception—the boats were not required to leave the dock.

All told, gambling boats appeared in six states between 1990 and 1993—Iowa, Mississippi, Illinois, Missouri, Indiana, and Louisiana—but Mississippi was the only state to launch waterway gambling with no limits on dockside operations. The advantages were two-fold. It reduced costs by obviating the need to hire a pilot and other maritime workers who by law had to be Coast Guard approved. And it translated into faster turnover as patrons could come and go as they pleased rather than being forced to set aside a block of time for a cruise.

In February of 1992, four months prior to the opening of the first legal casino in Mississippi, the first Native American casino, called Foxwoods, opened in Connecticut on the Mashantucket Pequot reservation near the town of Norwich, roughly halfway between New York City and Boston. The drumbeats of this dawning—a development with huge ramifications—were U.S. Supreme Court rulings affirming that Indian reservations were sovereign nations, and the child born from these rulings, the Indian Gaming Regulatory Act of 1988, which authorized full-fledged casinos on reservation lands in states where some form of gambling was already permitted. The law required a tribe to establish a compact with the state in which it was located and allowed outside companies to come in and manage casino operations.

Originally a high-stakes bingo hall, Foxwoods was transformed into the largest and most profitable casino in the world with financing from Chinese Malaysian billionaire Tan Sri Lim Goh. A formidable competitor, the Mohegan Sun casino, opened ten miles down the road in 1996 and eventually became the larger complex as measured by square feet of casino space. By the end of the century, the average number of daily visitors at both properties combined was about seventy thousand.

By 2011, 236 Native American tribes operated 422 gambling facilities in twenty-eight states.[8] The largest concentrations were found in Oklahoma, California, Minnesota, Washington, and Wisconsin. Some of the facilities were little more than trailers on patches of dirt along two-lane highways, but others were full-blown casinos in heavily populated areas. Riverboat and dockside casinos, now numbering more than a hundred, amplified the congestion. Looking across the Ohio River to the dockside casinos then sprouting on the Indiana side, a Kentucky racetrack executive likened the scene to an invading armada.[9]

RACINOS

In some states, casino games were welded to racetracks. Mountaineer Park in Chester, West Virginia, was the first out of the gate. In 1990, track operators received approval from the State Lottery Commission for 165 video lottery terminals. These weren't traditional reel-spinning slot machines with their iconic symbols, but computerized versions of scratch-off instant lottery games. The revenue they produced kept the operation afloat, no mean feat, as the track, originally known as Waterford Park, never had anything approaching a golden era and was situated in a band of the Rust Belt hit particularly hard by the downfall of the U.S. steelmaking industry. Four years after their introduction, the track's operators were permitted to install as many video lottery terminals as they wanted. The number grew to three thousand five hundred. West Virginia's other thoroughbred track, Charles Town, introduced video lottery terminals in 1996 and by the end of the century there were *racinos* in five other states—Rhode Island, Louisiana, Delaware, Iowa, and New Mexico—and in four Canadian provinces. Most offered a variety of gambling machines that mirrored those found at large stand-alone casinos.

Proponents of racinos had an easier row to hoe than proponents of more intrusive alternatives. Neighborhood opposition—"not in my backyard"—was tempered by the fact that racing plants, especially the newer facilities, tended to be situated outside residential areas. With their massive, underutilized parking lots, they had plenty of room to expand without extending their boundaries. A synthetic embodiment of America's growing acceptance of gambling, the riverboat that never leaves the dock was likewise the product of a felt need to harness the economic benefits of gambling without allowing it to fan out into residential communities.

To a far greater extent than simulcasting, casino games uplifted ailing racetracks. Mountaineer Park added racing dates, contravening the national trend, and their premier event, the West Virginia Derby, became a major stakes race. These enhancements were mirrored at Charles Town. The surge was under way before both properties were transfigured into resorts with lodging, concert halls, and a full-blown casino with table games.

An even more stunning turnaround occurred in Iowa. Prairie Meadows in the Des Moines suburb of Altoona opened in 1989, ironically the same year that Universal Pictures released *Field of Dreams*, a heart-warming baseball ghost story with an Iowa cornfield backdrop. The richly celebrated movie popularized the phrase "if you build it, they will come" and the racetrack, built on farmland, made a mockery of it. Prairie Meadows was a money pit from the get-go, entered bankruptcy in 1991, and suspended live racing the following year. Slot machines saved the track from the wrecking ball. Two years after their introduction, the county-owned facility was debt-free. The property was on firm financial footing when the racino was permitted to add table games in 2004, initiating a third round of expansion.

In 2002, a study funded by the Pew Center found that forty-three states were facing modest to substantial budget deficits. Within a few years, deficits in some of those states grew to catastrophic proportions. In this climate, the rush to exploit America's gambling bug came to resemble an arms race, and racinos began to penetrate heavily populated areas. In 2010, after a successful six-year trial with slot machines, Pennsylvania authorized table games. Within two years, the Keystone State, with twelve casinos, six at racetracks, leapfrogged New Jersey in gambling receipts, trailing only Nevada. The top earner, Parx Casino and Racing at Philadelphia Park (motto: "Get Lucky in No Time"), was located in a heavily trafficked area. In an earlier time, before the deluge, the place had a less cumbersome name: Keystone Park.

Legal slot machines diffused into metropolitan New York in October of 2006 with the opening of the Empire State Casino at Yonkers Raceway, and five years later, after innumerable delays, the first legal casino inside the boundaries of New York City opened at Aqueduct. Drawing as many as two hundred thousand visitors a week, the facility bubbled quickly into the top grossing emporium of its kind. The great irony was that Aqueduct sat barely ten miles from La Guardia Airport, named for the man whose essence was captured in a newsreel clip of him fiendishly attacking a mound of confiscated slot machines with a sledgehammer.

The Aqueduct operation was a public-private partnership, a common racino model. The diverse parade of electronic table games and video lottery terminals was linked to a centralized bank of computers controlled by the State Gaming Commission. The property was run by a subsidiary of the Genting Group, the multinational company founded in Malaysia by Foxwoods sugar daddy Tan Sri Lin Goh.

In the beginning, proponents of racinos placed heavy emphasis on the revitalization of horse racing, an industry cast as a vital segment of America's agricultural economy, the backbone of the nation. The bill that enabled racinos in Delaware was called the Horse Racing Preservation Act. The equivalent bill in Pennsylvania, signed into law at Philadelphia Park, was titled the Race Horse Development and Gaming Act. However, the rebranding of some racinos bore witness that live racing wasn't viewed as a useful accessory but as a burden to be tolerated. Bass Park, a venerable harness racing facility in Bangor, Maine, morphed into Hollywood Casino Hotel and Raceway Bangor. A sister property, the Charles Town track in West Virginia, was rebranded Hollywood Casino at Charles Town Races.

Racinos were a great boon to horsemen in the jurisdictions where racinos were found, but nationally the industry continued to lose ground. Between 2006 and 2010, purse money distributed to horsemen declined by $90 million despite spectacular gains in a few places, notably Pennsylvania.[10] Folks drawn to electronic gambling devices didn't mutate into dedicated horseplayers. There was virtually no crossover. The racino model failed to generate new fans and as this became apparent, there were grumbles that the horse racing subsidy drained away money that could be put to a better purpose.

24

OFFSHORE AND ONLINE

The last decade of the twentieth century witnessed the flowering of e-commerce, an upshot of the technological revolution that changed the world. Between 1996 and 2000, the number of worldwide Internet users grew tenfold, expanding to more than four hundred million, and the surge was just getting started. The personal computer, a novelty at the start of the decade, came to be embraced as an indispensable household tool.

In the lexicon of North American gamblers, the words "offshore" and "online" came to be used interchangeably, obscuring the fact that "offshore" came first. In 1988, Ron Sacco, a bookie with a long rap sheet in California, established a call center at a capacious villa in a gated community in Santo Domingo in the Dominican Republic, a move animated by technological developments that lowered the cost and expanded the scope of toll-free telephone service. (By some strange alchemy the Dominican Republic, despite grinding poverty, boasted one of the most sophisticated telecommunication systems in Latin America.) A few other bookmakers followed Sacco's example, moving the nucleus of their operations outside the United States. They had a leg up when the Internet arrived.

In 1995, there were reportedly three "bookie joints" with platforms on the World Wide Web. Two years later, the number was one hundred seventy. Most were housed in the Caribbean. During the second wave of off-shore development, San Jose, Costa Rica, emerged as the epicenter of the online sports betting universe.[1]

Although the cost of maintaining long-distance telephone lines became more affordable, the cost was still too high to allow for an influx of small-fry bettors, a valued component of the ecosystem. But when it became possible to transmit a wager with the click of a mouse, this was no longer an issue; the number of bettors that one could accommodate was virtually unlimited. On January 11, 1998, during the half-hour interim between the NFL conference championship games, a pioneering online book, Intertops, was reportedly processing two hundred fifty bets per second. Barring pernicious legislation, said Steven Crist, "the genie of global sports gambling is out of the bottle for good."[2]

Pernicious legislation was already in the works. The man at the forefront was Jon Kyl (R-Ariz) who was then in his first term in the Senate after serving his constituents for eight years in the lower house. A second-generation lawmaker who spent his formative years in a small farming town in Nebraska, Kyl could see that the Wire Act, now roughly four decades old, was fraught with loopholes born from advances in telecommunications. Stumping for his fixer-upper, named the Internet Gambling Prohibition Act, Kyl said "gambling erodes the values of hard work, sacrifice, and personal responsibility; [the Internet] brings this threat right into the living room, allows the kids to get hold of the family credit card and gamble away the mortgage."[3]

In the first version of his bill, introduced in 1997, Internet gambling operators were subject to a fine of $20,000 and two years in prison and the person making the bet could be fined up to $2,500 and confined to prison for a period of not more than six months. However, the bill as written threatened to cripple the horse racing industry, kept afloat by off-site wagering and, as detractors noted, might even be contorted to criminalize individuals competing for prizes in fantasy sports leagues. Subsequent modifications narrowed the focus, penalizing only Internet gambling providers, thus eliminating the Orwellian specter of a man being hauled off to jail for making a bet via his personal computer in the privacy of his home. However, it took nine years before Kyl finally had a bill that cleared every hurdle. By then, the horse racing industry was in the clear, protected by the 2000 amendment to the Interstate Horseracing Act. The amendment, tucked inside a mammoth appropriations bill, tidied up some hazy language to clarify the legality of wagering over the Internet provided that all of the extant preconditions were satisfied.

The original Wire Act may have been musty, but it was still cogent; so said the federal grand jury weighing the evidence in the case against Jay Cohen. In 2000, after a ten-day trial, Cohen was found guilty of violating the Wire Act for accepting bets over the Internet. The presiding judge sentenced him to twenty-one months in prison. A federal appeals court upheld the verdict.

A nuclear engineering major in his college days at Cal-Berkeley, Cohen and two coworkers, Steve Schillinger and Hayden Ware, left their jobs at the Pacific Stock Exchange in San Francisco to open an online book. They set up shop in Antigua. They were drawn to the island, a former British colony, because English was the official language; government officials welcomed businesses that diversified the tourism-centric economy; a recently established free-trade zone meant they could operate without paying corporate taxes; and, most important, Antigua was connected to the United States with an undersea fiber-optic cable that assured a good Internet connection, one of only two Caribbean nations that then satisfied this need.

They named their book World Sports Exchange. Launched in November of 1996, WSEX was one of the first books in cyberspace. The book was ahead of the curve in offering in-game wagers on sports popular in the United States, a variation on day trading.

Cohen and his partners and seventeen other offshore operators were named in an FBI complaint that charged them with conspiracy to violate the Wire Act. Cohen elected to contest the charges, whereas the others arranged plea deals or chose to ignore the charges, effectively renouncing their U.S. citizenship.

Cohen, the face of WSEX, had never shied from talking with reporters; the more he talked, the more confident he became that his business, by virtue of being licensed and regulated in a foreign country, was outside the grasp of the United States government. The jury disagreed, basically saying that a wager is a legal transaction only if it is legal at both ends of the transmission. (In a touch of irony, Cohen served his sentence at a federal detention camp on the outskirts of Las Vegas. WSEX went belly-up in 2013 several weeks before the death of cofounder Steve Schillinger, a presumptive suicide.)[4]

Despite the Cohen verdict, the stampede continued. Less than three years after his indictment, the number of companies taking bets on the Web had mushroomed to an estimated fourteen hundred. The deluge brought ancillary sites that functioned as communities where gamblers with offshore accounts and those working in the industry could share ideas and information. The forums at all of these websites served as consumer watchdogs—some were established specifically for this purpose—pointing players toward books that were solid and warning them away from those that were shaky.

For an online bookmaker circa 2000, inclusion on the Don Best screen was the best way to stand out from the herd. The screen displayed the odds at a select number of books and kept lurkers abreast of other pertinent information such as injuries and weather conditions. Buying the premium service put a betting man in league with the heavy hitters; line moves were updated instantly. With this tool, professional gamblers shopped with greater efficiency and bookmakers kept their finger on the pulse of the market, making it less likely they would be blindsided by a sharpshooter exploiting a rogue number.

The Don Best prototype was developed by Donald Bissette, hence the name. Bissette was part of a small colony of individuals who prowled the sports books of Las Vegas in search of favorable betting lines. He died before e-commerce took flight and likely without ever foreseeing that his contrivance would flower into a product used by people around the world. Las Vegas newcomer Al Corbo acquired the service in 1992. Working with his son Dana Corbo, he improved the product with new features made possible by more sophisticated software programs. The elder Corbo, a Philadelphia native, had prior bookmaking convictions and alleged mob connections, leading to his placement in the Black Book, a listing of individuals banned from Nevada's casinos. His son was a nonpracticing attorney with a law degree from the University of Miami.

The Don Best agency didn't formulate betting lines; they merely disseminated them. That set them apart from the dominant line services of earlier generations, notably Leo Hirschfield's Minneapolis Line, and from the contemporaneous Las Vegas Sports Consultants, which was born to serve the Nevada market and remained largely wed to that client base. A visit to the Don Best screen invariably entailed a gander at CRIS, which seized the distinction of originating the betting line, a key to becoming the first of a handful of offshore books with a volume greater than the *combined total* of all the books in Nevada![5]

The driving force behind CRIS (Costa Rica International Sports) was none other than Ron Sacco. The son of a San Francisco barber, Sacco found his first clients at Bay Area thoroughbred tracks. His name first hit the papers in 1971 when he was one of twenty-three persons arrested by federal authorities in a sweeping crackdown on bookmaking in San Francisco. He was identified as a twenty-eight-year-old bartender. In 1973, in a different case, he and a codefendant were found guilty of offering bribes to a San Mateo County police sergeant in return for advance tips on police raids. Sacco was quoted (or misquoted) as saying that during one six-month period his gross income was $1,340,000.[6]

More arrests would follow. There were three between 1980 and 1987 when Sacco's operation was headquartered in Los Angeles. The third arrest, which bubbled out of a series of raids at six fictitious business establishments, identified Sacco as the ringleader of a ring that used 800-prefix toll-free telephone numbers to accept wagers that amounted to an annual handle of $40 million.[7]

Since betting on sports was legal in the Dominican Republic, Sacco assumed that his employees at the call center in Santo Domingo were outside the clutches of U.S. authorities. He was wrong. On January 8, 1992, a phalanx of FBI agents and Dominican soldiers stormed the villa and arrested everyone there. The following year, a federal indictment unsealed in San Francisco accused Sacco and twenty-five associates of running a multinational bookmaking operation that took bets from "tens of thousands" of bettors across the United States. The main stash of ready money was reportedly kept in the vault of a San Francisco pawnshop in the city's scruffy Mission District.[8]

Costa Rica had long been a haven for expatriates with sketchy backgrounds. When Sacco arrived there, he had already spent a good portion of his adult life in prison. To someone outside his subculture, he was just another reprobate bookie with the ways of an outlaw embedded in his bones. The gruff exterior and omnipresent cigar would have reinforced the perception.

Whatever the perception, Ron Sacco was the most prominent U.S.-bred bookie ever, or at least the most prominent since Frank Erickson. A trailblazer who was quick to embrace new technologies, Sacco was the architect of a multilayered organization girded by neighborhood agents and runners in scattered precincts. For a time, he even had a branch office in Friendship, Ohio, of all places, an unincorporated hamlet near the Kentucky border. In San Jose, Costa Rica, his various enterprises occupied a seven-story building. At the core was CRIS, a book that could fairly boast that it had never barred a player for winning (albeit many players had their limits reduced). Sacco's saga was a dark version of the Horatio Alger story, a twisted rendition of the American dream.[9]

The mad scramble for customers as new books came online was a prod to innovation. With unlimited "shelf space," diversification was no problem. One manifestation was a flood of offbeat bets plumbed from popular culture. As the offshore scene was exploding, progressive elimination reality shows were becoming all the rage on television. Two shows in particular, *Survivor* and *American Idol*, attracted considerable wagering. Nevada's legal bookmakers couldn't tap into this sphere. They were hamstrung by the broadly defined stricture that prohibited them from taking bets on elections.

In England, bookmaking concerns, notably William Hill, had long embraced offbeat propositions as tools for generating free publicity. When Simon Noble, the young British marketing director of Intertops, seized upon *Survivor* as a brand enhancer, he was flabbergasted by the response. The show that stranded a group of strangers in a desolate locale attracted fifteen thousand bets during its debut season in 2000. The limits were low, but the volume of activity elevated the quirky offering into something more than window dressing.[10]

Another book, Bodog, exploited this niche to an even greater extent. Founded in 2000 by flamboyant Canadian entrepreneur Calvin Ayre, Bodog spent lavishly on advertising while virtually cornering the market on newbies: young, recreational players who hadn't previously had any dealings with a bookie. Often held up to ridicule for their unwillingness to accommodate arbitragers, Bodog diversified beyond bookmaking into music distribution and other forms of entertainment. It was the first book to mesh sports betting, casino games, and poker into an online portal that could be accessed with one account.[11]

In the offshore world, bonuses were the focal point of most marketing campaigns. Sign-up bonuses became near-universal. Rollover bonuses for replenishing a dwindling bankroll were also common. Books that didn't take this road were drawn to offer special bets with reduced odds. For bettors with multiple accounts, the offshore scene was the equivalent of happy hour at the neighborhood pub.

For some books, even some that were well-patronized, keeping up with the Joneses was toxic. The offshore terrain was quickly overbuilt and it was inevitable that there would be a falling out. Consolidations prevented massive liquidations. Funds were merely transferred from one book to another. However, a number of books collapsed, leaving account holders high and dry. Defalcations tended to cluster in the days following the Super Bowl when clients were disposed to shrink their balances or close their accounts.

The first high-volume book to go bust was Aces Gold. Headquartered in Curaçao, Aces Gold and its sister property Sports Market went belly-up in February of 2002. One of the pioneer books, Aces Gold had been among the industry leaders in generous bonuses and reduced-juice promotions. At websites where gamblers interacted on community forums, the book's sudden demise unleashed a storm of outrage that lasted for months.

There were telltale signs of impending trouble. Most books tightened up their betting lines in response to shifts reflected on the Don Best screen, a policy called "moving on air." Aces Gold was a maverick. Their prices often deviated from the consensus. In their end days, the deviations became more obvious. One could see that they were gambling, rather than working to achieve a balanced book. This continued into the Super Bowl when they hung a line certain to generate lopsided action. When the game played out the wrong way for them, any hopes of salvaging the business were lost. They could not interest rival companies in a buyout because their customer list was overloaded with savvy players. The principal owner of Aces Gold, identified as a resident of Lubbock, Texas, suffered no legal repercussions. He left the scene before the convulsions of 2006.

On July 16, 2006, David Carruthers, a Scotsman, was taken into custody at Dallas–Fort Worth International Airport while waiting for his connecting flight on a trip from London to Costa Rica. This wasn't a big news item in U.S. papers, but it was a major story in Great Britain. Reporters from three major London dailies traveled to Fort Worth for his bail hearing on July 31. Charged with fraud and racketeering in a twenty-two-count indictment, Carruthers eventually pleaded guilty and drew a thirty-three-month prison sentence.

Carruthers was the CEO of BetonSports. Prior to assuming this post, he had spent twenty-four years climbing the corporate ladder at Ladbrokes, the British betting behemoth. The growing influence of men like him in the world of offshore betting seemed to signify that the industry was moving beyond its shadowy roots, mirroring what had happened in Nevada where "corporate suits" came to rule the roosts at all the major properties, supplanting the streetwise characters that comprised the first generation of casino operators.

Headquartered in Costa Rica with branch offices in Aruba and Antigua, BetonSports was a major player before Carruthers came on board. With him, the firm became more aggressive, acquiring other Internet gambling brands and getting listed on the London Stock Exchange. The company's board of directors included a member of Britain's House of Lords. In public pronouncements, Carruthers touted BetonSports as the nascent Coca-Cola of the global online gambling industry.

Carruthers was one of eleven people named in the indictment. BetonSports founder Gary Kaplan, a Brooklyn native with prior convictions in the United States for cocaine possession, forgery, and bookmaking, was the big cheese. After eight months on the run, Kaplan was arrested by U.S. State Department officials and FBI agents in the Dominican Republic. He subsequently received a 51-month prison sentence and agreed to forfeit $43 million from his stash in foreign bank accounts. In addition, the judge ordered him to undergo substance abuse and mental health counseling and to earn a high school diploma.

The overwhelming majority of BOS clients, more than 90 percent, were U.S. residents. Most of them were required to fund an account before making a wager. Their accounts were frozen during the legal proceedings. When the assets of the company were liquidated, their claims were subordinated to the claims of creditors in the host countries. In July of 2011, five years after Carruthers's arrest, the watchdog site "Sportsbook Review" reported that refunds were trickling back to former clients. Recipients received settlement checks amounting to 4.63 percent of their balances.[12]

Ten weeks after Carruthers's arrest, the online gambling industry was rocked by news that the United States Congress had rewarded Jon Kyl's persistence with an antigambling law that portended big trouble for them. The legislation cleared the final congressional hurdle during the final hour of the final session before Congress adjourned for the upcoming elections. Titled the Unlawful Internet Gambling Enforcement Act, the bill was signed into law by President George W. Bush on October 13, 2006.

Kyl's chief allies were Senate majority leader Bill Frist (R-Tenn), who cooked up the perfect evasion to expedite the bill's passage, and longtime supporters Bob Goodlette (R-Va) and Jim Leach (R-Iowa). The bill they crafted differed from earlier drafts in that it zeroed in on the money movers. Banks, credit card companies, and eWallet services were prohibited from transferring funds between U.S. residents and offshore gambling firms.

The Unlawful Internet Gambling Enforcement Act (UIGEA), a 32-page rider to a 243-page bill, was guerilla legislation. It was noosed to an unrelated Homeland Security bill that tightened security at American seaports, a bill commonly called the Safe Port Act. Few people had time to study UIGEA's provisions, let alone debate them, but no one in the Senate dared advocate detaching the ill-fitting caboose for fear of derailing the Safe Port Act and being seen as soft on Islamic terrorism. Noting that UIGEA was rushed through with typos and vague terminology, Whittier Law School professor I. Nelson Rose, one of the world's leading authorities on gambling and the law, deemed it "a piece of garbage."[13]

Two years elapsed before the regulations were clarified. Financial institutions, required to "identify and block or otherwise prevent or prohibit restricted transactions," were given until December 9, 2009, to show that they were in compliance, a date that would be pushed back six months. But UIGEA had immediate repercussions. Within days of the bill's passage by the Senate, the market value of offshore gaming companies listed on the London Stock Exchange declined by more than $7 billion. The shakeout showed the extent to which betting firms with a global platform were dependent on the U.S. market.[14]

Among the companies that discontinued their U.S. operations, none inspired more handwringing by their leave-taking than did Pinnacle. The company stopped accepting wagers that originated in the United States on January 11, 2007. The stated reason was a tattered relationship with mainstream banks, the upshot of UIGEA.

Founded in 1998 on the island of Curaçao in the Netherlands Antilles, Pinnacle (no relation to casino operator Pinnacle Entertainment) eschewed bonuses for a reduced-juice wagering model that cut prices to the bone. An exhaustive betting menu (Swedish hockey, any-one?) reinforced comparisons with Walmart.

There is a school of thought that no bookmaker can deal with the bread-and-butter sports of football and basketball at odds of less than 11/10 as a routine practice and keep his head above water. Indeed, it has been suggested that with bettors becoming craftier and more well-informed each year, there will come a time when 11/10 will no longer cut the mustard, forcing bookmakers to nick up the odds to stay solvent. Pinnacle flouted this aphorism while taking on all comers and yet man-aged to develop an impeccable reputation for honest dealings and good customer service. Andrew Beyer, a fan of Pinnacle's head-to-head matchups in horse racing, noted in his *Washington Post* column that some people of his acquaintance, upon hearing the news that Pinnacle was vacating the U.S. market, reacted as if there had been a death in the family. Beyer's column ran under the headline "After Pinnacle, It's All Downhill from Here."[15]

Four days after Pinnacle's disclosure, there was more upheaval when U.S. officials arrested Canadian businessmen Stephen Lawrence and John Lefebvre. Lawrence, arrested in the U.S. Virgin Islands, and Le-febvre, arrested at his winter home in Malibu, California, were the founders of NETeller. Headquartered on the Isle of Man, NETeller was the world's leading processor of online gambling transactions with 75 percent of its revenue reportedly generated in the United States. Within days of the arrests, the company pulled out of the U.S. market. Lawrence and Lefebvre avoided prison by agreeing to forfeit $100 mil-lion plus two Malibu beach homes. During the negotiations, U.S. gam-blers with money in the NETeller pipeline had their funds frozen for six-and-a-half months.[16]

These actions hardly dried up Internet gambling. Resourceful bet-tors circumvented the embargo by bouncing transactions off computer servers in foreign countries. New third-party payers emerged to fill the void left by NETeller and subterfuges were concocted to disguise gam-bling transactions. A 2010 survey found 516 sports betting sites in Cy-berspace, a dwindling number of which continued to tempt fate by taking wagers from U.S. bettors.[17] By all accounts, many were being run on a shoestring.

Betfair, the world's leading destination for online horseplayers, was relatively unaffected by all this turmoil. The company never accepted U.S.-issued credit cards and proactively halted U.S. bank wire transfers.

Launched in London in 2000, Betfair embodied the vision of Andrew Black. The grandson of Sir Cyril Wilson Black, a staunch Baptist who campaigned against gambling during a lengthy career as a member of Parliament, Andrew Black had worked as a hedge fund trader, professional horseplayer, and computer programmer before cofounding the company that revolutionized Internet betting through peer-to-peer wagering.

Peer-to-peer wagering operates much like a stock exchange. Betfair matches sellers (backers) and buyers (layers), holds the stakes, and imposes a fee on winning wagers (as little as 2 percent) as their commission. The concept is as old as the hills. Brokering bets with the terms set down by the would-be action-seeker was a lucrative sideline for America's first poolroom operators, men like John Morrissey. Betfair adapted the concept to a divergent array of prediction markets and modernized the nuts-and-bolts with software that enabled bets to be aggregated into larger pools of liquidity. In 2010, a World Cup year, there were days when the company reportedly processed more than six million bets—more daily transactions than all of Europe's stock exchanges combined.[18]

Anticipating a loosening of constraints in the not-too-distant future, Betfair set about establishing a footprint in the United States. The company purchased TVG, the first TV network in the United States dedicated to horse racing, bought the naming rights to Hollywood Park and partnered with Atlantic City gambling casinos in developing online games for New Jersey residents. A rival betting exchange called Matchbook, born in 2004, concentrated on team sports, eschewing horse racing, and established a strong following, but that company, licensed in Antigua and Barbuda, pulled out of the U.S. market in 2011, another casualty of UIGEA.

25

WHALES

During the years straddling the opening of the twenty-first century as racetrack attendance was declining at an alarming rate, the pari-mutuel handle actually went up. Between 1996 and 2003, the total commingled worldwide handle on U.S. thoroughbred races increased every year. It was as if the sport was becoming healthier and more fragile at the same time. This rather odd development owed to more than the expansion of simulcasting; it reflected the impact of rebates.

Gamblers with offshore accounts could negotiate the best rebates. Racing and Gaming Services, a company based in St. Kitt's, and Elite Turf Club, operating out of Curaçao, emerged as the powerhouses, servicing the highest of the high-rollers, the so-called whales. In 2004, eleven betting syndicates affiliated with Elite—their entire roster of players—reportedly accounted for 10 percent of the North American pari-mutuel handle![1]

Whales weren't like the big plungers of Pittsburgh Phil's era. In those days, most of the plungers owned race horses and their biggest bets were on horses they owned. Some were bookmakers who had a financial interest in every race, but most lurked in the weeds until a good thing came along and then chunked it in. Judging by reports in the papers, their subculture revolved around betting *coups*. Their method of operation (or perhaps a skewed perception of it) gave rise to an aphorism: "a man can beat a race, but he can't beat the races." In other words, the key to winning is to be highly selective.

For a certain group of whales of the author's acquaintance, this is no recipe for winning whatsoever; it's merely a condescending admonition to horseplayers of modest means to control their impulses. Exploiting sophisticated algorithms with an eye toward grinding out a long-term profit, these individuals, collaborating as a team, are liable to make more than a thousand bets of various kinds and sizes across more than a hundred races on a particularly busy day. By the nature of the beast, volatility is inevitable, but the plungers of Pittsburgh Phil's day, with a few exceptions, seem to have had relatively steeper highs and lows.

For racetrack operators, the introduction of rebates was a thorny issue because they discriminated against the true fans of the sport. The racegoers that funneled their hard-earned dollars into ancillary revenue streams—parking, programs, refreshments, and so on—received none of the succor; they paid full fare. Moreover, since the players with rebates were sharper than the average horseplayer, less money was distributed in winnings to those without rebates. Taking the most conservative estimate, the distributions were reduced by 1.5 percent. A winning wager that would have paid $100 in the old days—assuming no change in the pari-mutuel tax—was reduced to $98.50. Another problem, even more troubling, was that the money from rebate shops tended to show in the final flashes of the tote board. It could not be otherwise, as the whales bet robotically through computer programs and the robot had to wait until the odds were fairly stable before it could calculate the advantage. However, a horseplayer at the track was sorely aggravated whenever a rush of late money pushed down the odds on his selection. The disarrangement just as the horses were leaving the gate was interpreted as evidence of skullduggery.

In an earlier era, track operators, in the main, were discomfited by comeback money. If they welcomed it, they were in bed with illegal bookies, but if they didn't they showed a "reckless" disregard for the bottom line. Rebate shops posed a similar dilemma. Some track operators took the high road and kept their pools pure, but they were in the minority. It wasn't easy to turn away business, especially when their industry was fraying.

The rebates brought fresh money into the game. At a meeting of the National Horsemen's Benevolent and Protective Association, Rob Terry, a representative of Racing and Gaming Services, a rebate shop described as the largest secondary pari-mutuel organization in the world, testified that horseplayers at his property would have lost about 6 percent of their wagers in 2011 if not for rebates. The rebates enabled them to sculpt a losing proposition into a positive-expectancy game.[2]

THE ST. KITT'S WHALE POD: A GLANCE
AT THREE BIG FISH

Kirk Brooks, the founder and president of Racing and Gaming Services, recalls that his first job was picking up dog feces. That was his job but it wasn't his calling.

One of ten children of a Denver print shop owner, Brooks got hooked on greyhound racing after taking a job as a kennel janitor. While still in his early twenties, he had his own kennel and was winning meets at leading tracks in New England. The sport was then flourishing in Florida and in New England but, akin to horse racing, there were dark clouds on the horizon. By 2010 greyhound racing would cease entirely in New England, halted for lack of business or outlawed by legislation advanced by animal rights activists.

At the Wheeling Downs greyhound track in West Virginia, Brooks developed a friendship with Don Lanners, the track's young racing secretary. Lanners left the Mountaineer State for Las Vegas, quickly climbed the ladder in the race and sports industry, and paved the way for Brooks, who followed closely behind.

Brooks arrived in Las Vegas at a time when hotel-casinos were rushing to add race and sports books. In this swirling environment, workers had opportunities for upward mobility that would ebb away as the industry matured. Brooks began as a lowly board man at the Sahara where the odds were displayed on an old-fashioned blackboard and had stops at three other properties before taking the reins of the freshly minted book at the Imperial Palace where he developed a well-earned reputation as an innovator.

The Imperial Palace was the first book in Las Vegas with a drive-thru window, the first with a color television at each individual seat, and was ahead of the curve in recognizing the resurgence of golf as a betting sport and the growing popularity of auto racing. What really set the book apart, however, were exotic Super Bowl wagering propositions, pages and pages of them, all but the oddest of which became Super

Bowl staples. These freak bets, as they were initially called, were developed almost exclusively in-house. Unlike his counterparts at other books, Brooks wanted his top supervisors to do more than mind the store; he expected them to pitch in and help formulate the odds.[3]

In 1995, after an eight-year stint at the Imperial Palace, Brooks was lured away to run the new book at the Holiday Inn Boardwalk. It was a curious move. The Imperial Palace wasn't swanky, but it was a larger Strip property with many more amenities than the tacky Boardwalk with its Coney Island–themed exterior and its Lilliputian casino sitting smack against the sidewalk. When the Boardwalk was reduced to rubble in June of 2006 to make way for the mammoth City Center project, the implosion went largely unnoticed.

At the Boardwalk, Brooks operated out of a nondescript seventy-five-seat race and sports book. A tourist would have never guessed that it catered to some of the biggest horseplayers on the planet. At the peak, over 50 percent of the Boardwalk's casino earnings accrued from horseplayers taking advantage of generous rebates.[4]

Rebates weren't new. Casinos routinely allowed high-stakes blackjack and baccarat players to write off a portion of their losses. Several properties had private arrangements with high-end horseplayers. Brooks raised the bar, offering kickbacks that his competitors were unwilling to match. He couldn't advertise this fact, but word got around. High-end horseplayers have a strong grapevine.

When the book at the Boardwalk opened, racetracks received about 3.5 percent of the money wagered off-site with simulcast partners. Money wagered at the track produced roughly five times as much "hold." In truth, the tracks underestimated the value of their simulcast product and sold it too cheaply. And when their best customers were wooed away by rebates, they decried it as poaching and demanded reparations to level the playing field.

Rebates were at the crux of a dispute over simulcast fees that led to an eight-month blackout of California races in Nevada, an impasse that began in November of 1996. Without pari-mutuel pooling, the books reduced their limits and turned away wagers with high payouts. Several race books closed during the stalemate, some permanently. Nevada gaming authorities subsequently outlawed rebates in hopes of forestalling another episode. The decision met with the approval of most of the bigger players in the casino industry. They too wanted a level playing field. They resented the fact that a book as small as the Boardwalk could outperform a book with more amenities and much higher overhead.

Brooks circumvented the proscription by cooking up special wagers with highly advantageous odds for qualified players. He knew that the regulators would shoot this down, but the book couldn't survive without rebates of one sort or another—there just wasn't enough foot traffic—and he was buying time while he plotted his next move. By the time the Boardwalk was imploded, Brooks was long gone. On the island of St. Kitt's, he accommodated many of his old customers and cultivated new ones. His best customer, the Parham-Benter syndicate, caught up with him there, establishing an office in such close proximity that it was as if the two operations had merged, which in a sense they had. For legal reasons, Brooks stayed completely clear of sports, concentrating exclusively on serving as the middleman between horseplayers and the racetracks with whom he had forged agreements.

Brooks settled on St. Kitt's after exploring other islands. Once the world's leading exporter of sugar cane, St. Kitt's had lost its signature industry and welcomed new investment. Other plusses were a highly literate English-speaking population, good phone service, and an affordable business license. Several bookmaking operations were already established there.

Beginning with three employees working in the living room of a rented house, Brooks grew Racing and Gaming Services to where it would employ thirty-five people in a state-of-the-art facility situated on the fringe of the capital city of Basseterre near the fashionable Frigate Bay Beach area. By 2004, his ever-growing handle had increased to a daily average of $1.3 million. For this Brooks could thank the modification to the Interstate Horseracing Act. Hidden inside a mammoth appropriations bill, the 2000 touch-up made clear that common pool parimutuel wagering across international boundaries was within the law if certain stipulations were met and, no less important, immunized Brooks and his associates from the virus of UIGEA.

If you had ventured into the book at the Holiday Inn Boardwalk during the Brooks era, you might have noticed a fellow sitting at one of the tables working on his laptop. That would have been Dana Parham. And if the scene struck you as odd, you were not alone. Parham was accustomed to having strangers look at him with an air of bemusement.

Attempting to beat the races with the aid of a portable computer made the quest appear all the more quixotic.

Born in 1951, Parham was raised largely by his maternal grandmother after his parents divorced when he was a toddler. As a boy growing up in Columbus, Ohio, he had an affinity for board games; a common finding in the biographies of professional gamblers. At age seventeen, he was betting the races at Beulah Park and Scioto Downs. The legal age was twenty-one; betting at the $50 window made him look older. In hindsight one could see that he was heading down a different path than his younger half-brother, who entered the ministry and is currently the senior pastor at a large Baptist church in Vermont.

Growing up in the shadow of Ohio's flagship university, it figured that Parham would enroll there where his natural aptitude for math would smooth the way to a bachelor of science degree. Ohio State University students were a constant presence in his life—his mother, who worked at the statehouse, cultivated a fertile avocation typing term papers and theses—and he was an avid fan of the school's athletic teams, the Buckeyes. But Parham was in a hurry to make his mark in the world and college became impractical when he had three mouths to feed. Married at nineteen, he was a father twice over by age twenty-two.

In 1986, now a divorced man in his mid-thirties, Parham moved to Las Vegas. Blackjack, poker, and sports betting paid the bills. In 1990, he outlasted fourteen competitors in a winner-take-all NFL handicapping contest at the Stardust. The prize was $37,500 and a free $25,000 bet on the Super Bowl. He made a bigger score one football weekend betting parlay cards at places that were over-generous with their odds on 5-, 6-, and 7-teamers. A baseball betting project was a loser, but several of his partners in this barren venture played instrumental roles in new endeavors. Prominent among them was Bill Benter. A quiet, unassuming man whose life has been one big adventure, Benter was known within a tight community of gamblers as the most successful horseplayer in the history of man.

Born in Pittsburgh in 1956, the son of a metallurgical engineer and a schoolteacher, Benter majored in physics and philosophy at Case Western Reserve University and spent a year abroad studying at the University of Bristol but quit school without ever earning a degree. (There would be honorary degrees in his future.) The incentive for breaking away from the life of a college student was provided by Professor Edward O. Thorp, the mathematical genius who devised a method for beating the game of blackjack.

For a certain set of people, Thorp's 1962 best seller *Beat the Dealer* was a clarion call. It invoked the famous saying "There's gold in them thar hills." The most fertile hills were found in Las Vegas. By the time that Benter arrived, casino operators were alert to card counters, but blackjack teams and a few lone wolves were still beating the game. With the aid of disguises and a micro-computer worn around his waist that operated on impulses sent from the toes of his shoes, Benter had a nice run before he was barred from every casino in town. His blackjack gambling forays would eventually take him to five other continents.

Some of the best card counters, including Thorp himself, went on to become prominent hedge fund managers. Benter went in a different direction. In 1984, while playing in Macau, he and his blackjack partner, Alan Woods, an Australian, made a side trip to Hong Kong to explore the possibility of taking a crack at beating the races. At the Happy Valley track, Benter recognized some of the faces in the crowd. They were people he had seen playing high-limit blackjack in Macau; people acting in ways that betrayed a belief in superstitions, a trait commonly attributed to Chinese gamblers. Benter inferred that there was a lot of sucker money in the pari-mutuel pools.

The pools were enormous. In Hong Kong, a city of about seven million, thoroughbred racing dwarfs all other sports in popularity. Racing is typically held on Wednesday nights and weekends only, but the annual betting handle is roughly six times that of the United States. With pools this large, a massive bet doesn't disturb the odds. Given that there were only two racetracks and a manageable number of race horses—horses didn't ship in or out—Benter could see that Hong Kong racing was ideally suited to computer analysis. It was imperative that he could establish an account and wager off-site, a precondition that was satisfied. The odds on each race could be monitored as they streamed across the bottom of a video screen and a new technology allowed the closing prices to be captured and stored electronically. Finally, it mattered greatly that a Westerner could meet his daily needs in Hong Kong without being fluent in Chinese. English and Cantonese were the official languages.

Benter spent thousands of hours harvesting and testing data before he made his first bet. The past performances of horses, jockeys, and trainers, data culled from old copies of annual reference guides, proved to be much more useful than the systems and angles that permeated much of the how-to-handicap literature. Tweaking the model—adding variables, discarding others, and recalibrating the weight assigned to each variable—was a never-ending process. And eventually he had an algorithm that identified overlays with a high degree of accuracy and went beyond that by calculating the optimal bet size for each type of wager.

Benter was reluctant to take on another horse betting project. The U.S. racing scene was far more jumbled than Hong Kong. Building an effective algorithm was a more daunting assignment. What sold him was the rebate factor—he would be competing against a manageable "house vig"—and the fact that good downloadable databases already existed; he wouldn't be starting from scratch. The company in which he and Parham are principal stockholders is licensed in Florida, employs twenty people in St. Kitt's where all the wagering is done, and maintains an office in Las Vegas.

Horse racing has provided Brooks, Parham, and Benter with the capital to pursue other business opportunities. When Brooks's children took an interest in ice hockey, he encouraged their involvement by buying a roller skating emporium and fashioning it into an ice center. Affectionately dubbed the coldest place on the desert, the Las Vegas Ice Center houses two regulation-sized rinks, a pro shop, and a bar and grill where patrons can watch hockey through a wall of Plexiglas. Brooks subsequently purchased a minor league hockey team and their multi-purpose arena. The team, the Tri-City Storm, is based in Kearney, Nebraska. Parham developed a more eclectic portfolio. After buying a company that designs, manufactures, installs, and maintains aquariums, he branched into related businesses such as custom cabinetmaking and pet supply stores. (His company created the twin 450-gallon salt water fish tanks that festoon the Miami Marlins baseball park.) Other enterprises include custom home building, a recording studio, and a hundred-acre horse farm, no longer operational, that housed his considerable stable of standardbreds.

Bill Benter used a portion of his Hong Kong winnings to purchase a medical transcription company. With headquarters in Pittsburgh and

Bangalore, India, and an outpost in the Philippines, the company, with roughly a thousand workers, serves doctors and other health professionals across a wide span of the globe. But Benter has reached the stage in his life where making money is less gratifying than giving it away. An enthusiastic supporter of Rotary International, particularly the organization's work in establishing programs that promote world peace, Benter's philanthropic endeavors have ranged from building schools in impoverished regions of China to funding projects that make Pittsburgh more bicycle friendly. In 2010, he started the William Benter Prize in Applied Mathematics, a biennial award with a cash prize of $100,000. The petty hustlers that inspired the die-hard horseplayers in Damon Runyon's short stories had nothing in common with Bill Benter.

The rebate controversy led track operators to initiate their own customer reward programs. Twin Spires, a subsidiary of Churchill Downs Inc., whose family of racetracks included Arlington Park and the Fair Grounds, emerged as the leader among the conglomerates offering Advance Deposit Wagering. Participants earn points for each dollar wagered that can be redeemed for wagering credits or handicapping products. Another ADW program, NYRA Rewards, introduced in 2007, pays account holders a rebate if the sum of their wagers reaches a certain threshold within a stipulated block of time. At long last racetrack bosses were drawn to pay more than just lip service to their steady customers.

26

PUSHING THE ENVELOPE

In 1908, Governor Charles Evans Hughes of New York was inundated with congratulatory calls, letters, and telegrams after signing off on a bill outlawing betting at racetracks. Among those paying tribute was Governor John Franklin Fort of New Jersey. Fort called the anti-betting law "a great victory for righteousness and morality."[1]

Fort was a Republican, as is Chris Christie, who easily outdistanced his opponent to win a second term as governor of New Jersey in 2013. There the similarity ends. Under previous administrations, New Jersey became the second state to legalize full-fledged gambling casinos and was in the forefront of the lottery push. With Christie leading the charge, New Jersey became the second state behind Delaware to expand comprehensive gambling into the digital age, offering a full range of popular casino games 24/7 to in-state residents playing on the Internet.[2] New Jersey during the Christie administration would also be the first state to mount a serious challenge to the Professional and Amateur Sports Protection Act which prohibited New Jersey and forty-five other states—all but Nevada, Delaware, Oregon, and Montana—from taking bets on sporting events. The four exceptions were "grandfathered" by virtue of having a law on the books that allowed sports betting in some form. Betting on individual games was legal only in Nevada.

The spearhead of the Professional and Amateur Sports Protection Act, commonly referenced by the acronym *PASPA*, was a New Jersey man with roots in Missouri, Bill Bradley. A basketball Hall of Famer and Rhodes Scholar, Bradley, a Democrat, was in his third term in the

Senate when President George H. W. Bush signed PASPA into law in October of 1992. Bradley had set out to make the ban universal, but was induced to accept a compromise that allowed sports betting to continue in states that already allowed some form of it. Because a bill to legalize sports betting in Atlantic City was under consideration in New Jersey, the Garden State was accorded a one-year window (until January 1, 1994) to activate an exemption. The state's failure to take the carrot would come to be seen as a colossal blunder.[3]

In 2009, the year that Chris Christie unseated New Jersey's incumbent governor, Atlantic City casino revenues were off 13.2 percent. At the end of his first term, things had worsened. Casino revenues were the lowest in twenty-four years and a drop of more than 45 percent from the peak year of 2006.[4] The revitalization of Atlantic City, a key component of Christie's platform, became a larger and larger priority.

Reversing Atlantic City's slide was complicated by a national oversupply of convention space. Sports betting had long been proposed as a good tonic. In November of 2011, Christie took up the cudgel, endorsing legalized sports betting in a speech at the University of Delaware, the school where he earned his undergraduate degree. That same month, voters in New Jersey approved a referendum to amend the state constitution to allow sports betting at racetracks and Atlantic City casinos. The legislature reacted quickly, passing a bill that Christie immediately signed into law. Within six months, the Division of Gaming Enforcement finalized a list of sports betting regulations.

"Let the games begin" whooped long-serving state senator Ray Lesniak, New Jersey's most vociferous sports betting advocate. But it wasn't that simple. The National Collegiate Athletic Association and the four major professional leagues—the NFL, NBA, NHL, and Major League Baseball—sued to block the law from taking effect. In December of 2012, a federal judge let the injunction stand. He rejected New Jersey's claim that the leagues failed to demonstrate that legal sports betting would irreparably harm their product. His ruling was upheld by a federal appeals court. The Supreme Court subsequently declined to review the case.

Senator Lesniak would not be deterred. He devised a plan that he thought would circumvent the roadblock. A bill drawn up by him would have kick-started sports betting in advance of state oversight by allowing private companies to offer sports betting without state interference.

Lesniak found common ground on the marijuana front. When he submitted his proposal, there were twenty-three states where marijuana was legal for medicinal use. This was contrary to federal law. Colorado and Washington had taken it further, decriminalizing the recreational use of the drug. Federal crime fighters, obeisant to the principal of state sovereignty, turned a blind eye.

Both chambers of the legislature approved Lesniak's bill. Christie signed it into law on October 17, 2014. A jubilant Lesniak announced that sports betting would commence on Sunday, October 26, at Monmouth Park, where the William Hill organization had invested millions in a state-of-the-art sports bar built to function as a sports book when the state gave the go-ahead. He would be there to make the ceremonial first wager. But again Lesniak was jumping the gun. The blastoff was put on hold when the leagues obtained a temporary restraining order. On November 20, federal judge Michael Shipp made the injunction permanent. But the battle was far from over. "We are going to continue pushing every legal option available," vowed the president of the New Jersey State Senate.[5]

Citing constitutional concerns, Christie was initially reluctant to approve Lesniak's bill. His about-face was prompted by the deepening crisis in Atlantic City. In the first nine months of 2014, four casinos—Atlantic Club, Showboat, Revel, and Trump Plaza—shut their doors. The demise of the Revel was particularly noteworthy. The city's newest and most lavish beachfront resort, Revel, at fifty-seven stories, was the tallest structure in the city. Despite a thriving nightclub scene, casino receipts were so weak that the property filed for bankruptcy twice in the first two years of operation.[6]

The four dead casinos employed 25 percent of Atlantic City's casino workforce. Their goodbyes, clustered within such a short period, were a devastating blow to Atlantic City's corroding tax base. As the surviving casinos were winning appeals for lower tax assessments, homeowners were being lashed with rising property taxes to pick up the slack. Many simply couldn't afford it. In the first quarter of 2015, the Atlantic City Statistical Area, which included all of Atlantic County, had the nation's highest rate of metropolitan home foreclosure activity.[7] Casino operators, the first generation of whom were extolled as white knights, came to be increasingly viewed as plunderers.

Casino gambling was supposed to spur economic development outside the casino corridor, uplifting the entire city. Dilapidated housing would give way to housing compatible with a middle-class lifestyle. Despite a surtax imposed on casinos for citywide refurbishments, this never happened. Visitors entering the city from the expressway were greeted with abandoned buildings and litter-strewn vacant lots. The failure to clean up the front porch of the casino district came to be seen as one of the triggers of the carnage. Tourists exposed to the bleak cityscape embraced gambling with a little less enthusiasm and were less likely to return.

Sports wagering wasn't likely to significantly inflate casino revenues. Throughout Nevada's history, sports books never accounted for more than 2 percent of statewide casino earnings. Moreover, recent research contradicted the conventional wisdom that sports books were a significant driver of other casino revenues. Sports bettors didn't migrate to slot machines in any appreciable numbers.[8] However, there was yet good reason to think that Nevada-style sports betting, *if exclusive to the region*, would be a game-changer for the troubled resort city.

Atlantic City's casino-hotel operators had lagged behind their Las Vegas counterparts in plumbing the non-gaming assets of their properties; as late as 2014, gambling accounted for 70 percent of their revenue, roughly double that in Las Vegas. But the gap was narrowing, and if sports bettors didn't gravitate to slot machines, that was becoming increasingly less of an issue. Sports bettors in town for the weekend still needed a place to sleep and a place to eat and could perhaps be induced to buy things in the myriad shops in and around their hotel.

A survey conducted in 2012 showed that 60.1 percent of visitors to Atlantic City were fifty years of age or over. The comparable figure for Las Vegas was 37 percent.[9] It was imperative that the casinos in Atlantic City attract a younger crowd and sports bettors fit the demographic. The games that attracted the most action—the Super Bowl and the first two rounds of the NCAA basketball tournament—played out during traditionally slow times when casino operators were in need of a lever to goose the hotel occupancy rate. In Nevada, these events didn't merely fill rooms, but filled them at jacked-up prices consistent with the law of supply and demand. Moreover, in Nevada sports betting was the only casino game exhibiting an upward trajectory! Other casino games weren't just flat, but were actually shrinking.[10]

Proponents of legal sports betting were cheered when NBA commissioner Adam Silver came out in favor of it. In a *New York Times* op-ed piece that ran on November 14, 2014, Silver wrote: "Times have changed since Paspa was enacted. . . . Gambling has increasingly become a popular and accepted form of entertainment. . . . In light of these domestic and global trends, the laws on sports betting should be changed. . . . Congress should adopt a federal framework that allows states to authorize betting on professional sports, subject to strict regulatory requirements and technological safeguards. . . . I believe that sports betting should be brought out of the underground and into the sunlight where it can be appropriately monitored and regulated."[11]

Silver elaborated on his bombshell in an interview with ESPN's gambling beat writer David Purdum. In this interview he revealed that the other major professional sports leagues were studying the matter, "actively planning" in his words, "for the new gambling reality."[12] But that reality, as they saw it, wasn't compatible with a piecemeal push. As Silver made clear, he believed that this was a job for Congress, not the courts. Hence, although the professional leagues had softened their stance on gambling, they were not about to break ranks with the NCAA in beating back New Jersey's plan for circumventing PASPA.

Silver's op-ed piece ran the day after it was announced that the NBA had purchased an equity stake in FanDuel. The NHL and Major League Baseball were already involved with Draft Kings, the other big cheese in the exploding fantasy sports market.

Fantasy sports were initially identified with baseball rotisserie leagues. These were season-long competitions that allowed participants to vicariously become the owners of major league teams. A participant built his team from active rosters during an auction in which each of the bidders worked from a finite bankroll, real or imagined. Various statistics were deployed to determine the standings. The exemption for fantasy sports carved into UIGEA was based on this model. It was a model that evoked the image of a Norman Rockwell painting: friends and coworkers sitting around a kitchen table sharing their love of the American pastime as they conducted their annual player draft. FanDuel and Draft Kings and the newbies that came down the pike in their wake compressed the competitions into tournaments lasting one day or one week. Participants paid to play and winners received cash prizes, the value of which was depressed by the operator's commission, typically 10 percent. The framework had many features in common with online poker and bookmaking operations.

Fantasy sports gave the attorneys for New Jersey a chip that lent more weight to their argument. By partnering with daily fantasy leagues, they argued, the leagues had unclean hands. To claim that legal sports betting threatened the integrity of their product was the height of hypocrisy. They presented their case before a three-judge panel at the Third Circuit U.S. Court of Appeals in Philadelphia on March 17, 2015.

A victory for New Jersey in this latest round of court battles was expected to create a domino effect. It would be transformative. And many people figured that the odds were in New Jersey's favor when they learned the composition of the panel. Julio Fuentes, Maryanne Trump Barry, and Marjorie Rendell were picked to hear the case.

Judge Fuentes had sided with the majority in denying New Jersey's previous appeal. For sports betting proponents, his reappointment was a bad sign. But all that was required was a 2–1 majority and there was reason to think that his peers on the panel would be sympathetic. Judge Barry was the sister of Donald Trump, a man often referenced as a casino mogul. Judge Rendell was the spouse of former Pennsylvania governor Ed Rendell. There was a touch of irony there. Back on July 5, 2004, Judge Rendell's husband stood in the winner's circle at Philadelphia Park and signed two bills into law. The first authorized slot machines, 61,000 in all, more than existed in all of Atlantic City. The second bill, to take effect after all the slot parlors were up and running and raining money into the state treasury, was a property tax abatement measure. The decline of Atlantic City, one could argue, began at that very moment. Now Ms. Rendell had the opportunity to undo some of the damage, albeit it wouldn't be her decision alone.

On August 25, nine days before the start of the college football season, the appeals court finally made known its verdict. Judge Fuentes had an about-face. He felt that Senator Lesniak's plan—to allow bookmaking without explicitly authorizing it—didn't violate the tenets of PASPA. But he was outvoted and New Jersey was shot down once again.

There was still a crack in the door. The state could request an en banc review. If granted, the case would be heard by all the active judges of the Third Circuit, of which there were then twelve. The chances that this request would be honored were considered remote—en banc reviews were seldom granted—but the state's attorneys were duty-bound to keep plugging away until every avenue was exhausted.[13] And, left unsaid, the cost would continue to escalate. An Associated Press investigation, made public in May of 2014, revealed that New Jersey taxpayers were on the hook for $2.8 million in legal fees for work performed on the sports betting project in 2012 and 2013 alone.[14]

Had New Jersey won the case, the state's sports betting providers would have entered a red-hot market. Delaware reintroduced sports betting in 2009. An attempt to broaden the menu to include single-game wagering was shot down by a federal judge, who ruled that the state was locked in to what it had offered in 1976, namely NFL parlays, but despite this encumbrance, the game was well received. Abetted by a wider and more diverse network of vendors and the addition of teaser and over/under parlays, participation increased in leaps and bounds. In 2014, the sports lottery pumped $7.1 million into the state treasury, an increase of $1.4 million over the previous year.[15]

The Nevada experience was more telling. From 2011 to 2014, the sports betting handle increased 35.6 percent. Propelled by a record-setting Super Bowl—$119,400,822 was wagered on the game between the Seattle Seahawks and Denver Broncos, an increase of $20 million over the previous year—Nevada's 2014 sports wagering handle rose to $3.9 *billion.*[16]

There were several factors at work. The big game attracted a record number of six-figure bets, virtually all of which were placed at the "M." A casino-resort at the far south end of Las Vegas Boulevard, the "M" housed the flagship book of the eight book Cantor Gaming chain. Under the direction of maverick CEO Lee Amaitis, the former chairman of the London branch of the Cantor Fitzgerald global investment firm, the Cantor Gaming operation (which would be rebranded CG Technology) adopted an aggressive posture that set it apart from the competition. Las Vegas golf course developer Billy Walters, America's most prominent sports gambler, and the aptly nicknamed boxer Floyd "Money" Mayweather were conversant with the policies of the sports book at the "M." Their titanic wagers, in the lingo of an old-time gambling man, would choke a horse.

UIGEA undoubtedly played a role in the surge. As U.S. bettors were left with only a few reliable online books, domestic providers, legal and (overwhelmingly) illegal, acquired a larger market share. The introduction of mobile betting applications was a huge propellant. Several of Nevada's largest sports betting chains rolled out apps that allowed in-state residents to wager from their computer, iPad, or smart phone. But another factor may have been even more salient: the mainstream media had become more open to the subject of sports gambling.

For years, the talking heads on the big national sports shows danced around the point spread with sly allusions. Mentioning the words on the air was a no-no. Things started to change in the mid-1990s. Jovial radio personality Armand "Papa Joe" Chevalier was in the forefront. From 1994 to 2005, his show was heard on hundreds of stations. But things really started to percolate when Chad Millman assumed a larger role with ESPN. Millman started a sports betting blog for *ESPN the Magazine* in 2009. The next year the blog was adapted to a podcast. Gambling-related content on all of the ESPN platforms became more plentiful after he was named editor-in-chief of the magazine in 2011. At *ESPN Chalk*, the most prominent spawn, journalists covering the sports betting industry, reside with handicappers, expounding upon their "value plays."

For Las Vegas journalist Matt Jacob, the year 2013 was the tipping point, the year that the betting line became part of the national conversation.[17]

The spike was presaged by developments in the Westgate Super-Contest, the most talked-about NFL handicapping contest. Launched in 1987 when the property was known as the Las Vegas Hilton, the SuperContest, with a $1,500 buy-in, requires contestants to pick five games against a midweek point spread each week of the regular season. Contestants must sign up in person but may designate a proxy to turn in their picks. As the number of contestants grew, enterprising individuals established proxy services for out-of-state contestants.

In 2011, the SuperContest attracted a record 517 entries. Three years later the number had zoomed to 1,403, inflating the prize pool to $2,104,500 with the winner receiving $736,575. Season-long coverage of the competition by ESPN radio personalities and by Las Vegas correspondents for ESPN.com and other websites boosted enrollment to new levels.

HORSE RACING

As New Jersey was fighting her lonely battle for legal sports wagering, the sport of horse racing fell into a deeper rut, notwithstanding a scattered gust of glorious moments. The 2014 Belmont Stakes attracted a record crowd, 102,198. More than a third, nearly 36,000, arrived by train, a record high for the Long Island Railroad. A sidebar to the story was the logjam at the rail station and the massive traffic jam that awaited those leaving the track. There was a precedent for it. The first day of racing at Belmont Park, May 4, 1905, produced the first newspaper report of a traffic jam. It was as if someone had turned back the clock to recapture the tumult of a more prosperous day.

This was no ordinary Belmont Stakes. California Chrome was bidding to become the first Triple Crown winner in thirty-six years. There was a fairy-tale air about the quest that made the story more compelling. The horse had a humble pedigree. The seventy-seven-year-old trainer had never experienced such a rush. The co-owners were "everyday folk," plebeians in a blue-blood sport. With these hooks, a strong turnout was assured, but the turnstile count was yet extraordinary.

California Chrome finished fourth. The drought would end the next year when a horse with a misspelled name, American Pharoah, ended the dry spell. The first two legs of Pharoah's triumphant journey brought out record crowds: 170,153 at the Kentucky Derby; 131,680 at the Preakness. The turnout for the Preakness was especially noteworthy as the ancient Baltimore racing plant had been poorly maintained, the weather forecast was ominous—the race was run in a torrential downpour—and the host city was still reeling from four nights of civic unrest following the death of an unarmed black man in police custody, a worrisome issue for tourism. There would be no record crowd at the Belmont Stakes. Attendance was capped at 100,000 to prevent a recurrence of the gridlock that soiled the 2014 event. Later that summer, Pharoah ran in the Haskell Invitational at Monmouth Park and in the Travers Stakes at Saratoga, competing before capacity crowds.

These lush moments were deceiving. The big events were getting bigger and bigger, particularly the Kentucky Derby, but getting folks to show up for an ordinary day of racing was getting harder and harder. The lush moments came late during an era of contraction and consolidations.

Hollywood Park, the national leader in daily average attendance for the decade of the 1950s, shut down in 2013. The last race at the storied California racing plant was run on December 22. Ten months later, Suffolk Downs, the last remaining thoroughbred track in New England from a list of seventeen, gave up the ghost after failing to win a casino license.

Bedeviled by changing consumer tastes in gambling, racetrack operators faced a potentially lethal challenge in the elimination of subsidies. Twenty states diverted a slice of gambling revenue to the horse racing industry. The subsidies allowed tracks to offer bigger purses, which in theory meant better horses, bigger crowds, and more jobs for racetrack workers and those in related fields. The appropriations saved jobs but didn't create new ones, and state lawmakers were increasingly disposed to shut off the spigot.

Long gone were the days when the top jockeys were as well known as the top athletes in other sports. Only 1 percent of the respondents in a 2013 Harris Poll survey named horse racing their favorite sport. Other racetracks would inevitably join Hollywood Park, Suffolk Downs, and their many antecedents in the catacombs of history. Aqueduct was a leading contender. The original Aqueduct, born in 1894, had been completely rebuilt, a four-year project completed in 1959. The reconstructed Aqueduct, dubbed the "Big A," was ballyhooed as the largest, costliest, and most modern racing facility in the world, the last word in elegance, but the property didn't age well. The track was blasted as an unsanitary dump in a series of reports in the *New York Daily News*.[18]

Governor Andrew Cuomo, who seized control of the New York Racing Association and charged the agency with developing a strategic plan for reprivatizing the state's horse racing industry following his election in 2010, saw no reason why racing should continue at Aqueduct, which, like Hollywood Park, sat on valuable land near an airport that was coveted by developers. But Cuomo couldn't simply wave his magic wand and do away with racing there. That would have endangered the golden goose lashed to it. By law, a non-Indian gaming establishment in New York could not exist without being tethered to a racetrack.

The death of a racetrack doesn't necessarily abbreviate the racing calendar. Racing dates are shifted to other tracks. But each time that a racetrack dies the sport loses adherents who, for convenience or other reasons, were loyal to that particular venue. Moreover, many individuals feel a sense of loss when a familiar sporting venue is no more, a feeling that often smolders into resentment.

FOOTBALL

The 2015 college football season commenced on September 3; the NFL kicked in a week later. During this period, those tuning in on television and radio were inundated with ads for fantasy sports. A visitor from a foreign land exposed to the deluge would have thought that playing fantasy sports was a national obsession. Lawmakers took notice, many expressing concerns that fantasy sports were diverting money away from state lotteries and casinos.[19] Tax revenues from these sources were generally flat and in many cases actually declining, exacerbating worries about new threats, real or imagined, to this money supply.

In Las Vegas, the 2015 Westgate SuperContest, a strong barometer of football betting trends, set another record, attracting 1,727 entries. Proponents of legal sports betting in New Jersey looked on in dismay. But there would soon be a light at the end of the tunnel. On October 14, 2015, in a surprising development, it was announced that the state had won its appeal for an en banc review. This vacated the August 25 decision rendered by judges Fuentes, Barry, and Rendell. It was, pardon the cliché, a whole new ballgame.

Getting that many judges to clean up their schedules and convene as a group was logistically challenging, and the best guess—and it was only a guess—was that the reexamination would take place in mid-February 2016. Regardless, in the opinion of most legal experts, in agreeing to rehear the arguments the court shifted the odds in favor of the plaintiff. A new chapter was about to unfold in this long-running saga that spoke to America's love/hate affair with sports gambling.

GLOSSARY

action. a wager, e.g., "I have action on the Mets today."

beard. an agent who bets for someone else to disguise the source of the money.

chalk. the favorite; a chalk player has a penchant for betting favorites. Labeling someone a chalk player is most often meant as a term of derision.

churn. the number of times that a gambler turns over his bankroll; when a horseplayer cashes a ticket and then commits all or part of his winnings to another bet, he is said to be churning. Bookmakers were elated when the NFL pushed back the starting time of most of the games in the second tier of Sunday contests to 4:15 and then 4:25 EST. The later starts reduced the number of overlapping games, stimulating more betting on the second batch, increasing the churn.

circle game. a game with a reduced betting limit. In the days when the odds were chalked on a blackboard, a circle game had an actual circle around the betting line.

cover. to beat the point spread.

dime. a $1,000 wager. In football and basketball, a dime typically means risking $1,100 to win $1,000. In sports such as baseball, where one bets into a money line, a dime equals a flat $1,000 on the underdog or a wager structured to win $1,000 on the favorite. When calling in their bets, the heaviest hitters typically frame their wagers in multiples of dimes: five dimes, ten dimes, etc.

dog. the underdog as shown in the betting line.

dollar. a $100 wager (see dime).

exposure. the amount of money that a bookmaker stands to lose on a game. Lopsided action compels a bookmaker to make adjustments to correct the imbalance, thereby reducing his exposure; i.e., his liability.

fade. to bet against, e.g., "I'm fading the Rams today."

get down. to make a wager.

handicapper. originally a horse racing term; a track handicapper attempts to give each horse in a race an equal chance of winning by making the stronger horses take on more weight. More generally, a handicapper is a person who analyzes variables to arrive at his selections. The opposite of a hunch bettor.

hold. what the bookmaker or pari-mutuel operator gets to keep after paying off the winners.

hook. a half-point affixed to a betting line. The word is often mouthed by disgruntled bettors, as in, "Damn, I gave four-and-a-half points with the Steelers and they won by four; I lost by the hook."

hoops. the sport of basketball; also referenced as baskets.

laydown. a bet.

limit. the maximum wager that a bookmaker will accept; it varies by sport. A bookmaker will accept a larger wager on an NFL game than on a generic college basketball game because NFL lines tend to be tighter (i.e., less volatile) and because it's easier to attract a matching bet on the other side.

line. the odds or point spread on a particular event; a commonly used synonym is "price."

lock. a bet that can't lose; the word is associated with unscrupulous touts.

middle. winning both sides of a game that uses a point spread by exploiting an alteration in the betting line. In the 1976 Super Bowl between the Pittsburgh Steelers and Dallas Cowboys, the line favoring the Steelers vacillated between "3½" and "4½." Many professional bettors played both sides and "hit the middle" when the Steelers won 35–31. In sports betting circles, this game would be remembered as a great bloodbath for the bookies.

money line. the amount one must risk to win $100, signified by the minus sign (−), and the amount one stands to win if risking $100, signified by the plus sign (+). Let's take the example of a baseball game that is priced –220/+180. In this example, a bet on the favorite structured to win $100 requires a laydown of $220. A $100 bet on the underdog stands to win $180. In this proposition, the "true odds" on the favorite are 2/1. But if the bookmaker offered true odds (–200/+200) and succeeded in balancing his action, he would have nothing to show for it. In setting the line, he must create a straddle between the price on the favorite and the price on the underdog to clock in a profit.

nickel. a $500 wager.

off the board. a game without a betting line. A common reason for taking a game off the board is an injury of uncertain severity to a key player.

out. a place or person that takes wagers. Sharp players shop for the best lines, dictating multiple outs. Those that bet very large sums need multiple outs because their wagers are too large for any individual bookmaker to handle.

outlaw line. a betting line made available to a select few before it is released to the public. Old-time bookies adopted this practice to sharpen their lines before taking large wagers.

parlay. a multi-horse or multi-team wager. A parlay offers a much higher rate of return than if each team was bet separately, but it only takes one losing selection to torpedo the bet.

past post. in horse racing, a wager on a race that has already been run. In sports, most commonly a wager on an event that has already started, inside of which were developments that increased the likelihood of a particular outcome.

price. the odds or point spread on a particular event.

prop bet. the root word is proposition, but while every kind of wager is in essence a proposition, the contraction "prop" has a more specific meaning, referencing an unconventional wager. The bigger the sporting event, the greater the number of props attached to it. An example from the Super Bowl: Will there be a kickoff or punt returned for a touchdown?

punter. a British term that is slowly filtering into the United States; a synonym for "bettor," albeit often mouthed with a supercilious tone.

push. an event that for betting purposes is graded a tie. In football and basketball, a push occurs when the margin of victory is congruent with the point spread. If the bet was made on credit, it's "no action." If money was left with a stakes holder, i.e., a bookmaker, the money is refunded.

round robin. a multi-team wager that does not require the bettor to win all of his picks. For example, if one fancies four teams, he could box them into six two-team parlays. If three of the four picks win, one would show a larger return on investment than if he had bet each team individually for an identical amount.

rundown. a reading of the lines for a particular day or sport. Bookies call their line consultants for a rundown; bettors call their bookies. To facilitate an efficient rundown of a large set of games, it is imperative that the person providing the line and the recipient use the same schedule; there must be uniformity in the rotation. In a large office on a day with a multiplicity of games, a rundown is delivered at a rapid pace. The process might begin with the provider saying, "All bottom teams unless I specify otherwise. Here we go: four-and-a-half, six, eleven, two on the top, eight-and-a-half . . ." The schedules that sports bettors use list the home teams on the bottom. In football, the bulk of the home teams are giving points, so it isn't necessary for a line service provider to name every team; that would slow things down. The words "on the top" signify a road favorite. It goes without saying that oral rundowns are fading away as bookies and bettors increasingly harvest this information online.

sandwich game. a game on a team's schedule that is less meaningful or less attention getting than the games that come immediately before and after. As a rule of thumb, a handicapper shies away from a team giving points that is "caught in a sandwich."

scalp. to lock in a profit by betting both sides of a proposition. In competitions where there is a pronounced favorite, one typically sees late money on the underdog, compelling the bookmaker to shorten the odds, sometimes to the point where an early-bird bettor holding a ticket on the underdog can bet the other side and lock in a profit. A bettor whose radar is constantly attuned to scalping opportunities is called an arbitrager or an advantage gambler.

square. an unsophisticated bettor; an Englishman might describe a square as a mug punter.

steam. a surge of money on one side of a betting proposition, exemplified by a radical change in the odds.

store. a bookie or a place where one can get down a bet.

straight bet. the most common wager; a stand-alone wager into a proposition typically framed with only two sides.

teaser. a parlay that allows players to add points on the underdogs or subtract points on the favorites (one can mix or match) in return for a lower payout.

totals. also known as over/unders. A wager where one bets whether there will be more or less of a specified thing, such as the number of points scored in a football game. The sport of pedestrianism (long distance race walking) gave rise to the first over/unders. One wagered on whether a runner could complete the course before a specified amount of time had elapsed.

vigorish. the commission charged by a bookmaker for accepting a wager, commonly abbreviated "vig." Thought to be a corruption of the Russian word *vyigrysh,* meaning winnings or profit, a word transported to the United States by Yiddish-speaking immigrants. Before diffusing into sports gambling, the word referenced the interest charged by illegal moneylenders.

whale. a person that bets enormous sums; in olden days a big plunger.

wiseguy. a sophisticated bettor; a person who is well informed and well versed in the art of handicapping. In the plural, men of this description are more commonly referenced as "sharps."

NOTES

I. LEONARD JEROME

1. John Eisenberg, *The Great Match Race: When North Met South in America's First Sports Spectacle* (New York: Houghton Mifflin, 2006), ix.

2. "The Race," *New Orleans Times-Picayune*, 21 May 1845, 2.

3. "Great Match Race for $20,000," *Brooklyn Daily Eagle*, 8 May 1845, 3.

4. Anita Leslie, *The Remarkable Mr. Jerome* (New York: Henry Holt and Company, 1954), 52.

5. "Wall Street's Wit Dead," *Boston Weekly Globe*, 30 March, 1887, 5.

2. SARATOGA AND JEROME PARK

1. Rev. Theo L. Cuyler, "Life at Saratoga," *Independent*, 21 July 1870, 1.

2. Quoted in Bernard Livingston, *Their Turf: America's Horsey Set and Its Princely Dynasties* (New York: Arbor House, 1973), 230.

3. Edward Hotaling, *They're Off! Racing at Saratoga* (Syracuse, NY: Syracuse University Press, 1995), 48. (According to historian Steven A. Riess, the first use of the word "poolroom" in the *New York Times* referenced Underwood's operation in Saratoga.) *Daily Racing Form*, "America's Racing Center," 15 August 1918, 1.

4. "The Races Second Annual Meeting of the Saratoga Association," *New York Times*, 8 August 1865, 1.

3. POOL SELLERS, BOOKMAKERS, AND PARI-MUTUELS

1. "John F. Chamberlin Dead," *New York Times*, 24 August 1896, 2.
2. "The Turf; The Paterson Spring Race Meeting Programme of the Sport," *New York Times*, 2 June 1867, 5.
3. "Track Bookies Likely to Go," *Salt Lake Tribune*, 4 June 1911, 49, 50. Pierre Lorillard IV would eventually view bookmakers as counterproductive to the best interests of racing. In an 1888 interview, he called them an unscrupulous pack of scoundrels. "Down With Bookmakers: Pierre Lorillard Speaks Out," *New York Tribune*, 8 May 1888, 7.
4. "About Bookmaking," *Portland Morning Oregonian*, 5 September 1894, 8.
5. John Dizikes, *Yankee Doodle Dandy: The Life and Times of Tod Sloan* (New Haven, CT: Yale University Press, 2000), 25–26.
6. "Rise of the Pari-Mutuel 'Mid Ruins of the Betting Ring," *Ogden Evening Standard*, 27 March 1911, 11.
7. Steven A Riess, "Horse Racing in Chicago," in Ralph C. Wilcox, David L. Andrews, Robert Pitter, and Richard L. Erwin, eds., *Sporting Dystopias* (Albany: State University of New York Press, 2003), 120.

4. OFF-TRACK BETTING

1. "Pool-Room Swindling," *New York Daily Tribune*, 14 November 1876, 1; "A Pool-Room Reformer," *New York Times*, 11 December 1876, 1.
2. "The Presidential Pools," *New York Times*, 12 December 1876, 1.
3. "All Bets Off," *New York Daily Tribune*, 11 December 1876, 4.
4. "The Pool-Room Nuisance," *New York Times*, 13 September 1881, 8.
5. David G. Schwartz, *Roll the Bones: The History of Gambling* (New York: Gotham Books, 2006), 335.
6. "The Gambler's Paradise," *New York Times*, 23 June 1880, 8.
7. Steven A. Riess, the leading authority on the racing scene in metropolitan New York from the Gilded Age through the Progressive Era notes that independent handbook operators were members of a covert subculture about which we know very little. They worked in the shadows and left no diaries or other remains that offered a window into their world. The same may be said of modern day commission agents who facilitate dealings between off-shore bookmakers and men approved to bet on credit.

8. *Portland Morning Oregonian*, 1 July 1891, 4; "Against the Ives Pool Act," *New York Daily Tribune*, 13 March 1893, 12.

9. "The Gambler's Paradise: They Make Thieves," *Chicago Daily Tribune*, 20 April 1890, 1.

10. "Gamblers' Mascots," *New Orleans Daily Picayune*, 31 May 1896, 28; Rev. Henry C. Vrooman, "Gambling and Speculation: A Symposium," *Arena*, 11, February 1895, 421–22. See also Arthur B. Lewis, "The Craze for Betting," *Fort Worth Morning Register*, 29 September 1900, 13. In a similar vein, a writer for a San Francisco paper declared that women had less control over their emotions and were thus more susceptible to a gambling addiction. The paper had launched a campaign to close the poolrooms that women frequented "to prevent their degradation" ("Poolsellers Meet with Signal Defeat," *San Francisco Call*, 22 March 1898, 7).

11. "Postal Telegraphy," *Los Angeles Daily Herald*, 1 March 1890, 3.

12. "Mr. Nicoll Takes a Hand: Indictments against the Poolsellers," *New York Times*, 22 May 1891, 5.

13. "Open Under Difficulties: The Western Union's Poor Service to the Poolrooms," *New York Times*, 30 May 1891, 5. "Races Reported from a Balloon," *Chicago Tribune*, 13 September 1891, 5.

5. NEW YORK'S
RACETRACK-BUILDING BOOM

1. "A Vast Crowd," *Brooklyn Daily Eagle*, 5 July 1881, 3.

2. The original Monmouth Park was built by John F. Chamberlin, an associate of John Morrissey. In the literature, Chamberlin is often portrayed as a scoundrel who got rich running dishonest games at his various gambling houses. A different image appears in his obituaries. Here Chamberlin is described as a man with genial manners and epicurean tastes who was widely esteemed by statesmen, military leaders, and scholars. Chamberlin died in 1896 while vacationing in Saratoga. By then he had transitioned into a Washington, D.C., restaurateur ("John F. Chamberlin Dead," *New York Tribune*, 24 August 1896, 7).

3. "The Season at Saratoga: A Look at the Hotels and the People in Them," *New York Times*, 2 August 1881, 2.

4. Charles B. Palmer, *For Gold and Glory: The Story of Thoroughbred Racing in America*. (New York: Garrick and Evans, Inc., 1939), 127.

5. "Proctor Knott's Futurity," *New York Times*, 4 September 1888, 3.

6. John J. White, *The History of the Louisiana Lottery* (master's thesis), Louisiana State University, May 1939, 1–6. See also Berthold C. Alwes, *The*

History of the Louisiana State Lottery Company (master's thesis), Louisiana State University, 1929.

7. "75,000 in Bowery for T.D. Sullivan's Funeral," *New York Tribune*, 16 September 1913, 1.

8. "Belmont Park Opened," *New York Tribune*, 5 May 1905, 1.

9. "Belmont Park Opened," 1.

10. "Scenes at Race Course on the Opening Day," *New York Evening World*, 4 May 1905, 1, 11.

11. "Empire City Starts Week under Optimistic Conditions," *Brooklyn Daily Eagle*, 19 August 1907, 16.

6. BOOKMAKERS AND THEIR MODUS OPERANDI

1. "Law's Distinction in Method of Gambling," *New York Times*, 1 April 1901, 16.

2. "Thoroughbred Topics," *New York Daily Tribune*, 22 September 1902, 8.

3. Joseph Freeman Marston, "The Maelstrom of the Betting Ring," *Munsey's Magazine*, 29, no. 5, August 1903, 708; "Problems for the Jockey Club," *New York World-Telegram*, 15 January 1899, 1.

4. "The Winnings of Troubadour," *San Francisco Evening Bulletin*, 12 June 1896, 3. Many bookmakers were ruined when Black Gold won the 1924 Kentucky Derby. The one-horse stable of Rosa Hoots, a recently widowed Osage Indian woman from Ardmore, Oklahoma, Black Gold went to post the favorite in a field of nineteen but was so lightly regarded when the nominations were announced that an early-bird bettor could have locked in odds of 100/1 ("Tom Kearney, Bet Commissioner, Dies," *Washington Post*, 24 February 1936, 14). The foreign book at the Caliente track in Tijuana reportedly lost $750,000 in future book wagers when the California-bred filly Winning Colors won the 1988 Kentucky Derby (Bill Christine, "Caliente Bets Its Life on the Appeal of All-Sports Wagering," *Los Angeles Times*, 2 October 1989, J1B).

5. A. J. Liebling, "The Line," *New Yorker*, 24 July 1937, 20–25.

6. "Imp's Great Race in the Suburban," *New York Times*, 18 June 1899, 1.

7. "Betting Commissioners," *Washington Post*, 14 August 1904, 3. At Terrazas Park in Juarez in 1910, pari-mutuels were installed in the grandstand after women complained they were not receiving a square deal from the messengers that carried their wagers to the bookmakers ("Passes Up Pari-Mutuel," *Pittsburgh Post-Gazette*, 26 December 1910, 10).

8. "Poor Luck at Aqueduct: Starter Pettingill Left the Favorite Rey Del Tierre at the Post," *New York Times*, 27 July 1897, 3.

9. "John Cavanagh, Racing Official," obituary, *New York Times*, 24 November 1937, 23.

7. TIPSTERS AND TOUTS

1. "Monmouth Park Looking to Bar Touts," *New York Times*, 18 February 1888, 3.

2. "Tipsters in Trouble," *New York Daily Tribune*, 9 June 1904, 2.

3. Seebohm Rowntree, ed., *Betting and Gambling: A National Evil* (London: Macmillan, 1905), 225–27.

4. Rowntree, *Betting and Gambling*, 233; Frank G. Menke, "Horse Racing Certain Bet," *Fort Wayne News*, 13 January 1915, 8; Mark Clapson, *A Bit of a Flutter: Popular Gambling in English Society, 1823–1961* (Manchester, UK: Manchester University Press, 1992), 117.

5. "Racing Tipsters Have Superseded the Old Tout," *St. Louis Republic*, 30 November, 1902, 12(II).

6. "Getting 'Tips' on the Races: Touts Who Sell Sure Things," *Washington Post*, 30 June 1907, 3(M). This article first appeared in the *Chicago Record-Herald*.

7. "Post Office Downs Racing Tipsters," *New York Times*, 24 June 1908, 1.

8. George Graham Rice, *My Adventures with Your Money* (Boston: Corham Press, 1913), 38.

9. "Arnold's Career on the Turf Brilliant for a Brief Time," *St. Louis Republic*, 12 February 1903, 2; "Collapse of Turf Investment Bubble Wipes Out the Savings of Thousands," *St. Louis Republic*, 15 February 1903, 9.

10. "No Turf Bills Enacted," *New York Times*, 15 May 1936, 32.

11. "86 Are Indicted by Saratoga Grand Jury in Race Tip Racket," *New York Times*, 3 December 1935, 1; "Race Tipsters Held in Raids," *St. Petersburg Evening Independent*, 23 March 1938, 16; "Huge Raid: Tip Office Raided," *Los Angeles Times*, 24 March 1938, 8.

12. Michael Madden, "Slyly Touted, for Bettor or Worse, It's Big Business," *Boston Globe*, 28 November 1981, 1; Bart Barnes, "Friendly Wagers to Big Bookmaking," *Washington Post*, 18 January 1982, D1; Timothy Bannon and Gregory Gordon, "Illegal Sports Tipsters Scams," *Las Vegas Sun*, 31 March 1985, 1,2(A); Lawrence Van Gelder, "Practicing the Art and Artifice of Picking Winners," *New York Times*, 19 January 1986, 12(L).

13. Phil Mushnick, "Scamdicappers Hit with $40G in Fines," *New York Post*, 8 February 1990, 77.

14. Hal Lancaster, "Here's a Tip: Sports-Tip Services Rarely Fulfill a Gambler's Dreams," *Wall Street Journal*, 24 October 1985, 1; Frederick C. Klein, "On Sports: Tips on Tipsters," *Wall Street Journal*, 2 October 1982, 12(A); Arne K. Lang, *Sports Betting 101* (Las Vegas: GBC Press, 1992), 150–56.

15. Jerry Fox and Karl J. Mayer, "Assessing Sports Advisory Services: Do They Provide Value for Football Bettors?," *UNLV Gaming Research Journal* 11, no. 2, 25.

16. In 1987, an informal survey by sociologist James H. Frey and law school professor I. Nelson Rose placed the number of sports betting advisory services at between six and seven hundred (James H. Frey and I. Nelson Rose, "The Role of Sports Information Services in the World of Sports Betting," *Arena Review*, May 1987, 44–51). While documentation is lacking, the number has declined and concomitantly there's been a sharp reduction in the number of salesmen employed by the major boiler room firms. With a wealth of information and opinions galore available free on the Internet, fewer people are inclined to pay for picks. Firms of the stripe once prominent in Saturday morning cable TV infomercials have been subject to scathing reviews by disgruntled customers whose voices were muted before the advent of Internet forums.

8. BIG PLUNGERS AND OUTLAWS

1. "Betting Ring Fortunes," *New York Times*, 15 July 1900, 16; "Gossip of the Turf," *Daily Racing Form*, 22 July 1902. 1; "Racing on the Pacific Coast," *Washington Sunday Star*, 1 September 1907, 4(5). Perhaps these figures should be taken with a grain of salt. Bookmaking was a precarious profession but reporters may have exaggerated the thinning-out, just as they exaggerated the winnings of big plungers on their best days. There is an oft-repeated story of a racetrack bookmaker who was forever crying that he was losing his shirt. "Then why continue?" he was asked. "Well," he replied, "a fellow has to make a living."

2. "Made Biggest Book in Ring," *Brooklyn Eagle*, 28 February 1902, 17.

3. The term "plunger" originally denoted a person whose wagers were out of proportion to his means. In time the term was extended to anyone betting an enormous sum.

4. Lloyd Wendt and Herman Kogan, *Bet a Million! The Story of John W. Gates* (New York: Bobbs-Merrill, 1948), 243. See also J. B. Sheridan, "Great Bettors of the Running Turf," *Ogden Standard*, Sunday magazine section, 14 July 1917, 1.

5. Nixola Greeley-Smith, "Mrs. Drake Bets $5, Mr. Drake Bets More," *St. Paul Globe*, 5 October 1902, 16.

6. "Plunger 'Pittsburgh Phil,'" *Washington Post*, 7 August 1904, 66; "Plungers Go Down and Out," *San Antonio Gazette*, 30 March 1907, 5.

7. "Hollywood Turf Club Opens Summer Racing Here Today," *Los Angeles Times*, 10 June 1938, 15(A).

8. *New Orleans Daily Picayune*, "The Premier Plunger," 29 September 1895, 19.

9. Henry V. King, "Death Takes Noted Gambler When 'Chicago' O'Brien Dies," *Youngstown Vindicator*, 9 August 1931, 14.

10. E. J. Edwards, "Richard Croker as 'Boss' of Tammany," *McClure's Magazine*, volume 5, November 1895, 548.

11. Rev. John L. Scudder, "The Gambling Fraternity," *Independent*, 5 January 1893, 3.

12. "Under the Guise of Racing," *New York Times*, 17 September 1894, 3.

13. The primary owner of the Guttenberg track, Gottfried Walbaum, parlayed his earnings into the controlling interest of Saratoga, over which he rode herd for almost ten years. A good rendering of the Walbaum years at Saratoga appears in Jon Bartels, *Saratoga Stories: Gangsters, Gamblers, and Racing Legends* (Lexington, KY: Blood-Horse Publications, 2007), 107–24.

14. For a more thorough discussion see Steven A. Riess, "Politics and the Turf in New Jersey, 1870–94," in *The Sport of Kings and the Kings of Crime* (Syracuse, NY: Syracuse University Press, 2011), 101–36.

15. "Spurred by Electricity," *San Francisco Morning Call*, 8 April 1892, 2; "A Jockey's Scheme," *Maysville (KY) Evening Bulletin*, 26 November 1892, 4. Roby was a largely undeveloped sliver of land on the south shore of Lake Michigan in Lake County, Indiana. During the years immediately preceding and following the 1893 World's Fair, the county became known for sheltering illicit activities chased out of Chicago. Writing in 1892, a reporter described Lake County as "a center of infamy for the scum of a great city" ("An Insult to Indiana," *Chicago Inter-Ocean*, 16 November 1892, 10).

16. "Stewards Still Investigating New Orleans Steeplechase," *St. Louis Republic*, 22 February 1901, 4.

17. "Who Got the Pool Money?," *Boston Daily Globe*, 15 October 1883, 10.

18. "Tapping the Bookies Bar'l," *Omaha Daily Bee*, 4 April 1896, 12; "Pool-Rooms Lose $100,000 to Band of Wire-Tappers," *New York Evening World*, 5 July 1906, 1.

9. THE REFORMERS CRANK UP THE HEAT

1. Anthony Comstock, *Traps for the Young* (New York: Funk & Wagnalls, 1893), 111–23.

2. "Anthony Comstock Dies in his Crusade," *New York Times*, 22 September 1915, 1.

3. Anthony Comstock, "Pool Rooms and Pool Selling," *North American Review* 157, November 1893, 610.

4. Allan Carlson, "Pure Visionary: The Life and Times of Anthony Comstock, Moral Crusader," *Touchstone*, June 2009 (no pagination). Comstock's views enjoyed wide currency in England where long-standing anti-gambling societies were increasingly focusing their efforts on horse racing. In 1907, England prohibited off-course betting. The law was overturned in 1960.

5. "Mr. Comstock's Raid on Brighton Beach," *Philadelphia Times*, 25 September 1883, 2; "Suppressing Gambling," *Maysville (KY) Evening Bulletin*, 5 August 1886, 3.

6. "The Saratoga Season," *Brooklyn Daily Eagle*, 8 August 1886, 14.

7. "Gay Saratoga," *Philadelphia Times*, 15 August 1886, 9.

8. "Anthony Comstock's Service," *New York Times*, 23 September 1915, 8.

9. "Dr. Parkhurst Speaks Out," *New York Times*, 14 March 1892, 1.

10. Timothy J. Gilfoyle, *City of Eros: New York City, Prostitution, and the Commercialization of Sex, 1790–1920* (New York: W.W. Norton & Company, 1992), 252.

11. "Canfield's Place Raided by Mr. Jerome's Axemen," *New York Times*, 2 December 1902, 1; "Canfield Sues Jerome," *New York Times*, 16 December 1902, 1. See also "Canfield to Be Respected Father," *El Paso Herald*, 5 January 1911, 1, 3. The Canfield Casino was purchased by the village of Saratoga Springs in 1911. A treasured landmark, it houses the Saratoga History Museum.

12. Alexander Gardiner, *Canfield* (Garden City, NY: Doubleday, Doran, 1930); "Poolroom Raids Sweep City," *New York Tribune*, 21 May 1904, 1.

13. "Poolroom Raids Sweep City," 1.

14. Albert Shaw, "Policy-Shops and Pool-Rooms," *American Monthly Review of Reviews* 29, no. 6 (June 1904), 756–57.

15. "Partnership with Crime," *Boston Evening Transcript*, 12 May 1904, 9.

16. Richard O'Connor, *Courtroom Warrior: The Combative Career of William Travers Jerome* (Boston: Little, Brown and Company, 1963), 5.

17. O'Connor, *Courtroom Warrior*, 5.

18. O'Connor, *Courtroom Warrior*, 14.

19. "Election Bets Denounced as Indirect Propaganda," *New York Times*, October 17, 1926, 10(XX).

10. RACETRACKS IN THE CROSSHAIRS

1. "Attack on Race Tracks," *New York Daily Tribune*, 23 May 2007, 14.

2. "Sterilized Betting to Rule Race Tracks," *New York Times*, 17 March 1906, 2.

3. See *Reform Bulletin*, 1, no. 13 (1 April 1910), 4

4. "Preparing for the Races," *New York Times*, 21 May 1877, 8.

5. "Monmouth's Little Games," *New York Times*, 20 July 1893, 8; "Will Discourage Gambling by Women," *Chicago Daily Tribune*, 16 April 1905, S1; "Gossip of the Racing Game," *San Francisco Call*, 17 November 1907, 34; "Gossip of the Track," *San Francisco Call*, 2 May 1908, 13.

6. Edgar Fawcett, "A Paradise of Gamblers," *Arena*, November 1891, 641.

7. "Bingham Wants a New Force of Detectives," *New York Times*, 8 January 1907, 16; "Would Curb Immigration," *New York Sun*, 21 July 1907, 5.

8. "Wrong about Jews, Bingham Admits," *New York Times*, 17 September 1908, 16.

9. "English Betting Bill Abandoned; Gambling Spirit Hard to Curb," *New Orleans Daily Picayune*, 15 March 1913, 12.

10. "Racing Sport a Fixture," *New York Evening World*, 9 March 1906, 14.

11. *New York Evening World*, 5 January 1907, 7.

12. "Highball Wins American Derby," *Chicago Daily Tribune*, 19 June 1904, 1; "Big Race Track Closed," *Philadelphia Record*, 22 June 1904, 9.

13. "No Booking at Bennings, so Crowd Is Small," *New York Evening World*, 16 November 1906, 1.

14. "Governor Moore Signs Amis Bill," *Daily Racing Form*, 28 February 1907, 1; "Unique Hot Water Spa," *Waterloo Semi Weekly Reporter*, 19 November 1907, 6.

15. "No Racing in Tennessee," *Daily Racing Form*, 26 January 1907, 1.

11. NEW YORK RACING

1. "Betting on Thaw Verdict," *Meriden (CT) Daily Journal*, 16 February 1907, 9. These were the odds found at a poolroom in Chicago: acquittal, 3/1; convicted of first-degree murder and sentenced to death, 5/1; convicted of a lesser degree of murder or manslaughter, 2/1; declared insane, 2/1.

2. "New Jerome Crusade on Race-Track Betting," *New York Times*, 14 January 1907, 1; "Jerome's Hard Hand," *Boston Evening Transcript*, 21 January 1907, 9.

3. "Record Crowd Sees Nealon, at 20 to 1, win the Great Suburban," *New York Evening World*, 20 June 1907, 1.

4. "Racing Last Year Paid $246,429 Tax," *New York Times*, 13 January 1908, 5. See also *Daily Racing Form*, "Racing Statistics," 5 January 1908, 1.

5. "Gov. Hughes Declares War on Racetracks; Betting Must Stop," *New York Evening World*, 1 January 1908, 1, 2.

6. "No Tammany War on Racing Reform," *New York Times*, 4 February 1908, 3. See also Robert F. Wesser, *Charles Evans Hughes: Politics and Reform in New York, 1905–1910* (Ithaca, NY: Cornell University Press, 1967), 189–208.

7. "Hughes Talks to Crowd about the Anti-Racing Bill," *Lexington Herald*, 20 April 1908, 1.

8. Methodist and Presbyterian ministers were at the forefront of the movement. Roman Catholic and Jewish leaders tended to be lukewarm or indifferent. However, within these faiths one also found clerics who were fervently opposed to racetrack gambling. Hughes had staunch allies in the fight to overturn the Percy-Gray law in Rabbi Stephen S. Wise, the founder of the Free Synagogue, a pillar of Reform Judaism, and Martin Meyer, the head of a Reform congregation in Brooklyn. A later campaign directed at poolrooms was led by Rabbi Herbert Goldstein, the spiritual leader of an Orthodox synagogue in Harlem. Asserting that horse parlors were spreading like weeds in a thirty-block corridor of upper Manhattan, Goldstein called on the authorities to take action in "the interest of moral purification" ("Rabbi Goldstein Condemns Police," *New York Times*, 19 May 1922, 22). Cardinal James Gibbons, the archbishop of Baltimore, had cordial relations with several racetrack operators, James Butler and Col. Matt Winn among them. Gibbons, who famously sided with the wets on the issue of prohibiting the sale and manufacture of alcohol— he argued that Prohibition would cause more problems than it solved—would not lend his voice to the anti-racetrack-gambling movement. His posture was very useful in the fight to preserve thoroughbred racing in Maryland. James H. Blenk, the archbishop of New Orleans, had an altogether different perspective. In 1910, when the Louisiana legislature was considering a bill to restore racing in New Orleans, Monsignor Blenk declared that racetrack gambling was a plague worse than yellow fever ("Political Row over Racing Game," *Cincinnati Enquirer*, 4 June 1910, 9). The historian Samuel McSeveney noted that one reason why leaders of the Roman Catholic and Jewish faiths were rarely seen at antigambling rallies in New Jersey during the late nineteenth century was because they weren't invited (Samuel T. McSeveney, *The Politics of Depression: Political Behavior in the Northeast, 1893–1896* [New York: Oxford University Press, 1972], 47).

9. "Victory for Law and Order; Foelker a Hero, says Hughes," *New York Evening World*, 11 June 1908, 2; "Gambling Fight Won," *New York Daily Tribune*, 12 June 1908, 7.

10. "Police to Clear the Betting Ring," *Brooklyn Daily Eagle*, 13 June 1908, 1; "Bet Laws in Force," *Pittston Gazette*, 13 June 1908, 1.

11. "Keep Up Betting Ban," *New York Times*, 1 September 1908, 8; "Racing's Lost Revenue," *New York Times*, 14 December 1908, 7.

12. "Last Knell Sounded for New York Racing," *Washington Times*, 5 November 1908, 4.

13. "Racing in England," *Otago (NZ) Witness*, 26 May 1909, 56.

14. "Gossip of the Racetrack," *New York Sun*, 26 October 1908, 8.

15. "The Anti-Lottery Decision," *Chicago Tribune*, 3 February 1892, 4; "The Lottery Killed," *New York Times*, 5 February 1892, 4.

16. Henry Brolaski, *Easy Money* (Cleveland: Searchlight Press, 1911), 124-25.

17. "100,000 in New York Playing the Races," *New York Times*, 15 December 1909, 5; "Gives Mann List of Tennes Allies," *Chicago Daily Tribune*, 3 March 1911, 3. In his book, Brolaski conceded that some horseplayers actually did come out ahead, roughly 5 percent by his reckoning.

18. "Governor Hughes's Annual Message," *New York Daily Tribune*, 6 January 1910, 9.

19. "Racetrack Bills Passed," *New York Sun*, 27 May 1910, 2. Smith distanced himself from the sporting crowd as he moved up the political ladder. As governor of New York, he refused to sign a bill legalizing prizefighting until he was assured that it wouldn't provoke an assault on his character by Protestant church groups.

12. THE GOOD-BYE YEARS

1. "Affairs of Special Interest to Breeders of Thoroughbred Horses," *Lexington Herald*, 6 October 1908, 9.

2. "Losses Will Mount into the Millions," *New York Times*, 12 June 1908, 2.

3. "Big Shrinkage in Racers," *Daily Racing Form*, 13 January 1913, 1; see also Henry Sedley, "The Hard Case of the Thoroughbred," *Outing* 52, May 1913, 188–93, and "Woman Manages Famous Breeding Farm," *San Francisco Call Sunday Magazine*, 12 January 1913, 11.

4. "Betting Syndicate Menaces Baseball," *Washington Herald*, 28 February 1911, 9.

5. "Editorial Takes Whack at Betting on Baseball," *Scranton Republican*, 3 April 1912, 1; "Governor Trying to Free State of Baseball Gambling," *Pittston Gazette*, 3 April 1912, 8.

6. "30 Bettors Barred or Arrested at Baseball Fields," *New York World*, 16 June 1913, 1; "Bar Way to Gamblers at Polo Grounds," *New York World*, 17 June 1913, 1; "Capital Seems to Be Free from the Pools," *Washington Times*, 29 May 1915, 14.

7. "Ball Pool Chiefs Under Arrest," *Scranton Republican*, 16 July 1915, 2.

8. "Gambling Hits Game," *Chicago Eagle*, 25 August 1917, 7. Fullerton would be credited with unearthing the Black Sox scandal.

9. "Remount Needs of the Army," *Daily Racing Form*, 15 February 1912, 1.

10. "Thousands Cheer Revival of Racing," *New York Tribune*, 31 May 1913, 1. See also "Metropolitan Press Gives Its Hearty Approval to New Racing Era on New York Tracks," *Daily Racing Form*, 3 June 1913, 1.

13. REANIMATION

1. "Decision Is Far Reaching," *Daily Racing Form*, 23 February, 1913, 1.

2. Colonel Matt J. Winn with Frank Menke, *Down The Stretch* (New York: Smith and Durrell, 1945), 69–94.

3. For more on the evolution of totalizators, see Bob Doran, "The First Automatic Totalisator," *Rutherford Journal* 2 (2006–2007), available at http://rutherfordjournal.org/article020109.html.

4. "Gamblers Open Shop for First Play since Rosenthal Murder," *New York World*, 27 July 1912, 1.

5. Arthur H. Labaree, "Will Drinking Die as Gambling Did?," *New York Tribune Sunday Magazine*, 21 August 1921, 1; see also "Gambling 'System' Routed by Bingham," *New York Times*, 21 June 1908, 1.

6. "Billiards Blue Laws," *New York Times*, 6 March 1921, 85; see also Ned Polsky, *Hustlers, Beats, and Others* (Chicago: Aldine Publishing Company, 1967).

7. Doyle opened his billiards parlor in 1910 in partnership with New York Giants manager John J. McGraw and famous jockey Tod Sloan. Asked to name the biggest betting events of his lifetime, he named the 1916 presidential contest between Woodrow Wilson and Charles Evans Hughes, followed by the 1935 fight between Joe Louis and Max Baer (Jack Cuddy, "A Tribute to Jack Doyle," *Delaware County Daily Times*, 10 December 1942, 29).

8. "Comment on Current Events in Sports," *New York Times*, 20 October 1919, 19.

9. Elmer Davis, "Papyrus Fails from Start," *New York Times*, 21 October 1923, 1, 3; see also Braven Dyer, "The Sports Parade," *Los Angeles Times*, 22 May 1938, 13(A).

10. "Judge's Ruling Gives Chicago Racing; Decision Puts Official OK on Oral Betting," *Chicago Daily Tribune*, 20 April 1924, 1.

11. "Turf Revival Creates Race Center Here," *Chicago Daily Tribune*, 18 July 1926, 4(A); French Lane, "Finish Plans for Homewood Races, Betting," *Chicago Daily Tribune*, 27 June 1926, 1(A); "Race Bill Passed; Sent to Governor," *Chicago Daily Tribune*, 19 May 1927, 15.

12. "California on Turf Map," *Los Angeles Times*, 22 November 1923, 3(III).

13. "Ponies to Run Some Time Yet," *Los Angeles Times*, 9 December 1920, 1(II); "San Diego Has Police Fight on 280 Bookmakers," *Monroe News Star*, 16 April 1928, 18.

14. A VERDANT DEPRESSION

1. "Agua Caliente Course Opens," *Los Angeles Times*, 28 December 1929, 6.

2. R. L. Duffus, "Gambling Instinct Gets New Outlet," *New York Times*, 22 April 1934, 2(XX); "37,281 Attend Narragansett Track Opening," *Chicago Daily Tribune*, 2 August 1934, 24.

3. "Fans Wager $15,896,365," *Los Angeles Times*, 20 March 1935, 25, Bryan Field, "Definite Upturn Is Indicated by Success of Eastern Racing," *New York Times*, 2 December 1935, 29.

4. "The American Derby," *Chicago Daily Tribune*, 25 June 1893, 2.

5. Bob and Barbara Freeman with Jim McKinley, *Wanta Bet? A Study of the Pari-Mutuels System in the United States* (Loveland, CO: Freeman Mutuels Management, 1982), 240–43.

6. Westbrook Pegler, "Crowd Cheers Sande's Third Derby Victory," *Chicago Tribune*, 18 May 1930, 1(A).

7. "Like Repeal, Betting Reforms Are Coming," *Brooklyn Daily Eagle*, 20 December 1933, 22.

8. "Thousands Crowd Betting Ring, Swamping Jamaica Bookmakers," *New York Times*, 22 April 1934, 1, 3; Bryan Field, "Changes Planned in Betting Ring," *New York Times*, 23 April 1934, 23; "Here and There on the Turf," *Daily Racing Form*, 11 May 1934, 2.

9. "Report for 1934 Reveals Great Strides Made by Racing in New York State," *New York Times*, 26 November 1934, 22; Joe Williams, "The State's Duped," *Pittsburgh Press*, 18 December 1934, 31.

10. See Bob Ruck, Maggie Jones Patterson, and Michael P. Weber, *Rooney: A Sporting Life* (Lincoln: University of Nebraska Press, 2010), 117–35. In some of the retellings, it would be asserted that Rooney quit betting after his remarkable run. This is baloney. What is true is that the elimination of fixed-odds betting led him to severely curtail his wagers. A fixture at the Kentucky Derby for more than fifty years, Rooney yet maintained that racetracks lost their charm when the bookies left the scene.

11. See "Vote Yes to Horse Racing in New Jersey, 1939" *Colin's Ghost*, 26 January 2012, http://colinsghost.org/2012/01/vote-yes-to-horse-racing-in-new-jersey-1939.html.

12. "Bookies Out," *Washington Court House Herald*, 29 January 1934, 7.

13. "Racing Bill Draft Bars All 'Bookies,'" *New York Times*, 22 March 1940, 12.

14. Bryan Field, "Swope in Annual Report Hails New York Turf Gains Resulting from Mutuels," *New York Times*, 2 January 1941, 29. See also, Toney Betts, *Across the Board* (New York: Citadel Press, 1956), 52–53.

15. Field, "Swope in Annual Report," 29.

15. A SIDE TRIP TO THE WINDY CITY

1. "Gambling in Chicago," *Chicago Tribune*, 4 May 1871, 3.

2. "Betting as a Fine Art," *Chicago Daily Tribune*, 23 September 1877, 4.

3. "All Going to Roby," *Chicago Daily Tribune*, 16 January 1898, 4; "Militia May Storm Gamblers' Stockade," *Chicago Inter Ocean*, 3 May 1905, 1; "'Blind John' Condon Is Dead; Once Leader on Racetracks," *Chicago Daily Tribune*, 10 August 1915, 10.

4. "Gambling Ship Chased; Escaped," *Chicago Daily Tribune*, 4 August 1905, 1; "Gambling Boats Ruled off the Great Lakes," *Lexington (KY) Herald*, 11 July 1907, 8.

5. "Try to Foil Gamblers," *Grand Forks Daily Herald*, 10 August 1906, 2.

6. "Tennes to Start Rival Lake Boat," *Chicago Daily Tribune*, 1 July 1906, 7.

7. John Landesco, *Organized Crime in Chicago, Part III of the Illinois Crime Survey 1929* (Chicago: University of Chicago Press, 1968), 59.

8. "Tennes' Pal tells Inside Story of Chicago Gaming," *Chicago Daily Tribune*, 27 August 1911, 1; "Tennes Will Aids Boys," *New York Times*, 7 September 1941, 38; see also Richard Lindberg, *Chicago Ragtime* (South Bend, IN: Icarus Press, 1985), 177–213.

9. "Relief Board Boosts Costs as Funds Dwindle," *Chicago Daily Tribune*, 3 March 1934, 8; see also Roger Biles, "Edward J. Kelly: New Deal Machine

Builder," in *The Mayors*, ed. Paul M. Green and Melvin G. Holli (Carbondale: Southern Illinois University Press, 1987), 111–25.

10. "Weekly Fines Are Proposed for Bookmakers at Resorts," *Tipton Daily Tribune*, 22 March 1935, 1.

11. "Burgess Fights Club's Plea for Gambling Veto," *Chicago Daily Tribune*, 29 June 1935, 5; "Crime Fighters Back Bookie Licensing Bill," *Chicago Daily Tribune*, 1 May 1941, 19.

12. Percy Wood, "Handbook Bill Vetoed," *Chicago Daily Tribune*, 12 July 1935, 1. In 1957, Illinois governor William Stratton expressed a somewhat similar sentiment when he vetoed a bill that would have permitted pari-mutuel betting at jai alai frontons. Stratton said he could not condone an activity that might serve as the gateway to legal sports betting ("No Jai Alai in Illinois," *Chicago Daily Tribune*, 7 July 1957, 24).

13. "12,158 Arrested in Bookie Raids: 12,152 Set Free," *Chicago Daily Tribune*, 12 January 1938, 2.

14. "Horse Betting Jurors Free a Bookie Cashier," *Chicago Daily Tribune*, 7 December 1937, 1.

15. Brad Lewis, "Chicago State's Attorney Makes Smashing Drive on Rackets," *Edwardsville Intelligencer*, 25 August 1938, 1; "Political Fight Is Behind Ax Raids of Chicago Bookies," *Kansas City Star*, 30 August 1938, 7.

16. Many of these bulletins were informally known by the color of the paper on which they were printed. For example, race-goers referenced the *Chicago Daily Telegraph* as the "pink sheet." The sheets were cheap to manufacture and on a major racing day a vendor might sell a thousand. Annenberg's tip sheets were published by the printing firm owned by Charles W. Bidwell. A major stockholder in Annenberg's operations, the politically powerful Bidwell would be best remembered for the NFL team that he founded, the Cardinals.

17. Drew Pearson and Robert S. Allen, "Washington Merry-Go-Round," *Nevada State Journal*, 9 August 1939, 4.

18. "Handbook Making Called a Lottery in Annenberg Case," *New York Times*, 31 August 1939, 1, 13; "Annenberg Gets 3 Years in Prison for Tax Evasion," *Chicago Tribune*, 2 July 1940, 8. Books that delve into the life of Moses Annenberg lean heavily on a series of four articles that appeared in consecutive issues of *Collier's Weekly*. Written by John T. Flynn, the first installment of the "Smart Money" series ran on January 13, 1940. Annenberg agreed to a plea deal with the IRS to protect his then thirty-one-year-old son, Walter, who was dropped from the case as a codefendant. Walter Annenberg diversified his father's publishing empire. The youngest child and only son among Moses Annenberg's eight children, Walter devoted the last few decades of his long life to honoring his father's memory through philanthropy. The Annenberg School for Communication at the University of Pennsylvania and

the Annenberg School for Communication & Journalism at the University of Southern California stand as testaments to his largesse.

19. Westbrook Pegler, "Fair Enough," *Pittsburgh Press*, 9 July 1940, 17.

20. "Horse Race Betting Suffers Slump; Bookies Keep Plugging," *Lewiston (ID) Daily Sun*, 17 November 1939, 15; *Los Angeles Times*, "Race Broadcast Curb Sought," 23 April 1940, 7.

21. "Chicago Police Hunt Mobsters in Turf Shooting," *Belvidere Daily Republican*, 25 June 1946, 1; Clayton Kirkpatrick, "Gun Blasts That Killed Ragen Still Echo in Crime Annals," *Chicago Daily Tribune*, 10 October 1950, 1.

16. MID-CENTURY REFORMERS

1. Harold Conrad, "Pari-Mutuels Open to Eager Throng," *Brooklyn Daily Eagle*, 15 April 1940, 1; Joe Williams, "Jamaica Owners . . . Seem a Little Greedy," *Pittsburgh Press*, 16 April 1940, 21.

2. "Mayor Denounces Gambling in State," *New York Times*, 16 April 1940, 23.

3. "Lehman Ignored Facts in Geoghan Ruling, Jury Says in Protest," *Brooklyn Daily Eagle*, 26 September 1936, 1; "Geoghan Would Cut Kings From The City," *New York Times*, 13 May 1937, 27. The Grand Jury recommended that Geoghan be removed, but Governor Herbert Lehman took no action. Geoghan left office in 1939.

4. "Munns in Syndicate to Purchase Track," *Palm Beach Post*, 9 September 1941, 6.

5. Toney Betts, *Across the Board* (New York: Citadel Press, 1956), 108–11.

6. "La Guardia Appeals to Boys to Report Gambling Fathers," *St. Petersburg Evening Independent*, 16 September 1942, 2.

7. "645 Arrests Made in Gambling Drive," *New York Times*, 30 September 1942, 25; "Racing Sheet Ban includes 2 Dailies," *New York Times*, 6 October 1942, 25.

8. Walter Byers, "Big Ten Schools Winning in War against Bookies," *Sandusky Register*, 26 January 1945, 12.

9. "Crime Probe Gains More Support," *Daytona Beach Morning Journal*, 2 March 1950, 2.

10. Westbrook Pegler, "Fair Enough," *Reading (PA) Eagle*, 19 April 1950, 6.

11. Earl Brown, "The Racing Racket," *Life*, 5 May 1947, 112–14, 120–26; Ernest Havemann, "Gambling in the U.S.: *Life* Presents the Lowdown on the Nation's Biggest Racket," *Life*, 19 June 1950, 96–117, 121.

12. Thomas W. Hagan, "Syndicate of Cities vs. 'Syndicates,'" *Miami News*, 6 December 1949, 29. For a more thorough examination of the antecedents of

the Kefauver Commission see David G. Schwartz, *Cutting the Wire* (Reno: University of Nevada Press, 2005), chapter 2.

13. Thomas Patrick Doherty, *Cold War, Cool Medium: Television, McCarthyism, and American Culture* (New York: Columbia University Press, 2003), 115.

14. Drew Pearson, "Kefauver Clears O'Dwyer," *Daytona Beach Morning Journal*, 5 October 1958, 6(A).

15. Robert C. Ruark, "A Bum Rap," *Pittsburgh Press*, 18 August 1952, 13.

16. "Outlaw Race Wire Is Plan," *Milwaukee Journal*, 2 April 1951, 10.

17. Schwartz, *Cutting the Wire*, 124.

18. "Race Result News Curbs Are Hinted," *Reno Evening Gazette*, 28 February 1952, 8.

19. "The Law Serves You," *Chicago Daily Herald*, 10 December 1967, 24.

20. "Gambling Law Fails in Tax-Collecting Aim," *Salt Lake City Deseret News*, 21 May 1053, 6, Edward J. Mowery, "Wagering Act Is Sad Failure, Survey Shows," *Washington Post*, 1 April 1956, 1(A); "Gambling Tax Laws Ignored," *Wisconsin State Journal*, 24 August 1961, 24.

21. "Kefauver Raps Gambling Tax," *Eugene Register-Guard*, 19 December 1951, 2.

22. "Bookie Tax Crimps Racing-Paper Sale," *New York Times*, 17 November 1951, 1.

23. "The Mania to Bet on Sports," *Newsweek*, 6 June 1960, 41–45; see also Red Smith, "Exploring Some Myths about Sports Gambling," *Pasadena Independent*, 8 June 1960, 13.

24. President Kennedy's chief speechwriter and close confidant Theodore "Ted" Sorensen was the son of Christian Sorensen, an ardent foe of gambling. The elder Sorensen shut down Omaha's Ak Sar Ben track in 1929 while serving as Nebraska's attorney general. The track reopened in 1935 following Sorensen's failed gubernatorial bid. As was true of William Travers Jerome, Bobby Kennedy's preoccupation with gambling was grist for armchair psychoanalysts. Was his focus rooted in a felt need to distance himself and his siblings from his father, Joseph P. Kennedy, a notorious philanderer who had business dealings with ex-bootleggers and other questionable characters? During World War II, Joe Kennedy became the second-largest stockholder in Hialeah Park, a favorite hangout of alleged mobsters ("Joseph Kennedy Buys Bradley Hialeah Stock, Plans Little Activity," *Miami News*, 15 May 1943, 1B).

25. "U.S. Raids 30 Chicago Area 'Books,'" *Milwaukee Sentinel*, 10 April 1963, 1; "Gambling Raids in 13 States Net More Than 100 Arrests," *Tri-City (WA) Herald*, 3 May 1963, 11.

17. THE TAX MAN COMETH

1. "Legal Racing Bet Revenues Cited in Study," *Chicago Daily Tribune*, 12 November 1939, 20; "24 States Cut in on Race Betting," *Brownsville Herald*, 24 June 1948, 13.

2. "Memorial Day Race Crowds Set Records," *Salt Lake Tribune*, 31 May 1945, 8; Ralph Trost, "Betting Mark Set at Belmont," *Brooklyn Daily Eagle*, 23 September 1945, 23.

3. Joseph M. Sheehan, "Commission Asks Cut in Racing Tax," *New York Times*, 27 December 1946, 22.

4. "O'Dwyer to Fight Proposal by State Racing Commission for Repeal of Race Tax," *Oneonta Star*, 29 December 1948, 8; James Roach, "State Commission Again Asks Cut in Racing Taxes to Meet 'Alarming' Trend," *New York Times*, 22 December 1949, 32.

5. Quoted in Nelson Dunston's "Reflections," *Daily Racing Form*, 12 June 1953, 41. The National Association of Racing Commissioners was formed in January of 1934 at a meeting in Miami. Eight states were represented.

6. "Turf Betting Up," *Kansas City Times*, 21 December 1951, 25.

7. "Memorial Day Attendances Exceed Figure of 1951," *Daily Racing Form*, 31 May 1952, 48.

8. Stanley Levey, "Racing Now Virtual King of Sports, Topping Baseball in Gate Appeal," *New York Times*, 30 April 1953, 1, 23.

9. "Latest Type Totalisator Being Installed at Omaha," *Daily Racing Form*, 6 May 1953, 38.

10. "Race Betting Increases: U.S. Given Assist," *Chicago Daily Tribune*, 11 March 1952, 1(B); "Gambling Crackdown Credited with Boosting of Racing Attendance," *Oregon Statesman*, 11 March 1952, 9.

11. "Fla. Governor After Bookies," *Washington Post*, 19 February 1949, 13. (Fuller Warren was no friend of Estes Kefauver, who chastised him for taking large contributions from track operators with questionable business associates. In 1951, Warren vetoed a bill that would have made it unlawful to publish, sell, or possess wall charts, tip sheets, scratch sheets "or other items in furtherance of illegal gambling." As to charges that this was inconsistent with his anti-bookmaking posture, Warren countered that he could not support any legislation that would hurt racetrack profits. He was unseated in his bid for a second term by a candidate running on a reform platform.)

18. MULTIPLE-HORSE WAGERING
TAKES FLIGHT

1. "Flat Track Bets Set Record in '59," *New York Times*, 16 December 1959, 60.

2. Mary Matthew, "Santa Anita Opens, and . . . Nostalgia, Excitement, Reign," *Los Angeles Times*, 27 December 1960, 1(A).

3. "15% 'Take' Hit by Racing Board," *New York Times*, 24 December 1956, 11.

4. "Daily Double Restored by New York Race Courses, Effective Next Season," *New York Times*, 20 October 1948, 39. The last holdout was Santa Anita, which adopted daily double wagering at their 1961–1962 winter meet. Dr. Charles H. Strub, the general manager and co-owner of the Arcadia track, was opposed to daily doubles, quinellas, and "other contrivances designed to milk the last dollar out of the racing public" (*Los Angeles Times*, 14 September 1950, 4).

5. Charles Maher, "John S. Alessio, Shoe Shine Boy to Millionaire," *Los Angeles Times*, 20 April 1966, 1(C).

6. "Government Moves to Get Its Bite of Tax Winnings," *Ocala Star-Banner*, 20 September 1960, 7; "Multiple-Race Bets Popular," *Spokane Spokesman-Review*, 23 October 1960, 5; A. J. Snyder "Tax Hook Baited for Little Fish," *Frederick News*, 21 September 1976, 15. (Currently 25 percent is deducted from payouts of $5,000 or more if the odds were 300 to 1 or higher.)

7. "Bettors Anonymous Shun $46,177 Hore," *New York Times*, 4 October 1960, 1, 52.

8. Edward Ranzal, "Underworld Is Linked to Yonkers Raceway Fixing," *New York Times*, 9 January 1967, 28.

9. Lloyd E. Millegan, "State's Take Up; Bets, Crowds Down," *New York Times*, 13 December 1966, 80.

19. PRO FOOTBALL CORRODES
THE RACING GAME

1. Joseph Ator, "We Bet 5 Billion," *Chicago Daily Tribune*, 18 October 1936, 9(E).

2. Murray Schumach, "Betting: A $15 Billion Industry," *New York Times*, 15 January 1950, 9(E).

3. Emanuel Perlmutter, "250-Million 'Take' Laid to Bookie Rings in 5 Upstate Cities," *New York Times*, 21 April 1960, 1.

4. William Barry Furlong, "Of 'Lines,' 'Point Spreads,' and 'Middles,'" *New York Times Sunday Magazine*, 2 January 1977, 142; Robert H. Boyle, "The Brain That Gave Us the Point Spread," *Sports Illustrated*, 10 March 1986, 34; see also Boyle, "The Legal Whole's Legal Half," *Sports Illustrated*, 1 October 1956, 30–32, 59–63; personal correspondence with the late Louis Boasberg, the founding president of the New Orleans Novelty Company. (Among the rulings that have been traced to McNeil is the edict that a baseball pitcher must throw at least one pitch to be considered the starting pitcher for betting purposes. Over the years there have been several instances where a pitcher aggravated an injury while warming up and one bizarre case on July 17, 1960, when Cincinnati Reds hurler Don Newcombe got into a beef with the umpire during his warm-ups and was tossed from the game without facing a batter. Newcombe's name appeared in the box score that ran in all the papers, but this was adjudged a misprint.)

5. Henry McLemore, "Today's Sports Parade," *Harrisburg Evening News*, 24 December 1938, 8.

6. John Lardner, "Football Parlays Shown as Huge Gyp," *Lincoln Evening Journal*, 25 December 1934, 10; "What's Next in Skin Games," *Salem Daily Capital Journal*, 18 November 1939, 4.

7. Shirley Povich, "This Morning," *Washington Post*, 1 December 1944, 14. Nat Holman, the basketball coach at CCNY, waived off a free throw in the waning seconds of a 1945 match with Syracuse at Madison Square Garden so that it wouldn't land "7," the best-case scenario for the bookies. In those days, teams had the option of accepting a free throw or taking possession of the ball at mid-court ("Holman, CCNY Cage Coach, Beats Gamblers by Refusing Free Shot," *Amarillo Daily News*, 12 January 1945, 4).

8. Leo H. Petersen, "You Get 22 Points If You Like 'Skins,'" *Pittsburgh Press*, 11 December 1942, 8.

9. Carl Lundquist, "Sports Dopesters . . . Do Nothing but Read the Newspapers," *Nebraska State Journal*, 12 December 1948, 20; Bob Klaverkamp, "Sports Fans Cry, 'Smart Boys' Like Odds-Makers Odd System," *Lubbock Morning Avalanche*, 26 July 1957, 21.

10. Mort Olshan went on to found the venerable *Gold Sheet*, the granddaddy of all sports tip sheets. The unique twelve-panel newsletter, born in 1957, was designed to be concealed within the inside breast pocket of a suit jacket, standard working apparel for most of the early subscribers. Olshan willed the publication to longtime employees, who kept the operation going following his death in 2003.

11. Bill Shirley, "Gambling Information: It's a Tough Proposition: To Print It or Not to . . . ," *Los Angeles Times*, 4 November 1981, 1(D). Bobby Knight's take on this issue was widely quoted: "Right under the gambling line in the

paper, you ought to list whores' phone numbers. Call Cindy at 555-4410. Twenty-five dollars an hour. Then list all her strengths and weaknesses." The famously acerbic Knight spoke these words in 1981, the year that his Indiana team won the NCAA basketball tournament.

12. In the wake of the Kefauver hearings, Ed Curd was hounded for back taxes, ultimately agreeing to a $277,000 settlement. He took refuge in Quebec and then settled in the Bahamas, where he continued to make a daily baseball line. Before his troubles, Curd consorted openly with some of Kentucky's most prominent citizens. A. B. "Happy" Chandler, the Kentucky governor turned baseball commissioner, and Adolph Rupp, the iconic basketball coach, were frequent dinner companions. The author interviewed Curd when Curd was in his eighties and found him to be exactly as mutual acquaintances had depicted him: a courtly Southern gentleman.

13. Jack Hand, "'Equalization' Leads to NFL Boom," *Long Beach Independent Press-Telegram*, 8 February 1959, 42; Jack Cuddy, "Rumor Unitas Hurt Shakes Bookies," *Oakland Tribune*, 17 December 1959, 60; *Newsweek*, "$100 Million on One Game," 6 June 1960, 43.

20. NEW YORK WELCOMES OTB

1. "Legal Bookmaking again Introduced into Legislature," *Xenia Daily Gazette*, 21 November 1935, 16. "'Bookie' Bill Up to Governor," *Daily Racing Form*, 7 April 1937, 1; "Legalize California Books?" *Daily Racing Form*, 24 April 1937, 1.

2. Estes Kefauver, "Crime in America," *Kingsport Times-News*, 15 July 1951, 16(A). James J. Carroll was the second of three nationally prominent St. Louis bookmakers. He arrived on the scene after Tom Kearney and before C. J. "Kewpie" Rich. All three were heavily vested in future books and derived a large share of their play from wagers received by mail and telegraph. An employee of Rich, Bill Dark, went on to open a book in North Las Vegas where he would be credited with introducing totals—that is, over/unders, to Nevada's sports wagering menu.

3. Thomas P. Ronan, "Mayor Asks State to Legalize Bets on Sports Events," *New York Times*, 10 January 1950, 1; Leo Egan, "Dewey Denounces O'Dwyer Bet Plea as 'Immoral' Plan," *New York Times*, 17 January 1950, 1; "Dewey Kills Move for Off-Track Bets," *New York Times*, 1 April 1949, 1.

4. "Majority of Voters Favor Legal Off-Track Betting," *Troy Record*, 23 August 1951, 12.

5. "Swope Proposes New Betting Plan," *New York Times*, 20 June 1952, 25.

6. "Text of the Report on Off-Track Betting," *New York Times*, 7 February 1959, 9.

7. Steve Cady, "OTB's Telephone Room Good Line on the Future," *New York Times*, 23 June 1971, 33.

8. "Off-Track Bets Open Fast," *Spokane Spokesman-Review*, 9 April 1971, 2; Steve Cady, "Derby Action Swamps OTB," *New York Times*, 30 April 1971, 27.

9. Larry Simonberg, "Off Track Betting Booms in NYC," *Pacific Stars and Stripes*, 16 August 1972, 11.

10. Martin Tolchin, "5th Ave. Group Opposing OTB Parlor," *New York Times*, 21 April 1972, 78. OTB also encountered opposition in Harlem and other predominantly black neighborhoods where community leaders viewed it as an encroachment on the numbers game, a local institution ("CORE Attacks OTB Opening," *New York Amsterdam News*, 13 November 1971, 2C).

11. Steve Cady, "Portrait of an OTB Bettor: Male, Affluent, and Single," *New York Times*, 28 September 1971, 49; Gerald Eskenazi, "Rise in Illegal Gambling Linked to OTB Climate," *New York Times*, 10 January 1974, 1.

12. "Jimmy the Greek Says New York Off-Track Betting Bound to Succeed," *Dubuque Telegraph-Herald*, 11 November 1970, 26; Steve Cady, "Devastating Effects of OTB on Tracks, Tax Intake," *New York Times*, 18 November 1972, 45; Steve Cady, "Computerized Murder," *New York Times*, 2 January 1972, 8(S).

13. Thomas P. Ronan, "City Held Loser as Volume Falls," *New York Times*, 3 July 1974, 23.

14. Peter Kerr, "OTB's Bright Promise Fades to Uneasy Future," *New York Times*, 7 April 1986, 8(B).

15. Steve Cady, "Night Racing Breaks Into a Gallop at Meadowlands," *New York Times*, 7 September 1977, 98.

16. Eskenazi, "Rise in Illegal Gambling Linked to OTB Climate," 1.

17. Kerr, "OTB's Bright Promise"; Selwyn Raab, "O.T.B. Fails to Meet Revenue Goal and to Reduce Illegal Bookmaking," *New York Times*, 11 January 1979, 1(A).

18. "N.Y. OTB Is a Winner," *Washington Post*, 14 July 1995, 7(F).

19. Ryan Goldberg, "New York OTB: Remembering a City Icon," *Daily Racing Form* (digital edition), 7 February 2013. See also Irving Rudd with Stan Fischler, *The Sporting Life* (New York: St. Martin's Press, 1990), 172–86.

20. "Crackdown Nets a Bigtime Dade Bookie," *Miami News*, 19 December 1967, 5(A).

21. A SIDE TRIP TO OLD NEVADA

1. "What Reno Offers," *Meriden (CT) Daily Journal*, 9 March 1931, 5. (In 1910, according to the census bureau, 40,026 males of voting age resided in Nevada.)

2. George D. Cressey, "Gambling Law Bans Election Bets in State," *Las Vegas Age*, 15 November 1932, 1.

3. "Lower House Delays Vote on Race Bill," *Nevada State Journal*, 15 March 1941, 2; "Charge Hollen, Moore, Bowen Bookie Chiefs," *Bakersfield Californian*, 9 January 1941, 1.

4. "Editor Replies to Nevada Protest Letter," *Salt Lake Tribune*, 23 November 1948, 19. (See also Royce Feour, "Wagers on Nevada Banned in 1960," *Las Vegas Review-Journal*, 30 September 2002, 6C.)

5. "Tax Commission Lifts Licenses on Turf Clubs," *Reno Evening Gazette*, 2 December 1948, 1(B); "Tax Commission Aims to Clean Up Vegas Bookies," *San Bernardino Daily Sun*, 2 December 1948, 1, 4.

6. "Nevada Puts Controls on Bookmakers," *Salt Lake Tribune*, 17 December 1948, 33.

7. "Officials Own Interest in Nevada Joints," *Ogden Standard-Examiner*, 16 November 1950, 1. The state legislature expanded the duties of the Tax Commission to include overseeing gambling in 1945. The job of policing the industry was previously vested in the hands of county sheriffs.

8. "Vegas Race Book Robbed of $3800," *Nevada State Journal*, 30 May 1951, 8; "Lazy But Tough Thug Among 10 FBI Hunts Most," *Brooklyn Daily Eagle*, 27 June 1951, 7; "Extortion Plot Said to Explain Gang Execution," *San Bernardino County Sun*, 10 August 1951, 1.

9. "Most Nevada Bookies Quit," *Ogden Standard-Examiner*, 1 November 1951, 1.

10. "Nevada Politics by The Observer," *Nevada State Journal*, 9 December 1951, 13.

11. "Nevada Bookmakers May Stay in Business," *Nevada State Journal*, 9 April 1952, 10; "Nevada Bookies win a Victory," *San Rafael Daily Independent*, 29 December 1967, 23.

12. "Game Control Plan Faces Heavy Going," *Reno Evening Gazette*, 5 March 1953, 11.

13. "Old Nevada Statute Bars Election Betting," *Portsmouth Herald*, 3 November 1960, 1. According to published reports, the bookies opened Nixon a 7/5 favorite with Kennedy at even money. The early money was on Nixon, who was bet up to 11/5, but Kennedy money showed after each of the TV debates, notwithstanding the fact that most pundits thought Nixon won the second and third matches, overcoming a weak showing in the first of the three face-offs.

Shortly before betting was suspended in Nevada, Kennedy ruled the favorite at odds of 8/5 ("Election Bets," *Corpus Christi Caller-Times*, 1 November 1960, 15). JFK won the popular vote by a hair-thin margin but dominated the swing states, advancing to the White House with 58 percent of the electoral vote.

14. "Tax Cut Gives Legality a Chance Against Illegality in Nevada Betting," *New York Times*, 22 January 1975, 63.

15. "Bookmaking in Casinos; boon or 'can of worms'?" *Reno Evening Gazette*, 18 January 1975, 10.

16. "Gambler Fined for 'Fix' Try," *Delta Democrat-Times*, 8 December 1963, 5; Al Delugach and George Reasons, "Vegas Sheriff Aids Gambler," *Los Angeles Times*, 14 April 1977, 3, 27(B). (Rosenthal was ousted from his position as a Stardust executive in December of 1978 and placed in the Black Book, a list of individuals prohibited from setting foot in a Nevada casino. He died in 2008 at age 79 in Miami Beach.)

17. "Sports Betting Has Grown into a $1-Billion-a-Year Business," *Newburgh-Beacon (NY) Evening News*, 8 September 1985, 12(A). (The $8 million figure for 1974 should be taken with a grain of salt, as creative bookkeeping was rampant. A contributing factor in the declining "hold" was that some of the newer books were horribly mismanaged. The rapid proliferation of betting outlets outpaced the pool of competent people to run them.)

18. Stephen Nover, "Leroy's Expansion Raises Questions for Gaming Industry," *Las Vegas Review-Journal*, 21 April 1992, 1(E). See also Richard Zacks, "High-Tech Bookie: The Man who took Vegas by Computer," *Los Angeles Times Sunday Magazine*, 8 January 1989, 16. Salerno sold his operation lock-stock-and-barrel to British bookmaking company William Hill in 2011. The sale involved fifty-three books and nineteen self-service kiosks. Located primarily in taverns, the kiosks were outlawed in 2013 after successful lobbying by the Nevada Resort Association. Simultaneous with the acquisition, William Hill acquired two smaller betting chains, giving it 55 percent of Nevada's sports book market.

19. Chris Woodyard, "Simulcast Races Could Be Next Game Bonanza," *Gettysburg Times*, 8 June 1983, 25.

20. Bill Christine, "Simulcasts Fail to Hit the Jackpot," *Los Angeles Times*, 10 September 1985, 10(C).

22. SIMULCASTING

1. Steve Cady, "A Teletrack for Sports Betting," *New York Times*, 3 November 1979, 14.

2. "$135 Million Bet on Derby at Other Tracks, Off-Track Parlors," *Lexington Herald-Leader*, 6 May 1984, 1(A).

3. Andrew Beyer, "Laurel Renovations Signal Evolving Importance of Simulcasting," *Washington Post*, 13 October 1999, 12(D).

4. Steve Tartar, "OTB Parlor 'a dying situation,'" *Peoria Journal-Star* (digital edition), 23 September 2009.

23. LOTTERIES, CASINOS, AND RACINOS

1. "New Look in New Hampshire," *Corpus Christi Caller-Times*, 1 March 1964, 41.

2. "Delaware Makes Good on Cancelled Betting," *Lakeland (FL) Ledger*, 16 December 1976, 7(B); "Lottery Is Ordered to Pay Off," *New York Times*, 15 December 1976, 1(F).

3. "Delaware Lottery Closes in Uproar," *Ocala Star-Banner*, 19 December 1976, 4(C).

4. Kristin Goff, "Pro, College Representatives Talk against Lottery," *Hagerstown Daily Mail*, 17 November 1976, 48.

5. Ryan H. Sager, "Multi-State Lotteries Are a Bad Bet," *Wall Street Journal* (Eastern edition), 29 April 2001, 14(A). In 1983, University of Maryland philosophy professor Samuel Gorovitz proposed that a portion of lottery proceeds go to upgrading "the shamefully inadequate teaching in our schools about elementary probability and statistics" (*Los Angeles Times*, 31 March 1983, 7E). In Gorovitz's view, a person incapable of explaining and illustrating the principle of compound interest in simple layman's terms is suffering from a form of illiteracy.

6. "Clergy Back Casinos for New Jersey," *Milwaukee Journal*, 30 October 1976, 5.

7. Neil Milbert, "Do Casinos Pose Threat? You Bet," *Chicago Tribune*, 25 June 1992, 11.

8. Robert W. Wood, "Native American Casino and Tax Rules That May Surprise You," *Forbes* (digital edition), 11 October 2012.

9. "Kentucky Race Tracks Wary of Indiana Riverboats," *Logansport Pharos-Tribune*, 11 September 1995, 3(A).

10. Phil McManus, Glenn Albrecht, and Raewyn Graham, *The Global Horseracing Industry* (New York: Routledge, 2013), 69.

24. OFFSHORE AND ONLINE

1. Mark Asher, "On-line Bettors Take Their Chances, Reap the Rewards." *Washington Post*, 24 January 1998, 4(HO); David G. Schwartz, *Cutting the Wire* (Reno: University of Nevada Press, 2005), 181, 194.

2. Steven Crist, "All Bets Are Off," *Sports Illustrated*, 26 January 1998, 82.

3. Justin Matlick, "Green Felt Cyberspace," *Las Vegas Review-Journal*, 7 June 1998, 1(D).

4. Jack Boulware, "Online Pirates of the Caribbean," *San Francisco Weekly* (digital edition), 15 December 1999, 1–7; Tom Somach, "Fugitive S.F. Stockbroker Shot Dead in Caribbean," *San Francisco Examiner* (digital edition), 5 May 2013, no pagination. The Cohen trial is covered at length in Schwartz, *Cutting the Wire*, 204–15.

5. William Berlind, "Bookies in Exile," *New York Times Sunday Magazine*, 17 August 2003, 34–39; Angelo Cataldi and Glen Macnow, "Michael Roxborough Sets Bettors, Bookmakers, Handicappers, and Fans in Motion," *Philadelphia Inquirer* (digital edition), 10 December 1989; Matt Youmans, "Sports Betting: Guess Where the Big Bettors Spend Their Money?" *Casino City Times* (digital edition), 12 September 2005.

6. *San Mateo Times*, "7 Mateans Held in Gambling Net," 1 October 1971, 1; "Prison Term for Bookies in Bribery Case," *San Mateo Times*, 6 September 1973, 26.

7. Dorothy Townsend, "Mobile Bookie Ring Believed Broken with 12 L.A. Arrests," *Los Angeles Times*, 20 November 1982, 6(A); "Suspected Leader of Bookmaking Ring Arrested," *Los Angeles Times*, 28 June 1987, 30.

8. Seth Rosenfeld, "Alleged Bookie Is Charged," *Hutchinson News*, 16 August 1993, 18.

9. The author never met Ron Sacco. This brief portrait of him was drawn from interviews with former employees. When this book went to press, Sacco was no longer involved in the day-to-day operations of CRIS. He purportedly sold his equity in the company to his CEO, Michael Flynn III. A second-generation bookmaker from a prominent Pittsburgh-area family, Flynn is known by his alias, Mickey Richardson. Before this transition, CRIS's U.S. clients were moved to a sister company called Bookmaker.

10. Jeff Haney, "The New Face of Bookmaking," *Las Vegas Sun* (digital edition), 25 October 2000.

11. U.S. authorities seized the Bodog domain name in February of 2012. Several months prior to this action, Bodog's U.S. customers were transferred to its new Bovada brand.

12. Regarding the $43.65 million seizure, a prosecutor said the money properly belonged to U.S. taxpayers, since it would cost more than $44 million to

try the defendants (Hartley Henderson, "BetonSports Customers Can Expect Payments Starting in June," *Off Shore Gaming Association*, 23 December 2010). For a good rendering of the BetonSports soap opera, see Kristin Hinton, "Double Down," *St. Louis Riverfront Times* (online), 10 October 2007.

13. Dan Cypra, "Internet Gambling Expert Reacts to UIGEA Regulations Delay," *Poker News Daily* (online), 6 December 2009.

14. Michael McCarthy and Jon Swartz, "New Legislation May Pull the Plug on Online Gambling," *USA Today*, 3 October 2006, 18(A).

15. Andrew Beyer, "After Pinnacle, It's All Downhill from Here," *Washington Post*, 17 January 2007, 1(E).

16. Gilbert M. Paul, "Prohibition vs. Regulation Debated as U.S. Bettors Use Foreign Sites," *Washington Post*, 1 December 2008, 1(A).

17. David O. Stewart, "Online Gambling Five Years after UIGEA," American Gaming Association white paper, 1 May 2011, 4, available at https://www.americangaming.org/research/white-papers/online-gambling-five-years-after-uigea.

18. Patricia Kowsmann and Margot Patrick, "Betfair Shares Soar after IPO," *Wall Street Journal* (online), 22 October 2010.

25. WHALES

1. Joe Drape, "Horse Racing's Biggest Bettors Are Reaping Richest Rewards," *New York Times*, 26 April 2004, 1(A); Tom LaMarra, "Case Made for High-Volume Betting Services," *Bloodhorse.com*, 13 February 2012; see also Dan Seligman, "Revenge of the Horseplayers," *Forbes*, 2 April 2001, 90. (In Las Vegas, "whales" were predominantly Asian baccarat players.)

2. LaMarra, "Case Made for High Volume Betting Services."

3. Kirk Brooks's most prominent protégé is Jay Kornegay, who helms the race and sports book at Westgate, formerly the Las Vegas Hilton. Kornegay's longtime assistants, golf maven Jeff Sherman and NASCAR authority Ed Salmons, earned their spurs at the Imperial Palace where their oddsmaking skills were allowed to flourish. See Case Keefer, "Superbook's Jeff Sherman Makes Mark as Las Vegas Master of Golf Odds," *Las Vegas Sun* (digital edition), 10 April 2013.

4. An article in the *Review-Journal* said that 30–40 percent of the property's earnings came from the racing side of the book (Ed Vogel, "Another Mirage on the Strip," *Las Vegas Review-Journal*, 24 June 1998, 1). Brooks insists that the true figure was higher.

26. PUSHING THE ENVELOPE

1. "To Enforce the Laws," *New York Daily Tribune*, 12 June 1908, 2.

2. The extension of Internet betting beyond horse racing was made possible by a new reading of the Wire Act by the U.S. Department of Justice. The reinterpretation, announced in late December of 2011, said that the 1961 law was intended specifically for sports betting and that states were free to open other games to online wagering. Online gambling arrived in Delaware and New Jersey later that year. In New Jersey, a participant was required to establish an account with an Atlantic City casino.

3. For a look at the forces behind the immobilization, see Joseph F. Sullivan, "How Politics Nipped a Sports Betting Bill," *New York Times*, 2 January 1994, 25.

4. David G. Schwartz, *Atlantic City Gaming Revenue: Statistics for Casino, Slot, and Table Win, 1978–2013* (Las Vegas: Center for Gaming Research, University Libraries, University of Nevada, Las Vegas, 2014).

5. "Judge Rules Sports Betting Is Still Illegal in New Jersey," *New York Times*, 22 November 2014, 18(A).

6. Tom Corrigan, "Atlantic City's Revel Casino Files for Bankruptcy Again," *Wall Street Journal* (digital edition), 9 June 2014.

7. Harold Brubaker, "Casino Closings Have Big Impact on A.C. Property Tax Base," *Philadelphia Inquirer*, 19 January 2015 (digital edition); Brian Ianieri "Atlantic County Leads U.S. in Foreclosures," *Press of Atlantic City*, 16 April 2015 (digital edition); see also Eric O'Neill, "N.J.'s 'Zombie Foreclosure' Rate Highest in U.S.," *NJ Advance Media for NJ.com*, 11 June 2015 (digital edition).

8. Brett L. L. Abarbanel, Anthony F. Lucas, and Ashok K. Singh, "Estimating the Indirect Effect of Sports Books on Other In-House Gaming Volumes," *UNLV Gaming Research and Review Journal* 15, no. 2, 77–90.

9. Visitor profiles were culled from reports published online by the Convention and Visitors Authority of the respective cities.

10. David G. Schwartz, "Green Felt Journal: Sports Betting Hits It Big in the Casino Industry," *Vegas Seven*, 9 June 2015 (digital edition).

11. Adam Silver, "Legalize Sports Betting: Commentary," *New York Times*, 14 November 2014, 27(A).

12. David Purdum, "Silver: I'm Not Pro Sports Gambling, I'm Just a Realist," *ESPN the Magazine*, 16 February 2015, 55–58.

13. Joe Drape, "U.S. Court Rejects State Push for Betting," *New York Times*, 26 August 2015, 9(B).

14. Daniel Porter, "New Jersey Sports Gambling Suit Tab: $2.8 Mil, Rising," *Las Vegas Review-Journal* (digital edition), 4 May 2014.

15. Craig Anderson, "State Sports Lottery Keeps Running Up the Score," *Delaware State News* (digital edition), 2 February 2015. The odds were initially supplied by Brandywine LLC. Founded in 2008 by Delaware native Joe Asher, Brandywine operated a chain of Nevada books under the Lucky's brand. William Hill US inherited the Delaware operation when it acquired Brandywine in 2011. During the 2014 NFL season, the lottery experienced only one losing week.

16. College and pro football wagers accounted for 39.84 percent of the win. Parlay cards, devoted almost exclusively to football, accounted for an additional 9.84 percent (David G. Schwartz, *Nevada Sports Betting Totals: 1984–2013* [Las Vegas: Center for Gaming Research, 2014]); Hannah Dreier, "Fans Bet Record $119 Million on Super Bowl at Nevada Casinos," *Las Vegas Sun*, digital edition, 3 February 2014. There was a slight drop-off the next year when the Super Bowl pitted the Seahawks against the New England Patriots. The dip was attributed to the absence of a Money Line pool. The odds were even (11/10 "pick"), closing the door on this alternative method of betting the game.

17. Matt Jacob, "The Mainstreaming of Sports Betting," *Vegas Seven* (digital edition), 28 January 2014.

18. Pia Catton, "High Stakes for N.Y. Racing," *Wall Street Journal*, 31 May 2014, 15(A); Jerry Bossert and Michael O'Keeffe, "The Beaten Track: Aqueduct Was Once a Racing Jewel That Packed Them in, But Now the Big A Is a Den in Disrepair," *New York Daily News* (digital edition), 23 February 2014.

19. Eric Zorn, "The Grim Reality of Fantasy Sports," *Chicago Tribune*, 16 September 2015, 23.

BIBLIOGRAPHY

Adelman. Melvin L. *A Sporting Time: New York City and the Rise of Modern Athletics, 1820–70*. Urbana: University of Illinois Press, 1986.

Alexander, Michael. *Jazz Age Jews*. Princeton, NJ: Princeton University Press, 2001.

Alfange, Dean. *The Horse Racing Industry*. New York: Kensington Publishing Co., 1976.

Barker, Thomas, and Marjie Britz. *Jokers Wild: Legalized Gambling in the Twenty-First Century*. Westport, CT: Prager Publishers, 2000.

Bartels, Jon. *Saratoga Stories: Gangsters, Gamblers, and Racing Legends*. Lexington, KY: Blood-Horse Publications, 2007.

Bell, Daniel. *The End of Ideology*. New York: Free Press, 1960.

Beltran, David Jiminez. *The Agua Caliente Story*. Lexington, KY: Eclipse Press, 2004.

Betts, John R. *America's Sporting Heritage, 1850–1950*. Reading, MA: Addison-Wesley, 1074.

Betts, Toney. *Across the Board*. New York: Citadel Press, 1956.

Black, Conrad. *Franklin Delano Roosevelt: Champion of Freedom*. Cambridge, MA: Perseus Books, 2003.

Black, David. *The King of Fifth Avenue: The Fortunes of August Belmont*. New York: Dial Press, 1981.

Blanche, Ernest E. *Off to the Races*. New York: A.S. Barnes & Company, 1947.

Brolaski, Henry. *Easy Money: Being the Experiences of a Reformed Gambler*. Cleveland: Searchlight Press, 1911.

Broun, Heywood, and Margaret Leech. *Anthony Comstock: Roundsman of the Lord*. New York: A. and C. Boni, 1927.

Burbank, Jeff. *License to Steal: Nevada's Gaming Control System in the Megaresort Age*. Reno: University of Nevada Press, 2000.

Cameron, Colin. *You Bet: The Betfair Story and How Two Men Changed the World of Gambling*. London: HarperCollins, 2009.

Case, Carole. *The Right Blood: America's Aristocrats in Thoroughbred Racing*. New Brunswick, NJ: Rutgers University Press, 2001.

Chaftez, Henry. *Play the Devil: A History of Gambling in the United States*. New York: Bonanza Books, 1960.

Clapson, Mark. *A Bit of a Flutter: Popular Gambling and English Society*. Manchester, England: Manchester University Press, 1992.

Clark, Donald. *In the Reign of Rothstein*. New York: Vanguard Press, 1929.

Cole, Edward W. (ed.). *Racing Maxims and Methods of "Pittsburgh Phil."* Las Vegas: GBC Press, 1994 (reprint).

Cook, Fred J. *A Two-Dollar Bet Means Murder*. New York: Dial Press, 1961.

Crist, Steven. *Exotic Betting*. New York: DRF Press, 2006.

Dash, Mike. *Satan's Circus: Murder, Vice, Police Corruption, and New York's Trial of the Century:* New York: Crown Publishers, 2007.

Davidowitz, Steve. *The Best and Worst of Thoroughbred Racing*. New York: DRF Press, 2007.

Davies, Richard O., and Richard G. Abram. *Betting the Line: Sports Wagering in American Life.* Columbus: Ohio State University Press, 2001.

Eisenberg, John. *The Great Match Race: When North Met South in America's First Great Sports Spectacle.* Boston: Houghton Mifflin, 2006.

Figone, Albert J. *Cheating the Spread: Gamblers, Point Shavers, and Game Fixers in College Football and Basketball.* Urbana: University of Illinois Press, 2012.

Findlay, John M. *People of Chance*. New York: Oxford University Press, 1986.

Gardiner, Alexander. *Canfield*. Garden City, NY: Doubleday, Doran, 1930.

Gems, Gerald R. *Windy City Wars: Labor, Leisure, and Sport in the Making of Chicago.* Lanham, MD: Scarecrow Press, 1997.

Goldfarb, Ronald. *Perfect Villains, Imperfect Heroes: Robert F. Kennedy's War on Organized Crime.* New York: Random House, 1995.

Goodman, Robert. *The Luck Business*. New York: Free Press, 1995.

Gorn, Elliott J. (ed). *Sports in Chicago*. Urbana: University of Illinois Press, 2008.

Heimer, Mel. *Fabulous Bawd: The Story of Saratoga.* New York: Henry Holt and Company, 1952.

Hildreth, Samuel C., and James R. Crowell. *The Spell of the Turf: The Story of American Racing.* Philadelphia: J.B. Lippincott Co., 1926.

Hoffer, Richard. *Jackpot Nation*. New York: Harper, 2007.

Homer, J. Stanley, and Roger Dionne. *Homer's Las Vegas Sports and Race Betting Guide.* Las Vegas: Homer Gaming Publications, 1985.

Hopkins, A. D., and K. J. Evans (eds.). *The First 100: Portraits of the Men and Women Who Shaped Las Vegas.* Las Vegas: Huntington Press, 1999.

Hotaling, Edward. *They're Off! Horse Racing at Saratoga.* Syracuse, NY: Syracuse University Press, 1995.

Hoyt, Edwin P. *The Vanderbilts and Their Fortunes.* Garden City, NY: Doubleday, 1962.

Illman, Harry R. *Unholy Toledo.* San Francisco: Polemic Press, 1985.

Jeffers, H. Paul. *The Napoleon of New York: Mayor Fiorello La Guardia.* New York: Wiley, 2002.

Kahn, E. J. *The World of Swope.* New York: Simon and Schuster, 1965.

Katcher, Leo. *The Big Bankroll: The Life and Times of Arnold Rothstein.* New Rochelle, NY: Arlington House, 1959.

Katz, Leonard. *Uncle Frank: The Biography of Frank Costello.* New York: Drake Publishers, 1973.

Kefauver, Estes. *Crime in America.* Garden City, NY: Doubleday, 1951.

Landesco, John. *Organized Crime in Chicago, Part III.* Chicago: University Of Chicago Press, 1968.

Lankester, Marisa. *Dangerous Odds.* Stans, Switzerland: Cappuccino Books, 2014.

Lindberg, Richard C. *To Serve and Collect. Chicago Politics and Police Corruption from the Lager Beer Riot to the Summerdale Scandal, 1855–1960.* New York: Praeger, 1991.

Lindberg, Richard C. *The Gambler King of Clark Street: Michael C. McDonald and the Rise of Chicago's Democratic Machine.* Carbondale: Southern Illinois University Press, 2009.

Livingston, Bernard. *Their Turf: America's Horsey Set and Its Princely Dynasties.* New York: Arbor House, 1973.

Maeder, Jay (ed.). *Big Town Big Time. A New York Epic: 1898–1998.* New York: Sports Publishers, Inc., 1999.

Manteris, Art, with Rick Talley. *SuperBookie: Inside Las Vegas Sports Betting.* Chicago: Contemporary Books, 1991.

Mayer, Gary. *Bookie: My Life in Disorganized Crime.* Los Angeles: J.P. Tarcher, 1973.

McGowan, Richard A. *Government and the Transformation of the Gaming Industry.* Northampton, MA: Edward Elgar, 2001.

McManus, Phil, Glenn Albrecht, and Raewyn Graham. *The Global Horseracing Industry*. New York: Routledge, 2013.

McNickle, Chris. *To Be Mayor of New York: Ethnic Politics in the City*. New York: Columbia University Press, 1993.

Merchant, Larry. *The National Football Lottery*. New York: Holt, Rinehart, and Winston, 1973.

Messick, Hank, and Burt Goldblatt. *The Only Game in Town: An Illustrated History of Gambling*. New York: Thomas Y. Crowell Company, 1976.

Millman, Chad. *The Odds: One Season, Three Gamblers, and the Death of Their Las Vegas*. New York, Public Affairs, 2001.

Moehring, Eugene P. *Resort City in the Sunbelt*. Reno: University of Nevada Press, 1989.

Moldea, Dan E. *Interference: How Organized Crime Influences Professional Football*. New York: William Morrow and Company, 1989.

Mooney, Katherine C. *Race Horse Men: How Slavery and Freedom Were Made at the Racetrack*. Cambridge, MA: Harvard University Press, 2014.

Moore, Bob. *Those Wonderful Days: Tales of Racing's Golden Era*. New York: Amerpub Company, 1976.

Moore, William Howard. *The Kefauver Committee and the Politics of Crime, 1950–1952*. Columbia: University of Missouri Press, 1974.

Munchkin, Richard W. *Gambling Wizards: Conversations with the World's Greatest Gamblers*. Las Vegas: Huntington Press, 2002.

Murray, William. *The Wrong Horse: An Odyssey through the American Racing Scene*. New York: Simon & Schuster, 1992.

Nasaw, David. *The Patriarch: The Remarkable Life and Turbulent Times of Joseph P. Kennedy*. New York: Penguin Press, 2012.

O'Connor, Richard. *Courtroom Warrior: The Combative Career of William Travers Jerome*. Boston: Little, Brown, 1963.

Ogden, Christopher. *Legacy: A Biography of Moses and Walter Annenberg*. Boston: Little, Brown & Company, 1999.

Olshan, Mort (ed.). *The Best of the Gold Sheet*. Los Angeles: Nation-Wide Publications, 1988.

Parker, Dan. *The ABC of Horse Racing*. New York: Random House, 1947.

Parmer, Charles R. *For Gold and Glory: The Story of Thoroughbred Racing in America*. New York: Carrick and Evans, 1939.

Phipps, Herb. *Bill Kyne of Bay Meadows*. New York: A.S. Barnes, 1978.

Pilat, Oliver, and Jo Ranson. *Sodom by the Sea: An Affectionate History of Coney Island*. New York: Doubleday, Doran, 1941.

Poundstone, William. *Fortune's Formula: The Untold Story of the Scientific Betting System That Beat the Casinos and Wall Street*. New York: Hill and Wang, 2005.

Quinn, John Philip. *Fools of Fortune*. Chicago: G.L. Howe & Co., 1890.

Reizner, Sonny, and Martin Mendelsohn. *Sports Betting with Sonny Reizner*. Las Vegas: GBC Press, 1983.

Reuter, Peter. *Disorganized Crime*. Cambridge, MA: MIT Press, 1983.

Riess, Steven A. *City Games: The Evolution of Urban Society and the Rise of Sports*. Urbana: University of Illinois Press, 1989.

Riess, Steven A. *The Sport of Kings and the Kings of Crime*. Syracuse: Syracuse University Press, 2011.

Robertson, William H. P. *The History of Thoroughbred Racing in America*. Englewood Cliffs, NJ: Prentice-Hall, 1964.

Ruck, Rob, Maggie Jones Patterson, and Michael P. Weber. *Rooney: A Sporting Life*. Lincoln: University of Nebraska Press, 2010.

Rudd, Irving, with Stan Fischler. *The Sporting Life*. New York: St. Martin's Press, 1990.

Sasuly, Richard. *Bookies and Bettors: Two Hundred Years of Gambling*. New York: Holt, Rinehart, and Winston, 1982.

Sasuly, Richard. *The Search for the Winning Horse*. New York: Holt, Rinehart, and Winston, 1979.

Schmidt, John C. *Win. Place. Show: A Biography of Harry Straus*. Baltimore: Johns Hopkins University Press, 1989.

Schwartz, David G. *Cutting the Wire: Gambling Prohibition and the Internet*. Reno: University of Nevada Press, 2005.

Schwartz, David G. *Roll the Bones: The History of Gambling*. New York: Gotham, 2006.

Scott, Marvin B. *The Racing Game*. Chicago: Aldine Books, 1968.

Segrave, Kerry. *Wiretapping and Electronic Surveillance in America, 1862–1920*. Jefferson, NC: McFarland, 2014.

Sidney, Charles. *The Art of Legging*. London: Maxine International, 1976.

Simon, Bryant. *Boardwalk of Dreams: Atlantic City and the Fate of Urban America*. New York: Oxford University Press, 2004.

Somers, Dale A. *The Rise of Sports in New Orleans, 1850–1900*. Baton Rouge: Louisiana State University Press, 1971.

Steigleman, Walter. *Horseracing*. New York: Prentice-Hall, 1947.

Sterngass, Jon. *First Resorts: Pursuing Pleasure at Saratoga Springs, Newport, and Coney Island*. Baltimore: Johns Hopkins University Press, 2001.

Thompson, William N. *Gambling in America: An Encyclopedia of History, Issues, and Society*. Santa Barbara, CA: ABC-CLIO, 2001.

Turner, Wallace. *Gamblers' Money. The New Force in American Life*. Boston: Houghton Mifflin, 1965.

Vanderwood, Paul J. *Satan's Playground: Mobsters and Movie Stars at America's Greatest Gaming Resort*. Durham, NC: Duke University Press, 2010.

Vernetti, Michael. *Howard Cannon of Nevada, a Biography*. Reno: University of Nevada Press, 2008.

Vosburgh, W. S. *Racing in America, 1866–1921*. New York: Jockey Club, 1922.

Wadsworth, Ginger. *Farewell Jimmy the Greek*. Austin, TX: Eakin Press, 1996.

Welch, Richard F. *King of the Bowery: Big Tim Sullivan, Tammany Hall, and New York City from the Gilded Age to the Progressive Era*. Madison, NJ: Fairleigh Dickinson University Press, 2008.

Wesser, Robert F. *Charles Evans Hughes: Politics and Reform in New York, 1905–1910*. Ithaca, NY: Cornell University Press, 1967.

Wiggins, David W. (ed.). *Sport in America: From Wicked Amusement to National Obsession*. Champaign, IL: Human Kinetics, 1995.

Winn, Colonel Matt J., as told to Frank Menke. *Down the Stretch*. New York: Smith & Durrell, 1945.

Yeager, Matthew G. (ed.). *Illegal Enterprise: The Work of Historian Mark Haller*. Lanham, MD: University Press of America, 2013.

INDEX

ABOUT THE AUTHOR

A recognized authority on the history of boxing and the history of American sports gambling, **Arne K. Lang** has resided in Las Vegas for most of his adult life. He is the former Sports Information Coordinator for the fabled *Stardust Race and Sports* book. The position was invented specifically for him. Before transitioning into the world of sports betting, Lang was an instructor at UNLV and a visiting assistant professor at Tuskegee Institute, now Tuskegee University. He holds an MA in sociology from the University of Nebraska. This is his fourth book.